GENDER IN H

GH01044315

Series editors:
Lynn Abrams, Cordelia Beattie, Pam Shar   ....erield

+≻══⟨+

The expansion of research into the history of women and gender since the 1970s has changed the face of history. Using the insights of feminist theory and of historians of women, gender historians have explored the configuration in the past of gender identities and relations between the sexes. They have also investigated the history of sexuality and family relations, and analysed ideas and ideals of masculinity and femininity. Yet gender history has not abandoned the original, inspirational project of women's history: to recover and reveal the lived experience of women in the past and the present.

The series Gender in History provides a forum for these developments. Its historical coverage extends from the medieval to the modern periods, and its geographical scope encompasses not only Europe and North America but all corners of the globe. The series aims to investigate the social and cultural constructions of gender in historical sources, as well as the gendering of historical discourse itself. It embraces both detailed case studies of specific regions or periods and broader treatments of major themes. Gender in History books are designed to meet the needs of both scholars and students working in this dynamic area of historical research.

Housewives and citizens

Manchester University Press

HOUSEWIVES AND CITIZENS

DOMESTICITY AND THE WOMEN'S MOVEMENT IN ENGLAND, 1928–64

Caitríona Beaumont

Manchester University Press

The right of Caitríona Beaumont to be identified as the author of this work has been asserted by her in accordance with the Copyright, Designs and Patents Act 1988.

Published by Manchester University Press
Altrincham Street, Manchester M1 7JA, UK
www.manchesteruniversitypress.co.uk

British Library Cataloguing-in-Publication Data is available

Library of Congress Cataloging-in-Publication Data is available

ISBN 978 0 7190 9725 6 *paperback*

First published by Manchester University Press in hardback 2013

This paperback edition first published 2015

The publisher has no responsibility for the persistence or accuracy of URLs for any external or third-party internet websites referred to in this book, and does not guarantee that any content on such websites is, or will remain, accurate or appropriate.

Printed by Lightning Source

For my parents
Piaras and Margaret Beaumont

For my family
Patrick, Dónal, Rosa and Martha McDonnell

Contents

Acknowledgements

I owe a great many thanks to everyone who helped me at the various stages of the research and writing of this book. Firstly, thank you to the team at Manchester University Press for their professionalism and patience. It was a pleasure to work with them. This research began as a doctoral thesis at the Centre for Social History, University of Warwick and I am grateful to my supervisors, Tony Mason and Jim Obelkevitch, for their support and wise counsel. I would also like to thank Pat Thane, Maria Luddy and June Purvis for their advice and interest in my work over the years. I am grateful to the ESRC and to the University of Warwick Graduate Award Scheme for funding my doctoral studies and to the Weeks Centre for Social and Policy Research, London South Bank University, for awarding me a number of research grants since 2005, allowing me to complete my research.

Over the course of this project I have been helped by many librarians and archivists and would like to thank the staff at the Women's Library, Lambeth Palace Library, the London Metropolitan Archive, the British Library, the Modern Records Centre at the University of Warwick, the Public Records Office and Birmingham City Library. Thanks also to Daphne Glick of the National Council of Women and to the Mothers' Union for allowing me access to their uncatalogued collections. I would also like to thank David Doughan, formally of the Women's Library, for his interest and encouragement in my work from the outset.

Marisa Silvestri, Louise Ryan and Tanya Evans provided me with very helpful comments on the proposal for this book so thanks to them for their constructive criticism. I am grateful also to Matthew Hilton and to the anonymous readers of both the book proposal and final manuscript who provided me with invaluable comments and suggestions.

I would like to thank all of my colleagues in the Department of Social Sciences, London South Bank University, for their interest, support and comradeship over the years. Thanks to Dave Edwards, my Head of Department, for giving me the space and time to complete the book. In particular I would like to thank my colleague and friend Marisa Silvestri. Throughout this project she has listened to all of my concerns, doubts and anxieties and has provided excellent advice every time with endless patience and good humour.

Thank you to all of my friends and family who have listened to me talk about 'the book' for a number of years and asked how I was getting on. Without their interest and support life would have been very difficult and I hope they know how much they are appreciated. Thanks especially to all my friends in Tooting and to Tony Credland and Sceherazade Ameer for their help with formatting the cover image. Thank you to all of the McDonnells for putting up with me for so long and thanks to my sisters Clíona, Míde and Helen Beaumont for their love and friendship. I would like to thank my parents, Piaras and Margaret Beaumont for always believing in me and enabling me to pursue my interest in women's history. Thanks especially to Piaras for pinning the image of Mrs 1963 to our kitchen cupboard at home so that years later I could use it as the cover for this book.

A special thanks goes to my children, Dónal, Rosa and Martha, who have taken such an interest in this research and who have been very patient in allowing me to spend so much time working on it when they wanted me to play with them. I hope they think it was worth it. Last but not least, thanks to Patrick for just about everything.

List of Abbreviations

AEC	Association for Education in Citizenship
AGM	annual general meeting
ALRA	Abortion Law Reform Association
ARP	Air Raid Precaution
BCL	Birmingham City Library
BFBPW	British Federation of Business and Professional Women
BFUW	British Federation of University Women
BHL	British Housewives League
BL	British Library
CMW	Council of Married Women
CWL	The Catholic Women's League
ECCC	Equal Compensation Campaign Committee
EPCC	Equal Pay Campaign Committee
GFS	Girls' Friendly Society
LMA	London Metropolitan Archive
LPL	Lambeth Palace Library
MRC	Modern Records Centre
MSH	Mary Sumner House
MU	Mothers' Union
MWA	Married Women's Association
NBCA	National Birth Control Association
NBCW	National Board of Catholic Women
NCEC	National Council for Equal Citizenship
NCW	National Council of Women
NHS	National Health Service
NUSEC	National Union of Societies for Equal Citizenship
NUWSS	National Union of Women's Suffrage Societies
NUWW	National Union of Women Workers
NWCA	National Women Citizens' Association
ODC	Open Door Council
PRO	Public Record Office
SCWO	Standing Conference of Women's Organisations
SJCIWO	Standing Joint Committee of Industrial Women's Organisations
SJCWWO	Standing Joint Committee of Working Women's Organisations
SPG	Six Point Group
TG	National Union of Townswomen's Guilds
WAHC	Women's Advisory Housing Council
WAPC	Women's Auxiliary Police Corps
WCA	Women's Citizens' Association
WCG	Women's Co-operative Guild
WFL	Women's Freedom League

WGPW	Women's Group on Public Welfare
WI	The National Federation of Women's Institutes
WL	Women's Library
WLM	Women's Liberation Movement
WPCC	Women's Police Campaign Committee
WVS	Women's Voluntary Service
YWCA	Young Women's Christian Association.

Introduction

> For many housewives women's organisations provide the best access to cultural or educational pursuits ... resolutions are frequently passed by the branches to the national headquarters urging government intervention in matters where their particular knowledge and experience has shown that reform is both necessary and possible, and they exercise an undoubted influence upon the trend of domestic affairs.[1]

In 1964, *Women in Britain*, a survey published by the Central Office of Information, reported that there were 120 national organisations for women active within the UK. These groups were made up of a mixture of philanthropic, voluntary, feminist, political and religious women's groups.[2] Of the 120, only fifteen were classified as overtly feminist, reflecting the fact that groups openly espousing a feminist agenda were somewhat marginalised at this time.[3]

Historians of women in the twentieth century have explored the history of a wide variety of women's organisations active throughout the century.[4] These histories have included suffrage and post-suffrage feminist societies, women's sections of the established political parties and working-class women's organisations such as the Women's Co-operative Guild (WCG), all of whom engaged in political campaigns to extend female equality.[5] In the last two decades the scope of this scholarship has expanded to include voluntary women's organisations, religious groups, service clubs and professional societies seeking to bring women together over a wide variety of issues.[6]

Histories of the women's movement have however tended to focus predominantly on the trials and tribulations of suffrage and post-suffrage feminist societies. This has resulted in a narrative suggesting that after the passing of the 1928 Equal Franchise Act the movement lost momentum in the 1930s. Following a brief revival during the Second World War the movement once again slipped into decline, only to be revitalised by the emergence of the Women's Liberation Movement (WLM) in the late 1960s.[7] This orthodox interpretation has been challenged by a number of historians who have demonstrated that a vibrant and successful network of women's organisations remained active throughout the post-suffrage years and well into the 1950s, 1960s and 1970s.[8]

The inclusion of a more diverse range of women's organisations, for example middle-class housewives' associations such as the Women's

Institutes (WI) and the Mothers' Union (MU), has opened up debates amongst historians about the meanings of feminism and how the terms 'feminist movement' and 'women's movement' should be defined and applied.[9] Maggie Andrews, in her history of the WI, has argued that the organisation represented the 'acceptable face of feminism' allowing members to 'work out alternative meanings for the structure of their lives'.[10] In doing so it is suggested that WI members embraced their domestic roles but at the same time contested 'social constructions of gender'.[11]

Lorna Gibson argues that to include the WI in the history of the women's movement the term 'feminism' needs redefining. Feminism, Gibson suggests, 'is assumed to originate from women's dissatisfaction with domesticity'.[12] Moreover the concept of feminism also assumes some recognition of the imbalance of power between men and women and the desire to achieve equality between the sexes. As Karen Offen writes, 'feminism is the name given to a comprehensive critical response to the deliberate and systematic subordination of women as a group by men as a group within a given cultural setting'.[13] Such definitions make it difficult to comprehend the role played by voluntary women's groups who embraced domesticity, never challenged established gender roles and were reluctant to be associated with feminist beliefs.

To deal with this problem Gibson proposes a new definition of 'moderate feminism' or 'empowerment' so that organisations such as the WI can be included in the history of the women's movement. This is justified on the grounds that they allowed women to 'have fulfilled lives within the traditional social constructions of gender and acceptance of patriarchy'.[14] Offering a contrasting view, Cordelia Moyse, in her history of the MU, questions whether 'the lack of shared motivation and analysis of gender politics undermine the inclusion of some women's groups into the feminist movement?'[15]

Whilst the arguments put forward by Andrews and Gibson are persuasive it is important to remember that the five voluntary women's organisations included in this study, the MU, Catholic Women's League (CWL), National Council of Women (NCW), WI and National Union of Townswomen's Guilds (TG), never questioned traditional gender roles, nor did they ever envisage themselves as feminist throughout the years 1928–64. It would be wrong therefore to attempt to reconceptualise these groups so that they take on a more recognisable feminist identity. It would be equally misconceived to alter our understanding of feminist theory and the concept of patriarchy in order to secure a 'fit' for voluntary women's organisations, who it must be remembered were outspoken in their endorsement of women's domestic role and the centrality of mothers to family life.

Moyse's assertion that housewives' associations cannot therefore be included in the feminist movement appears logical but once again highlights the underlying confusion surrounding the terms 'feminist movement' and 'women's movement'. In most cases the two terms are conceived to be one and the same thing. However, when the diversity of the hundred or so organisations actively representing the interests of women throughout the years 1928–64 is considered, it is far too limiting only to view those with obvious feminist tendencies as part of the 'women's movement'.

Instead of attempting to locate feminist principles within all of these groups or developing a new understanding of feminism and patriarchy, what is argued here is that the term 'women's movement' needs to be revised. In a sense the women's movement needs to be liberated from its exclusive association with feminism. This will allow the movement to be recast as a social movement encompassing all women's organisations, including feminist, political and conservative women's groups, who campaigned to improve the position and status of women in society throughout the twentieth century.

Adopting this new, more inclusive definition, this book will assess the contribution of five mainstream and conservative voluntary women's organisations to the women's movement between the years 1928 and 1964. The five groups selected, the MU, CWL, NCW, WI and TG, were amongst the largest and most influential organisations representing housewives and mothers in twentieth-century Britain. Each group recognised the primary roles that women had as housewives and mothers. In doing so they set out to provide members with support and advice on domestic matters, marriage and motherhood. The origins and aspirations of each group will be outlined and discussed in Chapter 1.

In spite of their endorsement of domesticity, the MU, CWL, NCW, WI and TG insisted that housewives and mothers would be mistaken to devote themselves exclusively to family life. On the contrary this study will reveal that voluntary women's groups acknowledged the status of women as equal citizens and continually sought to inform and educate their members about the importance of democratic citizenship. Focusing on citizenship rights instead of feminism, these groups encouraged members to participate in local and national politics and campaigned to ensure that women benefited from the rights of equal citizenship bestowed upon them in 1928.

Publicly rejecting feminism made sense for these organisations as they wished to attract mass memberships through their recruitment of housewives and mothers. At this time the term 'feminism' was often used in a pejorative sense and feminist societies were assumed to be radical groups seeking to undermine traditional family life. Vera Brittain, writing in 1928, articulated these prejudices when she wrote that feminists were often portrayed as 'spectacled, embittered women, disappointed, childless, dowdy and generally unloved'.[16] Writing in a similar vein, Ray Strachey stated in 1936 that modern women 'show a strong hostility to the word feminism, and all which they imagine it to connote'.[17]

Chapter 2 will explore the ways in which voluntary women's organisations successfully utilised the rhetoric of citizenship, with all its adherent rights and duties, to articulate the needs of their members and to provide an effective public voice for women. The woman citizen was defined as a homemaker, but this did not mean, as Barbara Caine has suggested, that the housewife was 'not seriously involved in attempting to change the political and social framework in which she lived'.[18] Chapter 3 will discuss the ways in which these groups attempted to represent the views of women on the controversial and potentially divisive issues of divorce, birth control and abortion. Here it will be argued that despite the conservative views expressed by some groups, most notably the MU and CWL, the overall objective of housewives' associations in debating these issues was to protect the stability of the family and the role of the mother within the home. In doing so, voluntary women's organisations called upon the state to provide adequate public services so that women would be supported in their work as wives and mothers.

The involvement of the MU, CWL, NCW, WI and TG in a number of specific campaigns relating to social policy, for example the payment of family allowances to mothers, improved maternity services and the provision of social welfare benefits will be discussed in Chapter 4. Chapter 5 explores the contribution of these organisations to the war effort and their participation in two key wartime campaigns, the demand for equal pay and the employment of women police. The role played by voluntary women's groups in post-war reconstruction and their ability to successfully influence government policy on housing reform, as well as protecting the interests of women as housewives, workers and citizens, will be discussed in Chapter 6.

Chapter 7 considers how these mainstream women's organisations challenged traditional constructions of domesticity in the 1950s and early 1960s. It is argued that the MU, CWL, NCW, WI and TG, in continuing to highlight the importance of citizenship for women, presented a new, alternative and modern interpretation of women's domestic role. Rejecting the ideal of the 'perfect housewife' so pervasive during the 1950s and 1960s, voluntary women's groups argued that wives and mothers had more to offer society than just knowing 'how to keep a husband happy'.[19] Instead of condemning the increasing numbers of mothers going out to work in the 1950s, these groups focused their attention on the duty of the state and employers to provide more flexible work patterns and extended child-care facilities, allowing women to balance paid work with their domestic responsibilities.

This final chapter provides further evidence of the effectiveness of female agency during these years. Engaging in a wide range of campaigning activities, voluntary women's organisations were successful in bringing about legislative reform and influencing public policy. This presents a challenge to longstanding assumptions that the 1950s and early 1960s witnessed a women's movement overpowered by an ideology of domesticity. Accordingly, this study suggests that by 1964, the MU, CWL, NCW, WI and TG had proven themselves effective in providing housewives with opportunities to participate in social, leisure and educational activities. These groups campaigned on behalf of their members and informed women about the rights and duties of democratic citizenship. In doing so they did indeed exercise 'an undoubted influence upon the trend of domestic affairs'.[20] In light of all of these achievements, and their success in creating dynamic networks of women, these conservative women's organisations must now be included in any history of the women's movement.

In terms of methodology, the research for this book has been confined to England as the MU, CWL, NCW, WI and TG had separate administrative arrangements for Scotland, Wales and Northern Ireland. Although reference is made to the work of local branches, the principal objective here is to focus on the work and policy decisions of the five national organisations that represented the interests of hundreds of thousands of women throughout the years 1928–64. Sources used include the organisational archives as well the records of other societies, governmental departments and church bodies.

The archival material for each organisation is rich in detail. Annual reports, minutes of annual general meetings (AGMs), public questions committees, executive and sectional committees, all provide an excellent and insightful record of activity and achievement. In addition, the organisations produced their own journals, published reports and pamphlets and gave written and oral evidence to a large number of public enquiries and royal commissions. These records and the history of the five organisations included in this study have ensured that stories previously untold about the nature of female activism, and the agency of housewives and mothers, can now be heard.

Notes

1 Central Office of Information, *Women in Britain Reference Pamphlet 67* (London: HMSO, 1964), p. 25.

2 Cited in E. Meehan, 'British Feminism from the 1960s to the 1980s', in H. Smith (ed.), *British Feminism in the Twentieth Century* (London: Edward Elgar, 1990), p. 192.

3 See B. Caine, *English Feminism 1780–1980* (Oxford: Oxford University Press, 1997), pp. 234–240.

4 For a list of women's organisations see C. Law, *Suffrage and Power: The Women's Movement, 1918–1928* (London: I. B. Tauris, 1997), pp. 232–238. See also P. Gordon and D. Doughan, *Dictionary of British Women's Organisations 1825–1960* (London: Woburn Press, 2001).

5 See for example: *Law, Suffrage and Power*, G. Scott, *Feminism, Femininity and the Politics of Working Women: The Women's Co-operative Guild, 1880s to the Second World War* (London: UCL, 1998), K. Hunt, 'Negotiating the Boundaries of the Domestic: British Socialist Women and the Politics of Consumption', *Women's History Review*, 9:2 (2000), pp. 389–410, P. Thane, 'Women of the British Labour Party and Feminism, 1906–45', in Smith (ed.), *British Feminism in the Twentieth Century* and I. Zweiniger-Bargielowska, 'Explaining the Gender Gap: The Conservative Party and the Women's Vote', in M. Francis and I. Zweiniger-Bargielowska (eds), *The Conservatives and British Society, 1880–1990* (Cardiff: University of Wales Press, 1996).

6 See for example: C. Beaumont, 'Citizens not Feminists: The Boundary Negotiated between Citizenship and Feminism by Mainstream Women's Organisations in England, 1928–39', *Women's History Review*, 9:2 (2000), L. Perriton, 'Forgotten Feminists: The Federation of British Professional and Business Women, 1933–1969', *Women's History Review*, 16:1 (2007), M. Andrews, *The Acceptable Face of Feminism: The Women's Movement as a Social Movement* (London: Lawrence and Wishart, 1997), C. Moyse, *A History of the Mothers' Union: Women, Anglicanism and Globalisation* (London: The Boydell Press, 2009), C. Merz, *After the Vote: The Story of the National Union of Townswomen's Guilds in the Year of Its Diamond Jubilee 1929–1989* (Norwich: NUTG, 1988), H. McCarthy, 'Service Clubs, Citizenship and Equality: Gender Relations and Middle-class Associations in Britain between the Wars', *Historical Review*, 81 (2008) and P. Thane, 'Women and Political Participation in England, 1918–1970', in E. Breitenbach and P. Thane (eds), *Women and Citizenship in Britain and Ireland in the Twentieth Century: What Difference Did the Vote Make?* (London: Continuum, 2010).

7 See for example: S. Bruley, *Women in Britain since 1900* (Basingstoke: Macmillan, 1999), M. Pugh, *Women and the Women's Movement in Britain* (2nd ed.; Basingstoke: Macmillan, 2000), D. Beddoe, *Back to Home and Duty: Women between the Wars 1918–1939* (London: Pandora, 1989) and J. Lewis, *Women in England 1870–1950: Sexual Divisions and Social Change* (Brighton: Wheatsheaf, 1984).

8 See for example: Caine, *English Feminism*, C. Beaumont, 'The Women's Movement, Politics and Citizenship, 1918–1950s', in I. Zweiniger-Bargielowska (ed.), *Women in Twentieth Century Britain* (Harlow: Pearson Education, 2001), C. Beaumont, 'Housewives, Workers and Citizens: Voluntary Women's Organisations and the Campaign for Women's Rights in England and Wales during the Post-war Period', in N. Crowson, M. Hilton and J. McKay (eds), *NGOs in Contemporary Britain: Non-*

State Actors in Society and Politics since 1945 (Basingstoke: Palgrave Macmillan, 2009), pp. 59–76, S. Innes, 'Constructing Women's Citizenship in the Inter-war Period: The Edinburgh Women's Citizens' Association', *Women's History Review*, 13:4 (2000), V. Wright, '"Education for Active Citizenship": Women's Organisations in Inter-war Scotland', *History of Education*, 38:3 (2009), S. Clements, 'Feminism, citizenship and social activity: the role and importance of local women's organisations, Nottingham 1918–1969' (Ph.D. dissertation, University of Nottingham, 2008) and J. Freeguard, 'It's time for the women of the 1950s to stand up and be counted' (Ph.D. dissertation, University of Sussex, 2004).

9   For an overview of these debates see Clements, 'Feminism, citizenship and social activity', pp. 37–40 and L. Gibson, *Beyond Jerusalem: Music in the Women's Institute, 1919–1969* (London: Ashgate, 2008), pp. 42–48. See also Caine, *English Feminism*, pp. 222–240.

10 Andrews, *The Acceptable Face of Feminism*, p. 14.

11 Gibson, *Beyond Jerusalem*, p. 43.

12 *Ibid.*, p. 47.

13 K. Offen, *European Feminisms, 1700–1950* (Stanford: Stanford University Press, 2000), p. 20.

14 Gibson, *Beyond Jerusalem*, p. 48.

15 Moyse, *A History of the Mothers' Union*, p. 10.

16 *Manchester Guardian* (13 December 1928).

17 R. Strachey, *Our Freedom and Its Results* (London: Hogarth, 1936), p. 10. See also M. Pugh, 'Domesticity and the Decline of Feminism, 1930–1950', in Smith (ed.), *British Feminism in the Twentieth Century*, p. 147.

18 Caine, *English Feminism*, p. 202.

19 *Woman* (27 April 1963).

20 Central Office of Information, *Women in Britain*, p. 25.

1

Origins and aspirations: voluntary women's organisations and the representation of housewives, mothers and citizens

Between the years 1928 and 1964 the majority of British women married and had children.[1] Pat Thane writes that these years represent a 'golden age ... of the near universal, stable, long-lasting marriage'.[2] Responding to this resounding endorsement of traditional domesticity, housewives organisations sought to recruit wives and mothers by offering them support and advice to assist them in their domestic roles. In addition, members were given the opportunity to spend time outside the family home where they could engage in an interesting range of social, educational and leisure activities as well as mixing with other like-minded women in a friendly, relaxed and supportive environment.

The growing popularity of voluntary women's organisations during these years can also be attributed to the increasing number of women who now identified themselves as full-time housewives. Judy Giles has argued that during the first half of the twentieth century the term 'housewife' came 'to signify an apparently homogenous group of women who could be addressed as having common interests by the media, by politicians, and by designers and producers of domestic technology'. Giles views the 1920s and 1930s as the time when 'the idea of the housewife was offered as a highly valued and "modern" role for women albeit a conservative one, focusing as it did on women's traditional functions within the family'.[3]

This seemingly contradictory depiction of the modern woman as a traditional housewife underpins much of the work of the five voluntary women's organisations included in this study. These groups promoted housewifery as a skilled profession for women and argued that women's domestic expertise gave them the right to contribute to local and national affairs. As a result domesticity no longer demanded that women dedicate themselves exclusively to the demands of husband and children. On the contrary, domesticity was the means through which modern women could assert their right to participate in public life.

To attract mass memberships and in their desire to provide a welcoming environment in which women could meet, the MU, CWL, NCW, WI and TG presented themselves as avowedly non-feminist and non-party-political. To this end each group refrained from discussing topics deemed to be 'too political or too feminist' as this could prove divisive or deter new members from joining the organisation. This did not however prevent each of the five, who were respected and influential women's groups, from publicly voicing their concerns on a wide range of issues believed to impact on the daily lives of women. These organisations successfully utilised their popularity to represent the views of women on a national and local level. Like all large organisations not all members were either able or willing to engage in such campaigning activities but members were kept informed of action taken by the national organisation through the local branch meeting, in-house journals, annual reviews and reports of the AGM.

In analysing the origins and aspirations of these five popular and influential housewives' associations in this chapter, the intention is not to provide a detailed organisational history. Rather the aim is to contextualise the activities of each group in an attempt to explain what motivated them to engage in campaigning and how specific causes were identified as warranting support.

The Mothers' Union

Mothers' meetings, first established in Britain in the 1850s, were set up to provide support and advice for mothers on matters relating to public health and the care of their children. These meetings were of a distinctly religious nature and were run by middle-class women from the Anglican and Nonconformist traditions who hoped to improve the moral fibre of society by instructing working-class women in religious and domestic subjects.[4] Frank Prochaska has written that by the end of the nineteenth century as many as a million women and children were attending mothers' meetings, which he describes as 'the most pervasive female agency for bringing women together … outside the home in British history'.[5] It was in the midst of this growing popularity for mothers' meetings that Mary Sumner, a rector's wife living in Hampshire, set up a new organisation for mothers, the MU.[6]

Following the birth of her first child in the late 1840s, Mary Sumner recalled 'the awful sense of responsibility which seemed to overwhelm me as I took her in my arms, and realised that God had given an immortal soul into our keeping'.[7] Some thirty years later in 1876, with her own children grown up, Mary Sumner set up a mothers' meeting in the parish of Old Alresford, where her husband was the local rector. Sumner firmly believed that motherhood was one of 'the greatest and most important professions in the world' but one which had the poorest 'training for its supreme duties'.[8] The desire to unite women together through their common experiences as mothers was the second key objective for Mary Sumner. Writing in 1893 she celebrated the fact that the success of the MU had allowed women to come together 'to love and help one another'.[9]

In order to provide women with the support and guidance they needed in their role as wife and mother and to encourage women in their Christian faith, Mary Sumner began to hold mothers' meetings in her own home. These meetings for local mothers, who were members of the Church of England, soon became a regular feature of church work within the parish. Unlike other mothers' meetings, women attending Mary Sumner's meetings became members of the MU and were provided with a membership card on joining. The wording on the card clearly set out the Christian nature of the organisation and advised members on how to raise their children, reminding them that 'your Children are given up, body and soul, to Jesus Christ in Holy Baptism, and that your duty is to train them for His Service'.[10] As Cordelia Moyse suggests, the success of the MU was linked to Sumner's close ties to the Girls' Friendly Society (GFS). This organisation was set up in 1874 to train young women in 'religious principles and domestic duty', and Sumner had direct knowledge of its work through her role as an associate member. The GFS provided access to an active network of middle-class women already engaged in leadership roles within a religious organisation and it was hoped that former members of the GFS would join the MU following the birth of their first child.[11]

The idea of extending the MU to become a nationwide network of mothers' meetings for Anglican women was first proposed by Mary Sumner in 1885 when she addressed a meeting of clergymen's wives attending the Church of England Congress. In her speech Sumner suggested that wives and mothers had 'great work to do for our husbands, our children, our homes and our country, and I am convinced that it would greatly help if we could start a Mothers' Union, wherein all classes could unite in faith and prayer, to try to do this work for God'.[12] The following day the first Diocesan Section of the MU, with Mary Sumner as President, was established in Winchester. Within two years, fifty-seven branches of the Union had been established and the MU had become the recognised women's society within the Church of England. The speed of this expansion has been attributed to Mary Sumner's links with the GFS, her ability to draw on family networks within the Church of England to promote the MU, and the support of the clergy and episcopate for this new venture.[13]

The growth of the MU throughout the British Isles was rapid. In July 1889 the new organisation had attracted an estimated 157,668 members and associates.[14] In 1890 it was reported that branches had been established 'in practically every English diocese' as well as in the colonies where members of the Church of England had settled.[15] Separate sections of the Union were set up in Ireland, Wales and Scotland. By 1909 the total membership of the MU was calculated at 316,000 and branches had been established in 'all but one of the dioceses in England and Wales'.[16] This rapid expansion prompted the need for an effective organisational framework. Replicating the GFS model, a Central Council was set up in 1896 to co-ordinate the Union's work. The new council met twice a year in London, every June and December, and representatives from the various diocesan sections attended. It was here that decisions regarding the policy and administration of the MU were discussed and voted upon and every three years elections for the Central President and Executive Committee took place.

Although the MU was set up as an independent Church of England society, Union meetings could only be held with the approval of the local vicar, who also had the power to disband the branch in his parish even if this meant going against the wishes of the members.[17] Co-operation between the MU and the Church of England extended to the highest ranks of the hierarchy with bishops and archbishops invited to become patrons of the diocesan sections. The Central President consulted the Archbishop of Canterbury over matters of Union policy, most notably on the divisive issues of divorce and birth control. Although differences of opinion arose on such matters the MU always operated under the auspices of the Church of England and, unlike the NCW, WI and TG, was answerable to a higher male authority, in this case the Church hierarchy. The MU also assisted the Church in organising large gatherings, including the Lambeth Conference, when members offered to provide accommodation for visiting delegates and volunteered their services as caterers and tea-makers for the duration of the Conference.

Membership of the Union was open to women who belonged either to the Church of England or to a church in accord with the Church of England. These women were eligible to become official workers for the Union and could therefore stand for election to the Central Council and the Executive Committee. Ordinary membership was open to married women who were baptised and who undertook to have their children baptised. Unmarried women who supported the work of the Union were allowed to join as associate members. It is significant, though perhaps not surprising, that unmarried mothers were not eligible to join the MU, on the grounds that these women represented 'an infringement of the duties and ideals of Christian Motherhood'.[18]

This decision reflects the conservative and uncompromising nature of the society when it came to questions of moral behaviour. The MU saw itself as the guardian of traditional family life and any deviation from Christian principles was not tolerated. The Union worked within the confines of the 'three objects', drawn up by the Executive Council during the late 1890s, which defined the moral character and the ultimate aims of the organisation. These principal objects were:

> 1. To uphold the sanctity of marriage; 2. To awaken in all mothers a sense of their great responsibility in the training of their boys and girls, the fathers and mothers of the future; 3. To organise in every place a band of mothers who will unite in prayer and will seek by their own example to lead their families in purity and holiness of life.[19]

Upholding the 'first object' of the MU, which confirmed the organisation's belief in the indissolubility of marriage, dominated much of the national work of the MU during the 1920s and 1930s. Adherence to the principle of indissolubility and participation in national campaigns against the introduction of new grounds for divorce created controversy within the organisation and, for a short time at least, led to tension between the Union and some members of the Church of England hierarchy.[20]

The Union's belief in the sanctity of marriage and its opposition to divorce meant that divorced women were ineligible for membership of the MU. Any woman found to have been unfaithful to her husband ceased 'ipso facto to be a member of the Mothers' Union'.[21] The Union took a slightly less uncompromising position when it came to birth control. Members were encouraged to accept God's gift of a family but by the mid-1930s the leadership accepted that family limitation was a private matter for married couples and the rejection of birth control was not made a condition of membership.[22]

Moral issues such as divorce and birth control may have preoccupied the leadership of the MU but at the local level Union meetings gave women the opportunity to meet one afternoon a week and spend some time with other women who shared their religious beliefs and domestic concerns. In 1916 the Union had 8,266 branches with 415,354 members.[23] By 1930 half a million women had joined the MU, making it one of the largest organisations for women in Britain during the inter-war period.[24] Religious instruction was always a priority for the MU and members were expected to obey the moral and social teaching of the Church of

England. Union meetings began and ended in prayer and speakers were often invited to local dioceses to give lectures on topics ranging from the importance of temperance and religious education in the home, to the dangers of betting and gambling.[25] During the 1930s, local branches set up prayer groups for members who wished to devote more time to Christian observance.[26]

As an organisation for mothers, the MU meeting also offered practical advice to women about childcare, cookery, dressmaking and other domestic skills as well as encouraging women to set up knitting and sewing circles within the parish. The meetings gave women the chance to relax and enjoy each other's company with 'tea and a gossip', although leaders were warned to ensure that the religious and educational activities were not neglected.[27]

There is some evidence that working-class women found the tone of MU meetings patronising. In 1930, a woman who left the MU to join the WCG recalled why she favoured the guild's meetings. She explained that she 'had attended Mothers' Meetings, where ladies came and lectured on the domestic affairs in the workers' home that it was impossible for them to understand'.[28]

Although the membership of the MU included both working-class and middle-class women, there is no doubt that the organisation was very class-conscious and dominated by a leadership with middle-class sensibilities. *The Mothers' Union Journal* was first published in 1880 and was aimed specifically at 'cottage mothers', giving them advice on how best to care for their children and encouraging them to lead virtuous lives. Two years later the journal *Mothers in Council* was published to cater for ladies and 'mothers of the high classes', with tips on hiring domestic servants and articles on education and social work.[29] Whilst working-class women tended to be regarded as compliant members who were happy just attending the weekly meetings, middle-class women were encouraged to become official workers and play a more dynamic role in the running of the organisation.[30]

Active involvement in the organisation and administration of the MU branch was often regarded as part of the normal parochial duties of a clergyman's wife. This was certainly the case amongst the highest-ranking members of the Union. Nina Woods, for example, who served as Central President of the Union throughout the 1930s, was the widow of Theodore Woods, a former Bishop of Winchester. Frances Temple, elected Vice-President of the Union in 1942, was the wife of the Archbishop of Canterbury, William Temple. The close link with Canterbury continued in 1944 when Rosamond Fisher became Central President. Her husband, Geoffry

Fisher, was appointed Archbishop of Canterbury in 1945. Membership of the MU Executive, however, was not dependent on marriage to a high-ranking clergyman. Women elected to the Central Council were often well known for their interest in public welfare and their involvement in philanthropic work. Dame Beatrix Lyall, DBE, Vice-President of the MU during the late 1920s and 1930s, was well established as a public speaker on national, social and religious questions. Like many members of the MU leadership, Lyall was active not only in the MU but in a range of other organisations. A member of the Conservative Party, she was elected vice-chairman of London County Council in 1932. She also served on the Ladies Grand Council of the Primrose League and was an Executive member of numerous organisations for women including the NCW.[31]

As an organisation representing the interests of married Anglican women working within the home, the desire to protect the welfare rights of women and children was always an important consideration for the MU. In 1912 a Watch Committee was established to 'watch, give information and advise the Council as to desirable action with regard to legislative proposals in Parliament concerning matters affecting the welfare of the members of the Union'.[32] The setting up of this committee is significant as it signalled the willingness of the MU to participate in public debate and if necessary engage actively in campaign work in order to protect and enhance the quality of women's lives.

Although the MU is best known for its involvement in campaigning against divorce law reform, the evidence suggests that the Union, despite its non-party-political and non-feminist stance, was involved in active campaigning on a wide range of issues throughout the years 1928–64. The involvement of the Union in such campaigns, for example the payment of family allowances to mothers, better housing provision, improved maternity services and the appointment of women police, will all be explored in later chapters. Perhaps even more significant is the fact that the Union, despite its wariness of being associated with feminist or political groups, was willing to work alongside other women's organisations and to mount joint campaigns on issues of common interest. These organisations ranged from religious groups such as the Free Church Women's Council and the Young Women's Christian Association (YWCA) to voluntary women's organisations including the NCW, to which it was affiliated, and the WI.

Throughout its history there is no doubt that the MU endorsed traditional gender roles and that one of its central aims was to support women in their domestic role. The Union did however recognise that women had an important contribution to make not only to their families but also to their communities and to the nation. This belief was expressed in the

September 1934 edition of *The Mothers' Union Journal*, which stated that 'a mother's first place is in the home – not the only place, but the first. The mother is now a citizen of her country: she has a vote and with it a great responsibility.'[33] It is this aspect of the MU's work, its engagement with the notion of citizenship for women and its agency in participating in national campaigns to secure a better future for its members, which will be discussed and evaluated in the following chapters.

The Catholic Women's League

The increasing number of middle-class women participating in philanthropic, religious and educational work during the late nineteenth century resulted in the proliferation of mothers' meetings, new voluntary women's groups and organisations for young women. By the end of the century a number of national organisations had been established including the GFS, the MU and YWCA. In addition to the growing number of religious organisations, this period also witnessed a dramatic growth in the number of secular women's societies. For example the WCG, established in 1883 to draw attention to the interests of working-class housewives, was closely aligned to the co-operative and labour movement. The National Union of Women Workers (NUWW, later renamed the NCW) was set up in 1895 to promote the social, civil and religious welfare of women. The suffrage movement, active since the mid-nineteenth century, had spawned a myriad number of suffrage societies including the National Union of Women's Suffrage Societies (NUWSS), set up in 1866. The vast majority of these groups represented either the dominant Protestant tradition or were secular in nature. In 1906, in an attempt to redress the balance and raise the profile of Catholic women living in England, a new organisation, the CWL, was established.

The catalyst for the League's inauguration was news that a society for Catholic women in Germany had been set up by the Church hierarchy, as an alternative to the non-spiritual NCW.[34] This prompted Margaret Fletcher to make public her plans for an association of Catholic women in England. Fletcher, who became the League's first President, was the daughter of an Anglican vicar who in 1897 had converted to Catholicism. She was the editor of *The Crucible*, a journal promoting the importance of education for Catholic women and advocating greater participation in social work amongst middle-class Catholics.[35]

Addressing a meeting of the Catholic Ladies Conference in July 1906, Margaret Fletcher outlined her plans to develop a national organisation whose aim would be to encourage philanthropic work amongst Catholic laywomen.[36] Valerie Noble, in her study of the CWL, has suggested that the initial reaction of the Catholic clergy to the new organisation was one of suspicion. At a time when suffrage societies were demanding the parliamentary vote for women, parish priests expressed their disapproval and even horror at the thought of an association for educated Catholic women.[37] The bishops, however, are credited with taking a wider view in welcoming a new organisation for women in the belief that the Catholic hierarchy would be able to monitor and control the new organisation.[38]

The approval of the Catholic hierarchy was confirmed in December 1907, when the Archbishop of Westminster presided over the first general meeting of the League, and it was announced that Pope Pius X had given the organisation his blessing.[39] From the outset it was clear that the CWL was prepared to work within the parameters of Catholic social teaching and under the strict guidance of the Catholic Church. The League's constitution dictated that all policy decisions would be referred to the Cardinal for approval and that the work of the League would be carried out in a 'spirit of absolute and constant submission to the direction of ecclesiastical authority'.[40] It is important to note therefore that like the MU, the CWL was answerable to a male hierarchy and bound by the tenets of Church teaching. In both cases however adherence to religious belief and membership of a mixed-sex parent body did not prevent these two groups speaking out on behalf of their members and identifying areas of particular concern for housewives and mothers.

In January 1908, the first branch of the League was set up in Salford, followed by branches in Bournemouth and Leicester. Two years later CWL meetings were being held in Birmingham, Leeds and Preston. It was reported that twenty branches had been set up by the end of 1913, resulting in a total membership of 8,500 Catholic women.[41] The League appears to have been most successful in the Midlands and Northern England with Liverpool, Leeds and Birmingham attracting the greatest number of members throughout the inter-war period. In 1937 the Liverpool Archdiocesan Branch had 2,184 members, West Riding Branch (Leeds Diocese) 1,761 and the Birmingham Archdiocesan Branch 1,676 members.

Afternoon meetings consisted of debates, lectures and discussions on matters of Catholic and public interest as well as literary and historical subjects. Amongst the topics discussed during 1927 were 'The Early Training of Children' (Slough Section), 'Catholic Marriage' (West Riding Branch) and 'The Work of the League of Nations' (London Section).[42] Social evenings were organised to foster a sense of community spirit amongst Catholics and were doubtless welcomed by members as an entertaining night out. The CWL also encouraged its members to get involved in local community work. These activities included hospital and prison visits, setting up clubs and hostels for young female workers and raising funds for rescue homes to care for unmarried mothers. During the 1920s, the League set up hostels for unmarried women in Leeds, Liverpool and Woolwich.[43] In 1910 the CWL had affiliated to the newly established International Union of Catholic Women's Leagues (UILFC) and this link allowed the organisation to expand its interests beyond the borders of England and Wales and to unite with Catholic women around the world.[44]

Although membership of the CWL was open to all Catholic women, it is clear that these social and philanthropic activities appealed most of all to educated middle-class women. It was in an effort to persuade a greater number of working-class women to join the CWL that in 1914 the Union of Catholic Mothers (UCM) was established to cater for the needs of working-class mothers.[45] Mothers' meetings organised by the Union were intended to reinforce the traditional image of the Catholic mother who was 'by her nature fitted to home work … which is best adapted to preserve her modesty and promote the good upbringing of children and the well being of the family'.[46]

By the end of 1936, 18,000 mothers were members of the UCM and it was decided that the Union should become a separate society for Catholic mothers. As a result, the Union split from the CWL the following year and, as an independent organisation, affiliated to the National Board of Catholic Women (NBCW).[47] Although this division signified a major loss in membership for the CWL, the organisation survived and continued to represent the social and educational interests of over 22,000 Catholic women.[48] The stated aims of the organisation continued to be 'to unite Catholic women in a bond of common fellowship for the promotion of religious and intellectual interests and social and charitable work'.[49]

The women elected to serve on the National Executive of the League were prominent and wealthy members of the Catholic community known for their interest in religious and philanthropic work. Three of the League's National Presidents during the 1930s were recipients of the Papal Cross. Lady Petre (1930–32) was a former Divisional President of the League of Mercy and the Women's National Union Association. Mildred Hewitt (1933–35), a music critic and journalist, was a member of Chelsea Borough Council and Lady Winefride Elwes (1939–44) was a committee member of the National Adoption Society and a former President of the Lambeth Conservative Women's Association.[50]

One of the key national objectives of the CWL was to raise the profile of Catholic women and encourage its members to participate in social welfare work. During the First World War, the League provided huts and hostels at army camps in England and France for Catholic servicemen and women as well as sending a volunteer corps of nurses to Belgium. At home the League assisted the NUWW and the YWCA in setting up Women Patrols to safeguard the welfare of women and children during wartime, particularly young women who might be tempted to loiter around army camps and become involved in prostitution.[51] The League was also concerned about the health and welfare of mothers and their children during wartime and in 1915 opened a School for Mothers and Infant Welfare Clinic on the Old Kent Road in London.

At the end of the war the CWL, aware that women over thirty were about to be granted the parliamentary franchise, considered the implications of citizenship for women. In order to educate and inform Catholic women about their duties and entitlements as citizens, the League launched a citizens' campaign and published six citizenship leaflets dealing with questions of civil, social and moral responsibility.[52] It was also reported that twenty-seven study groups had been formed by the regional branches of the League to promote discussion on the importance of the vote for women.[53]

By 1924, the objectives of the League had expanded to reflect the growing political responsibility of women. The League now regarded itself as

> a national organisation for the formation and collective expression of Catholic public opinion among women, for securing the representation of Catholic interests upon all important public bodies and, for considering all civic and social responsibilities and duties of women in the light of Catholic principles.[54]

Although the League was anxious that women would make good use of their voting powers there is no evidence that the organisation was active in the suffrage campaign. Careful to avoid any political or controversial issue which might have offended the Catholic hierarchy, egalitarian feminist demands did not feature in the programme of the CWL. Instead, Catholic women interested in equal rights issues joined the Catholic Women's Suffrage Society (1911),[55] renamed the St Joan's Social and Political Alliance in 1928, whose aim was to 'secure the political, social and economic equality between men and women, and to further the work and usefulness of Catholic women as citizens.'[56]

In spite of the CWL's rejection of feminism, the organisation was willing to defend the welfare rights of women and mothers. In 1908 a Public Service Committee was formed to liaise with other women's societies and consider questions affecting the health and welfare of women and children. As a result of this co-operation the League became an affiliated member of the NUWW (later NCW) and worked with that organisation in campaigning for improved social services for women. Better housing, family allowances and adequate maternity services were amongst the legislative demands supported by the CWL during the inter-war period and into the 1940s, 1950s and early 1960s.

Throughout these years the League was never in any doubt that a woman's primary role was that of a wife and mother. In October 1936 Mrs Kemball, chairman of the Northern Province Public Service Committee, expressed this view when she stated that although it was

> no longer fashionable to believe that a woman's place is in the home ... I am old fashioned enough still to believe that the best work a woman can do is in the home ... and women who have the necessary time and training should come forward and take part in protecting it.[57]

In campaigning for the expansion of social welfare benefits for women, the intention of the League was to safeguard the traditional role of women as wives and mothers. But at the same time, it acknowledged that women were responsible citizens who had the right to demand these services from the state. In the following chapters it will be argued that the CWL, through its endorsement of woman's domestic role, was able to add its voice to that of other voluntary women's organisations seeking to ensure that the state provided adequate services and support to the hundreds of thousands of women who worked within the home.

The National Council of Women

The NCW, unlike the MU and CWL, was a secular society and independent of any parent body, but it shared with both of these groups the desire to 'promote the social, civil, moral and religious welfare of the community'.[58] The origins of the NCW date back to 1895 when a number of women involved in the Ladies Associations for the Care of Friendless Girls formed a national organisation to co-ordinate their philanthropic work amongst young working girls.[59] As a result the NUWW was established to 'provide a federation of women interested or engaged in philanthropy, in educational work, in industrial questions and social reforms'.[60] The organisation succeeded in attracting primarily middle-class women, some of whom were already involved in community work as Poor Law Guardians, lady visitors or as elected members of local councils.[61] Early members of the NUWW included Bertha Mason and Millicent Fawcett, both of whom were leading campaigners for women's suffrage.[62]

Although the NUWW supported the extension of the parliamentary franchise to women, the organisation did not wish to limit itself to one objective and remained committed to a diverse programme of charitable, educational and social welfare work. At its first Annual Conference held in 1895, the NUWW passed a resolution urging the government to repeal the 'reasonable cause to believe' clause in criminal law which allowed a man accused of assaulting a young girl to claim he believed she was over sixteen and had given her consent.[63] This decision marked the beginning of the society's involvement in extensive and wide-ranging campaigns for legislative reforms, the majority of which were intended to improve the legal, social and economic status of women.

Questions relating to the moral wellbeing of women and children preoccupied many of the women involved in the formation of the NUWW and within a year of its establishment a Moral Welfare Committee had been set up. This committee's objective was to investigate the international traffic in women and children, assaults on young women and children and the provision of 'rescue' homes for young prostitutes.[64] Education was also a high priority and in 1895 an Education Committee was set up to promote the teaching of domestic science in schools and to ensure good standards of training for women teachers.[65]

By 1900 the NUWW had set up twenty-eight branches in cities and towns around the country including Birmingham, Bristol, Oldham and Croydon.[66] As well as recruiting individual members, the NUWW hoped to unite a wide variety of women's groups with an interest in social welfare in order to form a national council of women. The ability of the National Union to create alliances between societies with diverse political, social and religious beliefs depended on its commitment to remain a non-party-political, non-sectarian and, perhaps most significantly, a non-feminist organisation. As a result of this the MU and CWL had both affiliated to the National Union before the outbreak of the First World War. Members of the WI were also free to represent their institute at local branch meetings of the NUWW. It was in this forum therefore that mainstream and conservative housewives organisations were able to mingle and work with feminist pressure groups and other societies representing women to achieve their common goal of publicly representing the interests of wives and mothers.

Affiliated societies were represented on the various sectional committees as well as the Representative Council and had the power to dissociate their organisation from any resolution passed by the National Union. This proviso was important as it allowed resolutions on controversial subjects, for example those in favour of divorce and birth control, to be discussed

without alienating groups opposed to these reforms. The affiliated societies could also submit resolutions to the Annual Conference and were
represented on the National Executive Committee, which met in London.

On the eve of the First World War, the NUWW had over one
hundred affiliated societies and the sectional committees had expanded
to include Legislation, Public Health, Insurance and Public Service.
Following the outbreak of war, the Union co-operated with government
ministries on projects such as the Food Economy Campaign, and the
President of the Union, Dame Ogilvie Gordon, was a regular speaker
at public meetings on matters such as food reform and the welfare of
women and children.[67] Another aspect of the Union's contribution to the
war effort was the recruitment, training and organisation of voluntary
Women Patrols. As mentioned earlier, the purpose of these patrols was to
supervise the behaviour of young women in public parks and streets to
ensure that 'khaki fever', the attraction of a man in uniform, did not lead
young women astray. Involvement in the Women Patrols also gave the
NUWW the opportunity to press for the employment of women police
officers, marking the beginning of a dynamic campaign which was to last
over thirty years.

Close co-operation between the government and the Union during
the war years presented an image of the NUWW as a patriotic and
responsible organisation willing to contribute to the war effort. This was
important at a time when suffrage societies campaigning for women's
equality were often regarded with suspicion and even hostility. The
increased participation of women in public life during the war years,
in the workforce and the armed services, also stimulated interest in the
activities of the NUWW. By the end of the war, 126 branches had been
set up and 156 societies had affiliated to the National Union.[68] In 1918 the
NUWW joined the International Council of Women (ICW) and changed
its name to the National Council of Women of Great Britain and Ireland.[69]
Having supported the suffrage campaign, the NCW welcomed the extension of the franchise to women over thirty and continued to work with
a number of other women's societies to secure the vote for women on
equal terms with men. For example, the Birmingham branch, which had
a membership of 600 women, co-operated with the NUSEC in organising Equal Franchise Meetings and sending letters to local MPs calling
on them to support the equal suffrage campaign.[70]

Throughout the 1920s the NCW campaigned 'for the removal of all
disabilities of women, whether legal, economic or social'.[71] However, the
Council stopped short of demanding dead-level equality for women or
publicly supporting a feminist agenda. Instead the NCW focused on the

contribution that women could make to national and local life. In 1929, Dame Ethel Shakespeare, President of the Birmingham branch of the NCW, reiterated this view when she said that 'while disclaiming a feminist attitude … women with their different points of view and functions have a special contribution to make towards the solution of public problems'.[72] In common with the CWL, the NCW appealed to educated middle-class women who were interested in the status of housewives and the positive influence that both housewives and professional women could have on public life. Although the Council did not provide the same level of practical weekly support to housewives as that given by the MU, WI and TG, its aim was to promote the interests of all women in society whether they be housewives or paid employees.

By the late 1920s, 145 societies had affiliated to the NCW, including egalitarian feminist groups such as the Open Door Council (ODC) and the Women's Freedom League (WFL). It is significant that working-class women's societies were not members of the Council, preferring to join the Standing Joint Committee of Industrial Women's Organisations (SJCIWO).[73] The unwillingness of the WCG and other working-class women's groups to work with the Council confirmed the fact that the NCW essentially represented the views of educated middle-class women. It is interesting to note that in 1929 a leaflet produced by the Birmingham branch described the Council as an organisation whose aim was to create 'a well informed public opinion among thinking women'.[74]

In 1928 individual membership of the Council in England and Wales was estimated at 14,289 and this remained fairly consistent throughout the 1930s along with an affiliated membership of some 135 societies. In common with the MU and the CWL, the leadership of the Council during this period included a large number of distinguished women who were well known in political and social circles. The Hon. Mrs Henrietta Franklin, President of the Council during the years 1925–27, was a former suffragist who in the 1930s served on the Executive of the National Council for Equal Citizenship (NCEC). A member of the Board of Management of the Liberal Jewish Synagogue, Mrs Franklin was also active in the League of Nations Union.

In 1929, Florence Keynes, former chairman of the Cambridge Board of Guardians, was elected President of the Council. A graduate of Newnham College, Cambridge, Keynes became Mayor of Cambridge in 1932. In 1935 another graduate of Cambridge, Eva Hartree JP, was elected Council President. Having worked as a town councillor for many years, Hartree was elected Mayor of Cambridge in 1924, the first woman to hold that position. She was also an Executive member of the WI and the ODC.[75]

Women MPs of all parties were invited to become honorary members of the Council. In 1934 Lady Astor, Thelma Cazalet, Florence Horsbrugh, Eleanor Rathbone, Megan Lloyd George, Mavis Tate and Irene Ward all served on the Executive Committee, establishing a useful link between the Council and the House of Commons.

During the years 1928–64 the NCW had two principal objectives: to increase the representation of women in local and national government and to campaign for legislative reforms which would protect and improve the status of women in society. Martin Pugh has suggested that the NCW was 'too widely drawn to be really coherent'.[76] This view can be challenged, however, when the impact of the Council's role in key campaigns, for example equal pay, the employment of women police, divorce law reform and legalised abortion, is assessed. These activities and the Council's determination to ensure that women enjoyed 'a freer life with wider opportunities'[77] will be explored to show that the NCW contributed in a meaningful way to the continuing struggle for women's equality throughout the mid-twentieth century.

The National Federation of Women's Institutes

One of the principal objectives of the WI Movement, an organisation for women living in rural areas, was to ensure that 'countrywomen need no longer lead lives of utter loneliness. They can form an Institute, they can meet and make friends, they can enjoy acting and dancing and singing, they can study the past and consider the present questions of the day.'[78] Modelled on the successful Canadian Rural Women's Institutes,[79] the WI was undoubtedly one of the most dynamic organisations for women during the period 1928–64.[80] Women's institutes came to Britain in 1915 when Mrs Alfred Watt, a Canadian woman involved with the Village Institutes in British Columbia, persuaded the Agricultural Organisation Society (AOS)[81] to set up a similar network of institutes in England and Wales.

As a result the first WI was founded in Anglesey on 25 September 1915.[82] The original purpose of the WI was to give women in rural areas the opportunity to study home economies and to stimulate their interest in agriculture and agricultural industries. Local institutes also provided centres for education and social intercourse, giving the hundreds of thousands of women living in relatively isolated communities the opportunity to meet with other women and spend some time away from the responsibilities of their homes and families.[83] By the end of 1916 forty local WIs had been established and the AOS appointed Lady Gertrude

Denman[84] to chair a committee set up to oversee the future development of the movement. Lady Denman, who was chairman of the WI for thirty years, played a major role in protecting the democratic nature of the organisation and highlighting the needs of rural women through the work of the WI Movement. It soon became clear that there was a huge demand amongst women for local WIs and by the end of the First World War 760 had been started up with an estimated membership of some 50,000 women.[85]

Throughout this period of rapid expansion, the WI Committee received financial backing from the Ministry of Agriculture. The Ministry regarded the work of local institutes as an ideal way to stimulate wartime food production in rural areas. By 1917, however, it had become clear that the Ministry hoped to incorporate the WI into its Food Production Department, thereby assuming control of the organisation. To avoid this certain loss of independence, Lady Denman called a meeting of representatives from 137 institutes and it was agreed to set up a National Federation of Women's Institutes.[86]

The organisation was to be non-party-political and non-sectarian with its administration set up on clear democratic principles. Membership of the movement would provide women with an education in the workings of democracy. Local institutes were to be run along democratic lines with elected officials and with resolutions passed to the national body for consideration. A postal ballot gave every member the opportunity to elect the National Executive Committee, whose duty it was 'to provide an organisation with the object of enabling women to take an effective part in rural life and development'.[87] Local institutes were represented on the County Federation which in turn appointed representatives to the National Consultative Council. This body advised the Executive Committee and selected which resolutions would be discussed at the Annual General Meeting.

With the extension of the parliamentary franchise to women at the end of the war, it was hoped that the democratic structure of the WI would prepare women for responsible citizenship and give them the opportunity to become familiar with the trappings of democracy. Inez Jenkins, in her history of the WI, wrote that members were always encouraged to 'understand the meaning and importance of resolutions and amendments, accurate minutes, correct accounts, secret ballots … and generally settle the affairs of the Institute to suit the wishes of the greatest number'.[88] At the local level the primary objective of WI was to cater for the interests and needs of women living in the countryside.[89] Membership was open to all women, subject to a two-shilling annual subscription, but it soon became clear that the majority of members were married housewives and mothers who appreciated the recognition given to their work by the movement.[90] The WI was successful in its aim of attracting both working-class and middle-class members. However, in keeping with the four other housewives' organisations included in this study, the leadership of the organisation remained firmly in the hands of educated middle-class women. Margaret Andrews writes that the majority of WI officials were middle-class women due to traditional class hegemony and because many working-class women, who managed without the help of domestic servants, had neither the time nor the energy to undertake administrative work for the movement.[91]

WI meetings were held monthly and usually took place in the local village or community hall. Records suggest that the most popular activities amongst local members were handicrafts, music, drama and agricultural pursuits, including bee keeping and fruit preservation. A typical meeting, which lasted about two hours, dealt first of all with business outstanding followed by a lecture or demonstration and concluded with the 'social half hour' of tea, music and conversation. During the 1920s, WI branches began to organise classes for their members to reflect particular interests developed at the local meetings. As Jenkins observed, 'having learned to meet together, work together and talk freely together, Institute members now wanted to learn more about many things'.[92] Classes in arts and crafts, domestic subjects such as cooking and dressmaking as well as dancing and singing became increasingly popular throughout the inter-war period. Adult education classes also became a feature of village life as a result of the association between the WI, the Workers Educational Association and the Adult Education Federation.[93]

Andrews, in her study of the WI movement, has argued that the provision of classes in handicrafts, cookery and sewing not only gave some recognition to the work performed by women in the home but demonstrated that their work was of value to the community. She suggests that WI classes, complete with graded examinations, exhibitions and competitions, acknowledged women's work as a worthwhile and skilled occupation and as a result did much to raise the status of housework during this period.[94] In common with the MU, CWL and NCW, the WI did not challenge the traditional role of women working within the home. Like other housewives' organisations active at this time, the WI represented women who accepted their domestic role and who wished to be part of an association whose aim it was to enhance the status of housewives within British society. An article published in the WI's journal, *Home and Country*, in June 1942, clearly illustrates this aspect of the organisation's work:

women doing their traditional and specific job of running a household and bringing up a family should be considered as important, as responsible and as much worthy of respect as women doing the kind of job ... done equally well by either sex ... their work is just as vital if not more so.[95]

In addition to promoting the role of women as housewives the WI also encouraged members to contribute to the life of their local communities because, as housewives, mothers and citizens, women had the potential to instil a 'richer sense of citizenship' within local and national life.[96] It was this understanding of the need for active citizenship amongst women that underpinned much of the work of the WI in the decades following the enfranchisement of women on equal terms with men.

In February 1928 *Home and Country* celebrated the fact that the movement now represented over 240,000 women. The editor observed that the WI was now a national organisation and that the 'educated opinion of 4,000 Women's Institutes can be the deciding factor in questions of far reaching importance'.[97] To this end the organisation promoted citizenship education for its members and throughout the years 1928–64 used its influence to campaign for a number of important legislative reforms, including the introduction of equal pay, the provision of adequate public housing, improved maternity services and health care for women. The involvement of the WI in all these campaigns will be discussed in more detail later and its links with the vibrant network of voluntary women's organisations including the NCW, MU, CWL the TG, will be revealed.

It may now seem somewhat incongruous that an organisation most often associated with handicrafts, jam making and the singing of the hymn 'Jerusalem' was active in the campaign to secure citizenship rights for women. However, when the background of some of the women involved in the organisation during this period is considered, these activities do not seem so surprising. Many of those elected to the National Executive had close connections with the suffrage movement and were involved in numerous campaigns to improve the health and welfare of women and children.

Lady Denman, for example, was a tireless campaigner on women's issues through her work with the WI Movement and her involvement in the National Birth Control Council. At a Memorial Service held in her honour in June 1954, she was recalled for her 'determination to do everything she could to help the women of her country ... to prevent them being trampled upon'.[98] Grace Hadow and Helena Auerbach, who served as Vice-Chairman and Treasurer of the National Federation respectively, had both been involved in the suffrage movement and supported the active participation of women in local and national affairs.

Grace Hadow, who was appointed national Vice-Chairman of the WI in 1933, hoped that joining the movement would give women the opportunity to 'realize their responsibility towards the community in which they live and, from an interest in their own village and their own country, come to see the connection between their affairs and those of the nation at large'.[99] Other prominent members of the WI National Executive included the former Liberal MP and feminist Margaret Wintringham and Megan Lloyd George, elected to Parliament as a Liberal MP in 1929. Both women were members of the NCEC and the TG, and Lloyd George also served as an honorary member of the NCW. These multiple memberships once again demonstrate the intricate associational networks existing amongst women active in voluntary women's organisations at this time.

Yet in spite of the involvement of many prominent feminist activists, the WI never regarded itself as a feminist organisation. Janet Courtney, in her history of the movement published in 1933, wrote that 'the Institute movement is a feminine movement, but so far it has not shown itself feminist. It contains too large a proportion of married women. No doubt a husband can be a poor thing but a wise wife is not going to tell him so.'[100] Rather than adopting a narrow feminist agenda, the WI catered for the hundreds of thousands of women who accepted their domestic role but who wished to engage in activities outside the home in an environment free from religious and political affiliations.

In terms of membership this policy proved incredibly successful and by 1937 the organisation had grown to 318,000 members, representing both working-class and middle-class women living in rural areas. In common with the MU, CWL and NCW, the WI was keen to establish international connections with like-minded women around the world and in 1933 joined the Associated Country Women of the World. This desire to support, educate and represent rural women in the broadest context possible resulted in the participation of the WI in a number of key campaigns to enhance women's lives at this time.

The National Union of Townswomen's Guilds

The success of the WI movement in attracting a mass membership by the end of the 1920s did not go unnoticed amongst the smaller post-suffrage feminist societies, most notably the NUSEC.[101] Whilst mainstream voluntary women's societies increased in size and popularity, the NUSEC had suffered a decline in membership with only forty-eight branches remaining in 1935.[102] Throughout the 1920s the NUSEC, under the leadership of Eleanor Rathbone,[103] continued to campaign for the extension of the franchise to women over the age of twenty-one, so that women would be entitled to the vote on equal terms with men. The NUSEC also championed egalitarian reforms such as equal pay, equal opportunities and an equal moral standard now that women's right to political citizenship had been won. At the same time, the NUSEC highlighted the specific needs of women as wives and mothers by supporting the introduction of family allowances, the right to birth control information and the principle of protective legislation for women.

The 1928 Equal Franchise Act signified the end of the suffrage campaign and left the NUSEC to consider its future role as a woman's organisation.[104] Margery Corbett Ashby,[105] who succeeded Rathbone as President of the NUSEC in 1928, expressed her concern about the five million newly enfranchised women when she asked 'what good is the fact that women have the vote, if they don't know how to use it?'[106] Corbett Ashby, along with Eva Hubback, former Parliamentary Secretary of the NUSEC, quickly surmised that some form of education in citizenship was essential if women were to play a more active part in democratic society. Impressed by the success of the WI, Corbett Ashby observed 'how marvellously they [the WI] have developed citizenship, initiative and self-reliance among the countrywomen. Our aim should be to combine the feminism of the National Union with the social activities of the Rural Women's Institutes.'[107] This statement is significant as it underlines the original intention of the TG Movement to merge feminist ideology with the more traditional and domestic interests of the vast majority of women.

The fact that the WI only established local institutes in towns and villages with a population under 4,000 gave the NUSEC the idea of setting up guilds for women in larger towns and cities. Although the NUSEC regarded the principal purpose of the proposed guilds as a way of instructing women in citizenship, the example of the WI made clear that to attract large numbers of women it was necessary to offer members a wide range of social and educational activities. As a result, the programme devised by the NUSEC for the work of TGs was divided into four major themes: civics, arts, handicrafts and home-craft.[108] Early in 1929, with funding from a £100 donation provided by Eleanor Rathbone, one of four experimental guilds was set up in the market town of Haywards Heath in Sussex.[109] The guild was established near to the home of Corbett Ashby, who became its first President, and over 120 women attended the inaugural meeting.[110] Following the success of the first guilds, the NUSEC set up a special committee in March 1929 to oversee the launch of a national TG Movement.

Gertrude Horton and Alice Franklin, who in 1933 were appointed National Secretary and Honorary Secretary of the movement respectively, were responsible for much of the early organisation of the TGs. Both women came from families with a strong suffragist tradition. Horton's mother had been an active supporter of Christabel Pankhurst and Franklin's brother Hugh was one of the few men to be arrested for militant suffragist activities.[111] At the age of twenty-eight Gertrude Horton, then an unemployed teacher, was appointed Parliamentary Secretary of the NUSEC whilst Franklin, a Care Committee worker in London, was invited by her cousin Eva Hubback to get involved in the establishment of local TGs. Both women went on to draw up the constitution and rules for the new organisation and supervised the administration of the TGs for over twenty years.[112]

By the end of 1929, twenty-six local TGs had been established. The new guilds provided women living in urban areas with a wide variety of activities including educational, social and leisure pursuits. Meetings were held once a month, usually in the early evening, and depending on the size of the guild and on local facilities, took place in members' homes, schoolrooms and church halls.[113] Early guild programmes included talks, lectures and debates on subjects ranging from the problem of maternal mortality, the need for international disarmament to the benefits of electricity in the home and the use of cosmetics. From the outset, handicrafts and home-craft proved to be the most popular activities offered by local guilds. In common with local WI, classes and demonstrations in glove making, cookery, dressmaking and embroidery were clearly favoured by members who attended these meetings in large numbers and who enjoyed the opportunity to develop their domestic skills in the company of other women.

In spite of the diverse programme offered, it would appear that there was some reluctance amongst women to join local guilds affiliated to the overtly feminist NUSEC.[114] To overcome this difficulty, Alice Franklin proposed that TGs should 'provide a common meeting ground for women irrespective of creed and party, for their wider education including social intercourse.'[115] In practice this meant that controversial subjects relating to religious, political and, most notably, feminist issues could not be discussed at guild meetings, thereby preventing the TG Movement from ever becoming an overtly feminist, party political or religious organisation. In 1949, A. A. Mitchell, a member of the Executive Committee of the TG, recalled, so many of us in the early days were already keenly interested in some social or national cause and were eager to enthuse fellow members with our views. It was soon, however, made clear to us that to provide a ready-made audience for the insistence upon one side of any subject was not the function of the NUTG.[116]

By 1932 it was obvious that TGs were more popular amongst women than the more traditionally feminist Societies for Equal Citizenship set up to continue the equal rights campaign work of the NUSEC.[117] This fact, coupled with the divergence between the political work of the NUSEC and the educational and social activities offered by TGs, left little doubt that the TG Movement had outgrown the narrower feminist agenda of the NUSEC. At its annual meeting in 1932, the NUSEC resolved to divide its work into two separate and independent organisations. The NUSEC was renamed the National Union of Guilds for Citizenship (later changed to the National Union of Townswomen's Guilds) and a new body, the National Council for Equal Citizenship (NCEC), was set up to co-ordinate the political and egalitarian work previously undertaken by the NUSEC.

Eva Hubback was appointed the first President of the NCEC and the new organisation pledged to continue the feminist agenda of the NUSEC to secure 'all such reforms as are necessary or may help to secure a real equality of liberties, status and opportunities between men and women'.[118] Conversely, the National Union of Guilds for Citizenship relinquished all feminist and egalitarian aspirations. Its principal function was to be educational not political, a fact reflected in its central objective 'to encourage the education of women to enable them as citizens to make the best contribution towards the common good'.[119]

The TG reorganisation on an educational basis and its commitment to provide women with a common meeting ground meant that it was unable to affiliate with organisations 'identified with any form of propaganda'. Because of this it was announced 'with regret' that the TG had to withdraw both from the NCW and the League of Nations Union and would not affiliate to the NCEC.[120] Women's Citizen's Associations (WCAs) and Societies for Equal Citizenship were not invited to join the new organisation on the grounds that 'there is … little room for societies whose objects include political and feminist activities, and the National Union is now for all practical purposes a Townswomen's Guild organisation'.[121]

The TG was therefore first and foremost an educational organisation, providing centres for women to study social and civic problems as well as handicrafts, arts, music and drama. Members were encouraged to 'educate themselves to take an effective part in national life, and to consider the problems of social welfare'.[122] Local guilds were non-party and non-sectarian and open to women and girls on payment of a two-shillings annual subscription.[123] Regional Federations co-ordinated the provincial work of the movement while the National Executive Committee meeting in London was responsible for administration and the enactment of policy agreed at the Annual Council Meeting. Like the WI the TG prided itself on the democratic nature of the organisation. It was argued that participation in guild life gave members the opportunity to gain 'practical experience in the science of self-government' and encouraged women 'to take their share as citizens in the management of their town and country'.[124] Although TGs were non-party, individual members were always encouraged to join political organisations as well as local pressure groups and urged to stand as candidates in local elections to increase the representation of women throughout the country.

The growth of the TG in the 1930s owed much to financial support from the Carnegie Trust and National Council of Social Service.[125] The fact that these funds were only available to non-political organisations was no doubt a further incentive for the TG's policy of remaining a non-feminist and non-party association. The TG also worked closely with the WI, which had provided the model for the guild movement and was regarded as a firm ally during this period. Occasional joint conferences were held to foster greater co-operation and continuing good relations between the two societies.[126] By 1939, 544 Guilds had been established nationwide representing an overall membership of 54,000 women. Above all, the Guilds hoped to attract the thousands of married women living in the new suburban housing estates on the outskirts of towns and cities. The TG recognised that many women who lived in these areas were often 'cut off from all interests' and spent 'a lot of the day alone in a labour saving house'.[127]

Becoming a member of a TG gave women the opportunity to meet 'new friends and acquire new interests' outside the home.[128] Although the movement claimed to represent a broad cross-section of urban women, the vast majority of officials and members were middle-class wives and mothers. In common with the MU, CWL, NCW and WI, the TG reflected a predominantly middle-class outlook and class divisions were not easily overcome within the organisation. Writing about her experience of guild membership during the Second World War, one woman explained that she was 'very disappointed with the cold, unfriendly attitude of middle-class women to their working-class sisters in the Guild. So far all attempts to mix these sections in Guild life have broken down.'[129]

Throughout the 1930s, arts, crafts and cookery classes remained the most popular activities, with citizenship education taking a poor second place. In 1935, the National Executive defended the 'study and practice of handicrafts' because it allowed members to 'develop their creative powers and enlarge their outlook on life, and so make a better contribution towards the common good.'[130] Tensions arose during the 1930s and 1940s as the organisation tried to balance its desire to provide a common meeting ground for women, offer education and support for wives and mothers and ensure that as a national organisation the TG spoke out on behalf of its members on public questions.

As a result the organisation was careful to support only campaigns considered to be of relevance to its members and which would not create any division within the movement. Yet in spite of this caution, the TG clearly understood the difficulties that women experienced in trying to balance their roles as wives and mothers alongside their interests outside the home. Margery Corbett Ashby expressed her hope that the new organisation would

> see members so confident of equality that they can devote themselves to the improvement of their homes without feeling shut in by them; the Guilds should rationalize cookery and home-craft as men rationalize their businesses, without fear of losing their university education or their claim to equal entry into industry and profession.[131]

In addition to Corbett Ashby the TG could boast of having large number of well-known activists within its ranks. In 1932, Lady Cynthia Colville JP, a former lady in waiting to the Queen, was appointed Honorary President of the Union and Lady Denman was appointed Vice-President.[132] Eleanor Rathbone and Edith Picton-Tubervill, both members of the NCEC Executive Committee, also served as Vice-Presidents of the TG during the 1930s. In 1933 Eva Hubback, President of the NCEC, was elected to the Executive Committee of the now-renamed National Union of Townswomen's Guilds and two years later she too was appointed Vice-President. The involvement of so many prominent feminists on the executive of the TG reveals the crossover in membership between the leadership of the mainstream TG and the egalitarian feminist NCEC.

Family allowances, improved maternity services, good housing, pension rights and universal healthcare were all included amongst the campaigns supported by the TG throughout the period 1930 to 1964. The evidence would suggest therefore that the TG did engage in political campaigns when the cause was deemed appropriate and where the intervention of housewives could make a difference. By exploring the role of the TG in these campaigns the orthodox view that the TG 'represented less an extension of the NUSEC tradition into the ranks of ordinary women than a diversion and a departure from it'[133] will be challenged.

This overview of the origins and aims of middle-class voluntary women's organisations reveals the extent of the diversity between these five popular and successful housewives' associations throughout the mid-twentieth century. The MU and CWL were conservative, religious groups operating within wider mixed-sex organisations and with the consent and approval of their respective church hierarchies. Conversely the NCW, WI and TG did not answer to any parent body and prided themselves on their non-sectarian stance but were always careful to distance themselves from party politics and what could be perceived as a narrow feminist agenda. Although these three organisations shared key characteristics they targeted different groups of women in terms of membership.

These differences are important and should not be overlooked. However, the similarities between the five organisations are even more significant. All five endorsed the domestic role of women and were united in their desire to sustain and protect traditional family life. The women who joined these organisations were given the opportunity to meet other women outside the home, to make friends and develop their interests in the arts and current affairs. These activities were an extension of women's work as wives and mothers and at no point did they challenge the division of labour within the home. This common aim to enhance women's lives and to promote domesticity for women allowed these five organisations to work together on common causes. As a result there is little evidence of any tension emerging amongst these groups despite the fact that they represented a wide diversity of women: urban, rural, professionals and housewives.

As a result, mainstream organisations offered more to women than egalitarian feminist groups. This was because their main objective was social and educational rather than political. But this focus did not result in a lack of engagement with politics or a failure to appreciate the power that the parliamentary franchise had bestowed upon their members. Each of the five groups recognised that women as wives, mothers and citizens had an important contribution to make to society. Women joining housewives' organisations were encouraged to use their vote, stand for election and to take an interest in public affairs. They were encouraged and expected to support national and local campaigns on issues affecting their lives, the lives of their families, their community and the nation.

What these five organisations also had in common was their ability to create an effective network of women's organisations in mid-twentieth-century Britain. The profile of each organisation reveals the strong links between the five groups as well as the affiliation of leaders and members to a range of other charitable, political, feminist and campaigning groups. All of this activism and agency on the part of women involved in voluntary women's organisations has at times been overlooked. This omission has been based on the assumption that housewives' associations dominated by middle-class sensibilities and eschewing feminism do not merit inclusion in the history of the women's movement. The following chapters will challenge this view and will begin by evaluating the significance of citizenship, citizenship rights and active citizenship, within the history of each of these five voluntary women's organisations.

Notes

1 The number of marriages in Britain began to rise in the 1930s and this trend continued until the 1970s. In the period 1931–35, 57.3 women (per thousand of the population) married. For 1936–40, 73.3 married and by 1956–60 this had risen to 82.6. See Pugh, *Women and the Women's Movement*, p. 223.

2 P. Thane, 'Family Life and "Normality" in Post-War British Culture', in R. Bessel and D. Schumann (eds), *Life After Death: Approaches to a Cultural and Social History of Europe during the 1940s and 1950s* (Cambridge: Cambridge University Press, 2003), p. 198.

3 J. Giles, 'A Home of One's Own: Women and Domesticity in England, 1918–1950', *Women's Studies International Forum*, 16:3 (1993), p. 239.

4 See F. Prochaska, 'A Mother's Country: Mothers' Meetings and Family Welfare in Britain, 1850–1950', *History, The Journal of the Historical Association*, 74 (1989).

5 *Ibid.*, p. 381.

6 For a detailed account of the origins of the MU see Moyse, *A History of the Mothers' Union*, pp. 17–43.

7 O. Parker, *For the Family's Sake: A History of the Mothers' Union 1876–1976* (Folkestone: Bailey and Swinfen, 1975), p. 5.

8 *Ibid.*

9 *The Mothers' Union Journal* (1893), p. 65, cited in Moyse, *A History of the Mothers' Union*, p. 32.

10 *Ibid.*, pp. 253–255.

11 *Ibid.*, pp. 18–28.

12 Parker, *For the Family's Sake*, p. 14.

13 Moyse, *A History of the Mothers' Union*, p. 28–29.

14 B. Harrison, 'For Church, Queen and Family: The Girls' Friendly Society 1874–1920', *Past and Present*, 61 (1973), p. 109.

15 Parker, *For the Family's Sake*, p. 15. For a full discussion of the MU's expansion overseas see Moyse, *A History of the Mothers' Union*, pp. 78–94.

16 *Ibid.*, p. 41.

17 In 1940 the Holy Cross St Pancras branch of the MU in London was disbanded by the local vicar because of its small membership in spite of protests from the members. Mary Sumner House Archive, London (hereafter MSH), *Holy Cross St Pancras Minute Book, 1931–40*.

18 MSH, Central Council Minutes, Vol. 9 (1930–32), 'Minutes of the Mothers' Union Central Council', December 1930, p. 58.

19 *The Mothers' Union Journal* (January 1926), p. 1.

20 The MU campaign against divorce will be discussed in detail in Chapter 3.

21 MSH, Central Council Minutes, Vol. 10 (1932–37), 'Minutes of the Mothers' Union Central Council', June 1934, p. 160.

22 Parker, *For the Family's Sake*, p. 91.

23 Prochaska, 'A Mother's Country', p. 383.

24 *The Mothers' Union Workers' Paper*, 204 (December 1930), p. 18.

25 MSH, Central Council Minutes, Vol. 10 (1932–37), 'Minutes of the Mothers' Union Central Council', December 1935, p. 314.

26 MSH, Central Council Minutes, Vol. 10 (1932–37), 'Minutes of the Mothers' Union Central Council', June 1934, p. 136.

27 *The Mothers' Union Workers' Paper*, 420 (January 1949), p. 4.

28 P. Hollis, *Women in Public Life: The Women's Movement 1850–1900, Documents of the Victorian Women's Movement* (London: George Allen and Unwin, 1979), p. 277.

29 Parker, *For the Family's Sake*, p. 15.

30 This predominance of upper and middle-class women amongst the leadership of the MU supports James Hinton's argument that middle-class women's organisations reinforced claims for middle-class authority at this time. J. Hinton, *Women, Social Leadership, and the Second World War* (Oxford: Oxford University Press, 2002), pp. 1–15.

31 *Mothers in Council*, 232 (September 1948), p. 116.

32 Moyse, *A History of the Mothers' Union*, p. 120.

33 *The Mothers' Union Journal*, 158 (September 1934), p. 11.

34 The German National Council of Women was affiliated to the International Council of Women (1888) representing associations of women working for the common welfare of the community.

35 M. Ryan, *Yesterday Recalled: A Jubilee History of the Catholic Women's League 1906–1981* (London: CWL, 1981), pp. 2–3.

36 V. Noble, 'A mission for women: a reflection on the history of women's organisations in the Catholic Church and their relevance within the contemporary Church' (Diploma dissertation, University of London, 1991), p. 5.

37 *Ibid.*, p. 9.

38 *Ibid.*

39 *The Catholic Women's League Magazine*, 251 (September 1932), p. 15.

40 Noble, 'A mission for women', p. 11.

41 *The Catholic Women's League Magazine*, 251 (September 1932), p. 15.

42 *The Catholic Women's League Magazine*, 195 (January 1928), p. 11.

43 *The Catholic Women's League Magazine*, 252 (October 1932), p. 21.

44 In 1952 the UILFC changed its name to the World Union of Catholic Women's Organisations (WUCWO).

45 Noble, 'A mission for women', p. 41.

46 Pope Leo XIII, *Rerum Novarum: The Condition of the Working Classes* (Encyclical, 1891), p. 58.

47 The National Board of Catholic Women (1937) acted as an umbrella organisation for catholic women's groups. The CWL and the Junior Catholic Women's League also affiliated to the National Board in 1937.

48 *The Catholic Women's League Magazine*, 306 (April 1937), p. 7.

49 *The Catholic Women's League Magazine*, 487 (January 1953), p. 5.

50 *The Hutchinson Woman's Who's Who* (London: Hutchinson, 1934).

51 The involvement of voluntary women's organisations in Women Patrols will be discussed in Chapter 5.

52 *The Catholic Women's League Magazine*, 90 (April 1919), p. 21.

53 *The Catholic Women's League Magazine*, 252 (October 1932), p. 23.

54 *The Catholic Women's Outlook*, 1:1 (April 1924), p. 1.

55 See F. Mason, 'The Newer Eve: The Catholic Women's Suffrage Society in England, 1911–1923', *Catholic History Review*, 4 (1986).

56 *The Catholic Citizen*, 14:10 (15 November 1928), p. 97.

57 *The Catholic Women's League Magazine*, 302 (December 1936), p. 102.

58 *Handbook of the National Council of Women of Great Britain 1931–32* (1932), p. 61.

59 In 1895 there were 125 Associations for the Care of Friendless Girls. The associations were made up of educated middle-class women involved in social reform work. M. Alfred, *During Six Reigns: Landmarks in the History of the National Council of Women of Great Britain* (London: NCW, 1955), p. 5.

60 *Ibid.*, p. 13. For a detailed organisational history of the NCW see D. Glick, *The National Council of Women of Great Britain: The First One Hundred Years* (London: NCW, 1995).

61 See P. Hollis, *Ladies Elect: Women in English Local Government 1865–1914* (Oxford: Oxford University Press, 1987) and Lewis, *Women in England 1870–1950*, pp. 92–97.

62 In 1897 Millicent Fawcett set up the National Union of Women's Suffrage Societies, the leading non-militant suffrage society, and in 1902 Bertha Mason was appointed Treasurer. See M. Pugh, *Women's Suffrage in Britain 1867–1928* (London: Historical Association, 1980).

63 The offending clause was finally removed with the introduction of the 1922 Criminal Law Amendment Act, signifying the end of a long campaign on the part of the NCW.

64 P. Adam (ed.), *Women in Council: The Jubilee Book of the National Council of Women of Great Britain* (Oxford: Oxford University Press, 1945), p. 58.

65 *Ibid.*

66 The branches were made up of individual members and representatives of local societies supporting the work of the Union.

67 Adam, *Women in Council*, p. 24.

68 *Ibid.*, p. 70.

69 In 1924 following the establishment of the Irish Free State, the Irish branches of the NCW broke away to form the National Council of Women of Ireland.

70 Birmingham City Library, Birmingham (hereafter BCL), MSS 841 B/31, Birmingham Branch Records (May 1925–January 1931), 'Minutes of the Birmingham Branch of the National Council of Women', 2 February 1928.

71 *Handbook of the National Council of Women of Great Britain 1931–32* (1932), p. 61.

72 BCL, Birmingham Branch Records, MSS 841 B/4 (May 1925–January 1931), 'Minutes of the Birmingham Branch of the National Council of Women', 20 April 1929, p. 129.

73 The Standing Joint Committee of Industrial Women's Organisations was set up in 1916 to 'represent the women of the political, industrial and co-operative movements of the workers'. The Committee was closely tied to the Labour Party and its offices were based at the Labour Party Headquarters. Gordon and Doughan, *Dictionary of Women's Organisations*, pp. 105–106.

74 BCL, MSS 841 B/4, NCW Birmingham Branch Records.

75 Adam, *Women in Council*, pp. 32–34.

76 Pugh, *Women and the Women's Movement*, p. 69.

77 *Women in Council*, 68 (May 1946), p. 2.

78 'Chairman's Address to the 1928 Annual General Meeting', *National Federation of Women's Institutes 12th Annual Report 1928* (1928).

79 Rural Women's Institutes were first established in Canada in 1897 at Stoney Creek, Ontario. J. W. Robertson Scott, *The Story of The Women's Institute Movement* (Kingham: Village Press, 1925), p. 8.

80 For a detailed account of the history of the WI see: Andrews, *The Acceptable Face of Feminism*, I. Jenkins, *The History of the Women's Institute Movement of England and Wales* (Oxford: Oxford University Press, 1953) and S. Goodenough, *Jam and Jerusalem* (Glasgow: Collins, 1977). See also Gibson, *Beyond Jerusalem*.

81 The Agricultural Organisation Society was set up in 1901, following the union of the British Agricultural Society and the National Agricultural Union. Robertson Scott, *The Story of the Women's Institute Movement*, p. 17.

82 *Ibid.*, pp. 20–32.

83 *Ibid.*, p. 51.

84 Lady Denman was the daughter of Viscount Cowdray, a liberal who supported women's suffrage, from whom she inherited an interest in feminism and a considerable fortune. Goodenough, *Jam and Jerusalem*, p. 27.

85 Pugh, *Women and the Women's Movement in Britain*, p. 227.

86 Andrews, *The Acceptable Face of Feminism*, pp. 17–40.

87 *National Federation of Women's Institutes Procedure at Meetings* (1949), p. 26.

88 Jenkins, *The History of the Women's Institute Movement*, p. 46.

89 To protect the rural character of the organisation, it had been decided that Women's Institutes should only be set up in villages with a population of less than 4,000.

90 Pugh, *Women and the Women's Movement in Britain*, p. 228.

91 M. Morgan, 'The acceptable face of feminism: the Women's Institute Movement 1915–1960' (Ph.D. dissertation, University of Sussex, 1992), p. 92.

92 Jenkins, *The History of the Women's Institute Movement*, p. 50.

93 In 1933 it was reported that fifteen institutes in the Bedfordshire Federation were associated with the Workers Educational Association and adult education classes had been set up in twenty-seven villages. *National Federation of Women's Institutes Annual Report 1933* (1933), p. 80.

94 M. Morgan, 'Jam Making, Cuthbert Rabbit and Cakes: Redefining Domestic Labour in the Women's Institute, 1915–60', in *Rural History*, 7:2 (1996), pp. 207–219.

95 *Home and Country*, 24:6 (June 1942), p. 114.

96 *Home and Country*, 10:8 (August 1928), p. 1.

97 *Home and Country*, 10:2 (February 1928), p. 1. The involvement of the WI in citizenship education is discussed in Chapter 2.

98 Cited in P. Kitchen, *For Home and Country: War, Peace and Rural Life as Seen through the Pages of the Women's Institutes' Magazine, 1919–1959* (London: Ebury, 1990), p. 159.

99 Cited in Goodenough, *Jam and Jerusalem*, p. 29.

100 J. Courtney, *Countrywomen in Council* (Oxford: Oxford University Press, 1933), p. 151.

101 Following the extension of the franchise to women over thirty in 1918 the National Union of Women's Suffrage Societies changed its name to the National Union of

Societies for Equal Citizenship (NUSEC).

102 Pugh, *Women and the Women's Movement*, p. 242.

103 In 1919 Eleanor Rathbone succeeded Millicent Fawcett as President of the NUSEC.

104 J. Lewis, 'In Search of a Real Equality: Women between the Wars', in F. Gloversmith (ed.), *Class, Culture and Social Change: A New View of the 1930s* (Brighton: Harvester Press, 1980).

105 Margery Corbett Ashby was a well-known feminist, pacifist and suffragist who had been appointed secretary of the NUWSS in 1907. She was also an active member of the League of Nations Union and the International Women's Suffrage Alliance. B. Harrison, *Prudent Revolutionaries: Portraits of British Feminists between the Wars* (Oxford: Oxford University Press, 1987), p. 193.

106 Merz, *After the Vote*, p. 8.

107 *Ibid.*, p. 17

108 *The National Union of Townswomen's Guilds Handbook 1938* (1938), p. 25.

109 The other three Guilds were set up in Burnt Oak, Moulsecoombe and Romsey.

110 M. Stott, *Organisation Woman: The Story of The National Union of Townswomen's Guilds* (London: Heinemann, 1978), p. 27.

111 *Ibid.*, pp. 11–13.

112 *Ibid.* See also Merz, *After the Vote*, p. 13.

113 *Ibid.*, p. 17.

114 The official aim of the NUSEC was 'to obtain all such reforms as are necessary to secure a real equality of liberties, status and opportunities between men and women'. *The National Union of Townswomen's Guilds Annual Report 1933* (1933), p. 10.

115 *The National Union of Townswomen's Guilds Handbook 1938* (1938), p. 1.

116 *The Townswoman*, 16:3 (March 1949), p. 1.

117 In 1930, 110 Townswomen's Guilds and 67 Societies for Equal Citizenship were affiliated to the NUSEC. Pugh, *Women and the Women's Movement*, p. 242.

118 *The National Union of Townswomen's Guilds Annual Report 1932* (1932), p. 4. The NCEC remained an active feminist pressure group during this period but failed to attract either the support or the funding available to the TG.

119 *The National Union of Townswomen's Guilds Annual Report 1932* (1932), p. 28.

120 *Ibid.*, p. 11.

121 *Ibid.*, p. 4.

122 *Ibid.*, p. 32.

123 Twenty-five members were needed to set up a guild with a maximum of 150 women joining any one guild.

124 *The National Union of Townswomen's Guilds Annual Report 1932* (1932), p. 12.

125 During the 1930s the Carnegie Trust awarded educational grants worth £2,200 and the National Council of Social Service provided £1,000 to fund the establishment of fifty guilds for women living in areas of high unemployment.

126 At these meetings the two organisations agreed about borderline areas with populations just above or below 4,000 and decided whether a guild or an institute should be established.

127 *National Union of Townswomen's Guilds Annual Report 1935* (1935), p. 28.

128 *Ibid.* For a detailed account of life for women living in urban estates during this period see D. L. North, 'Middle class suburban lifestyles and culture in England 1919–1939' (Ph.D. dissertation, Oxford, 1989). See also M. Clapson, 'Working-Class Women's

Experiences of Moving to New Housing Estates in England since 1919', *Twentieth Century British History*, 10:3 (1999).

129 Cited in Hinton, *Women, Social Leadership and the Second World War*, p. 48–49.

130 *National Union of Townswomen's Guilds Annual Report 1935* (1935), p. 28.

131 *The Women's Leader* (7 March 1930), p. 35.

132 Both women were close friends of Eva Hubback and had been involved in fund-raising for the TG since 1929.

133 Pugh, *Women and the Women's Movement*, p. 242.

2

Housewives and citizens:
the rights and duties of women citizens

Much of the political history of the twentieth century has been characterised by battles to extend, defend or give substance to political, civil and social rights of citizenship. Women played a central role in these struggles, not just for the vote but also for social citizenship rights, often explicitly using the ideal of citizenship as their lode star.[1]

As the previous chapter suggested, the five voluntary women's organisations included in this study represented a wide variety of women and had diverse aims and objectives. Yet in spite of these differences each organisation shared a commitment to support women in their traditional roles as housewives and mothers. What is perhaps less well recognised within the historiography is a second unifying characteristic. This was the prominence given by each of these groups to the concept of democratic citizenship, with all its adherent rights and duties, in the decades following the enactment of the 1928 Equal Franchise Act. This chapter will explore the ways in which the MU, CWL, NCW, WI and TG adopted the discourse of citizenship to provide a framework for women's participation in public life. Having rejected feminism as too radical and too political, the rhetoric of citizenship provided these groups with the means to articulate the contribution that women could make to local and national life. Moreover, equal citizenship gave women the power to demand civil and social rights for women. It was through the language of citizenship that these conservative women's organisations were able to justify their involvement in public debates and campaigns so that they could highlight the rights and needs of wives and mothers. The idea of citizenship as utilised by voluntary women's organisations reflects Kathleen Canning and Sonya Rose's argument that 'citizenship provides the languages, rhetorics, and even the formal categories for claims-making, sometimes in the name of national belonging or on behalf of specific rights, duties, or protections, or visions of political participation.'[2]

Gender and citizenship

The concept of citizenship within democratic societies and the different meanings of citizenship for men and for women have been topics of debate amongst political theorists and sociologists for many years. The vast majority of these theories draw on the work of T. H. Marshall (1950), who wrote that 'citizenship is a status bestowed on those who are full members of a community. All who possess the status are equal with respect to the rights and duties with which they are endowed.'[3] Marshall suggested that there were three distinct types of citizenship: civil, political and social. Civil citizenship referred to individual freedoms, political citizenship to the right to vote and social citizenship to economic and welfare rights.[4] Marshall's understanding of citizenship emerges from classic liberal traditions whereby citizenship is linked to individual freedom and membership of a community rather than a state. All those within the community are assumed to have the same rights. Marshall's theory, whilst acknowledged as key to our understanding of citizenship in modern western democracies, has been criticised by feminist writers on the grounds that it is 'gender blind'. Ruth Lister, Nira Yuval-Davis and Sylvia Walby have all argued that Marshall's assumption that political and social rights follow on from the extension of civil rights fails to acknowledge that men and women have achieved civil, political and social citizenship in different ways and at different times throughout history.[5]

Using the example of women's enfranchisement in Britain, Walby successfully challenges Marshall when she points out that women granted political citizenship in 1928 were still denied 'the "civil" right to work at the occupation of their choice, since there were so many restrictions in the forms of employment open to women'.[6] In addition women did not have the civil right to control their own fertility, to retain their nationality on marriage to a foreigner or to be paid the same rate as a man for the same job. Conversely, women in Britain had access to some political rights before the extension of the parliamentary franchise. From 1869 women were eligible to vote and stand in local government elections.[7] By 1914 there were 1,546 female poor-law guardians, 200 rural-district councillors and forty-eight women municipal and county councillors.[8]

The feminist critique of Marshall's theory of citizenship is helpful as it allows a greater understanding of why women's organisations, both feminist and mainstream, continued to campaign for women's civil and social rights once the vote had been won. As Walby suggests, 'in the case of British women, political citizenship was at least as often the power base from which women were able to win civil citizenship, as *vice versa*'.[9] This 'power base' of political citizenship is particularly useful in explaining why voluntary women's organisations, so often reluctant to be associated with feminist ideology, appropriated the concept of citizenship. Citizenship legitimated the involvement of mainstream women's groups in public debates and their demand for the extension of civil and social rights to women.

With rights come duties, and the MU, CWL, NCW, WI and TG were all aware that if they wished to speak out on behalf of their members they needed to ensure that housewives and mothers fulfilled their duties as active citizens. This duty required women to make a contribution not only to their own families but also to their local communities and to the life of the nation. This emphasis on the duty of citizenship stems from the republican civic tradition that 'constructs citizenship not only as a status but also as a means of active involvement and participation in the determination, practice and promotion of the common good'.[10]

The involvement of housewives in life beyond their own homes and families during the years 1928–64 was of critical importance to voluntary women's organisations. They recognised that in order for women to have a voice in public life and to have influence on public policy they had to have a presence outside the home. Walby reiterates the importance of female participation in public life, as 'it has only been by leaving the private sphere of the home that women have been able to gain some aspects of citizenship'.[11] Membership of a voluntary women's organisation offered women a new space outside the home, free from party politics or direct links to feminism, to engage in active citizenship and public life. Karen Hunt has identified the importance of new political spaces for women in European history which allows 'us to see politics happening not just in elected assemblies, in meeting rooms, in workplaces and in public squares but also in parlours in domestic homes'.[12] In the case of housewives' associations this new space was carved out in the weekly and monthly meetings of local women's groups.

One of the most interesting aspects of voluntary women's organisations was their acknowledgment that the private sphere of the home, which they so wished to protect, could also limit women's involvement in public life. Bryan Turner, in his analysis of citizenship, has focused on the dichotomy between the public/active and private/passive spheres with regards to the development of citizenship rights.[13] Like Marshall, Turner has been criticised by feminist theorists for ignoring gender and failing to recognise that the private sphere of the family has different implications for men and women. As Walby argues, 'the family is not private for women', and Turner's claim that '"the private is seen as the space of personal leisure and enhancement" thereby [denies] the salience of the household as a site of domestic labour by women.[14]

Organisations like the MU, CWL, NCW, WI and TG recognised that the private sphere of the home was the workplace for the majority of women throughout the early and mid-twentieth century. They also realised that in order to improve the lives of women who were full-time housewives and mothers, women would need support to venture outside of the home and engage in active citizenship. As Ruth Lister argues, women who have the status of citizenship are not always able to 'fulfil the full potential of that status' as they are constrained by their domestic or caring responsibilities.[15] What voluntary women's organisations sought to do was to enable and encourage women to benefit from their citizenship status by providing them with the space and support to fulfil their duties as citizens and in doing so, claim their rights of citizenship.

Where voluntary women's groups were most successful was in their ability to legitimate the private or domestic concerns of women as issues worthy of public debate. This was achieved through the effective mobilisation of female agency. Lister identifies agency as knitting 'together the different approaches to citizenship. It can be found implicitly in notions of "active citizenship" which have been promoted in the British context.'[16] Lister likens agency to community action that promotes the 'citizenship of individuals within those communities'. She argues that

> such action can boost individual and collective self-confidence, as individuals and groups come together to see themselves as political actors and effective citizens. This is especially true for women for whom involvement in community organisations can be more personally fruitful than engagement in formal politics ... often experienced as more alienating than empowering.[17]

Although writing in the context of the 1990s, Lister's argument holds true for the agency displayed by the hundreds of thousands of women who joined housewives' organisations some sixty years earlier. At a time when female representation in public life was so limited, membership of voluntary women's groups provided women with the opportunity to become political actors on their own terms.

In developing a feminist theory of citizenship, Lister argues that a 'synthetic approach' is required which combines elements of the liberal tradition of individual rights with the republican tradition of active citizenship and political participation. This synthesis allows for an understanding of citizenship as a dynamic concept in which process and outcome stand in a dialectical relationship to each other. Such a conceptualisation of citizenship is particularly important in challenging the construction of women… as passive victims, while keeping sight of the discriminatory and oppressive male-dominated political, economic and social institutions which still deny them full citizenship'.[18]

This feminist interpretation of citizenship is particularly useful in helping historians understand the way in which voluntary women's organisations engaged with the concept of citizenship between the years 1928 to 1964. It is clear that this focus on both the rights and duties of citizenship by housewives' organisations has much in common with Lister's more recent argument for a 'synthetic approach' to citizenship. Nonetheless it is important to recognise that the groups featured in this study did not draw upon such a feminist analysis for their discourse on citizenship. Instead they were influenced by contemporary understandings of citizenship prevalent during the inter-war years.

The concept of citizenship for women in inter-war Britain

Women in Britain had access to some of the civil and political rights of citizenship and were performing some of the duties of citizenship before the extension of the franchise on equal terms with men in 1928. Women were also active in the established political parties before they were granted the parliamentary vote. In 1906, the Women's Labour League was set up for women who supported the ideology of the Labour Party.[19] Women involved in the Primrose League (1883) undertook electioneering work for the Conservative Party and acted as an auxiliary force of party workers.[20] Similarly, the Women's Liberal Federation (1886) attracted considerable support and by 1912 had some 133,215 members.[21] Involvement in local government and political organisations gave women the opportunity to participate in the political process, although they were still excluded from national government.

From the mid-nineteenth century, becoming involved with voluntary and charitable societies facilitated active citizenship amongst upper- and middle-class women. Such activity was deemed respectable and a natural extension of women's caring responsibilities. Organisations such as the Charity Organisation Society (1869) and the Workhouse Visiting Society (1858) gave women the chance to get involved in public work and at the same time to campaign for social welfare reforms. By 1870 an estimated 500,000 British women were involved in public social welfare work.[22]

It was also during this period that middle-class voluntary women's organisations were established including the MU, YWCA and the NUWW. Recognising the importance of women's participation in charitable and voluntary organisations, Karen Hunt has argued that the involvement of elite and middle-class women in charitable societies 'not only gave them skills and networks that enabled them to move further into the public world, but also provided confirmation that the dominant discourse of domesticity need not be unsettled by such action'.[23]

For working-class women, involvement in the WCG provided them with the opportunity to engage in politics, and the Guild spearheaded demands for divorce law reform and improved maternity care for women throughout the late nineteenth century and early twentieth century. At the same time, members of the WCG were encouraged to stand for municipal elections and to familiarise themselves with the workings of a democratic society.[24]

In spite of these developments, women were still denied the parliamentary vote and the right to sit in parliament, basic rights of political citizenship, and were subjected to numerous social, legal and economic inequalities. The suffrage movement focused on the campaign for the women's franchise but was also part of a wider struggle for the rights of civil and social citizenship. These rights included access to education, an equal moral standard, divorce, equal pay and the right to sit on juries.[25] When, in 1918, the vote was extended to women over thirty and women became eligible to stand as parliamentary candidates, there followed a series of important legislative reforms. These measures, including the Matrimonial Causes Act 1923 and the Guardianship of Infants Act 1925, did much to improve the lives of women.[26] Finally, in 1928, the Equal Franchise Act granted the vote to women over twenty-one on equal terms with men.

The granting of formal political citizenship did not signify an end to women's social and economic inequality. This reality dawned on the feminist campaigner Eleanor Rathbone in 1936 when she remarked that 'no doubt ... some of us exaggerated [the power of the vote] ... progress has been rapid when it depended on political action and slow when it depended on changes in heart and habits'.[27] In the decades following 1928, women continued to be regarded as dependents of men, a fact reflected in the low levels of pay for women workers, the marriage bar and the lack of free healthcare for wives and mothers. It was necessary therefore for political, feminist and voluntary women's groups to demonstrate that women were citizens in their own right, entitled to claim civil and social rights from the state.

If men were able to qualify for citizenship rights through soldiering and working outside the home, would housekeeping and mothering entitle women to the same rights?[28] The notion that women could assert their citizenship through their work as wives and mothers is important when discussing women and citizenship in the period after enfranchisement. Carole Pateman has focused on the problem of equal versus different in claiming women's citizenship rights. She identifies Mary Wollstonecraft as the first liberal theorist to acknowledge that citizenship for women would be defined differently from that of men. Writing in 1792, Wollstonecraft claimed that women had 'specific capacities, talents, needs and concerns so that the expression of their citizenship will be differentiated from that of men.'[29]

This difference-based argument, which claimed that women's private domestic duty should be a basis for their right to citizenship, remained a salient theme within debates on women's rights throughout Europe from the 1790s onwards.[30] Karen Hunt writes that since the end of the nineteenth century, motherhood had been increasingly seen as a matter of national concern and this was certainly true in the British case.[31] This led to a focus on difference and maternalism, a trend that worked to women's political benefit and shaped women's politics for much of the twentieth century. Hunt surmises that this 'in turn affected how the possibilities for women's citizenship were imagined and practised as well as how women perceived politics and represented themselves as a political interest group'.[32]

Voluntary women's organisations became adept with using difference and maternalism to further their political objectives. These organisations engaged with a wide range of political debates and campaigns on the grounds that they represented women who as housewives and mothers had a different and unique contribution to make to the life of the nation. However, as Hunt and Pateman both identified, there is an inherent danger in pursuing a difference-based approach to citizenship as it can 'justify the marginalisation of most women from the exercise of real power over the management of the economy, foreign policy or national defence'.[33]

This dilemma in choosing whether or not to support equal or difference-based claims for women's citizenships was most evident amongst post-suffrage societies in the 1920s and 1930s. The 'difference-based' concept of citizenship for women dominated the thinking of Eleanor Rathbone, president of the NUSEC. Rathbone supported the introduction of welfare reforms, for example family allowances, which identified the specific needs of women as mothers. She argued that wives and mothers provided an important service to the community in caring for their husbands and children. In return for this work, women citizens were entitled to claim adequate social and welfare benefits from the state.[34] In 1925, Rathbone told members of the NUSEC that 'we can demand what we want for women, not because it is what men have got but because it is what women need to fulfil the potentialities of their own natures and to adjust themselves to the circumstances of their own lives.'[35]

Historians of the inter-war feminist movement have highlighted the debate over equality versus difference and viewed it as having a negative impact on the effectiveness of the movement.[36] In 1927 the NUSEC split as a result of disagreement on whether priority should be given to the equality or difference agenda. Women wishing to focus on so called 'dead-level' equal rights left the NUSEC to join organisations such as the WFL, the Six Point Group (SPG) and the ODC.

Those remaining in the NUSEC became known as 'new feminists' and began to concentrate on social welfare rights for women linked to their role as wives and mothers, for example family allowances, access to birth control information and improved housing conditions. Much has been made of this division within the feminist movement but it would be wrong to suggest that this split resulted in two diametrically opposed factions. The NUSEC continued to campaign for equal rights legislation such as the equal franchise and equal employment opportunities, and the SPG and WFL included issues such as child care and housing standards on their list of concerns.[37]

The WCG and the Women Sections of the Labour Party also used women's role as wives and mothers to demand the extension of civil and social rights of citizenship to women. As Pat Thane has suggested, labour women 'sought to ensure that work in the home was valued by enabling the largest occupational group in the country, the housewives, to assert themselves publicly, to contribute their voice to politics, and hence to advancement of their own status and causes'.[38] In much the same way, the MU, CWL, NCW, WI and TG highlighted the contribution that women working within the home made to society and used this to campaign for reform.

So rather than focus on the differences between feminist, political and mainstream women's organisations, it is more useful to recognise what these groups had in common. Throughout the 1920s and 1930s all of these groups sought to utilise the power base that political citizenship had granted women in 1918 and again in 1928 and to encourage their members to show that they could be responsible and active citizens. In return for their services as wives and mothers, women would be in a stronger position to claim support from the state.

During the inter-war period, the importance of active citizenship for women as well as men became increasingly significant. The rise of fascism in Italy and Germany and reports of the brutality of Stalin's regime in Russia focused attention on the need for participatory citizenship if democracy was to survive. The model of the 'good' and 'active' citizen adopted by women's organisations during the 1920s and 1930s can be linked to a number of different sources. Elizabeth Darling, writing in the context of the inter-war housing debate, has argued that the ideas of British Idealists, popular in the late nineteenth century, were influential to understandings of citizenship during these years. Writers such as T. H. Green and Bernard Bosanquet argued that central to the relationship between the state and the individual was the concept of active citizenship. To achieve this a reciprocal relationship between the state and its citizens must be developed. The state would provide social and political rights in return for which citizens would perform certain duties, including full participation in the life of their communities.[39]

Contemporary writings on citizenship during the 1930s adopted some of these ideas with regard to active and informed citizenship. The Association for Education in Citizenship (AEC), set up in 1934 to promote the ideal of the good and active citizen, stated that a good citizen was someone who 'had a sense of social responsibility, a love of truth and freedom, the power of clear thinking, and a knowledge of political and economic facts'.[40] The AEC's objective was 'to advance the study of and training in citizenship, by which is meant training in the moral qualities necessary for the citizens of a democracy'.[41] The work of this group, founded by Sir Ernest Simon and Eva Hubback, who at this time was a leading member of both the NCEC and the TG, provides a useful insight into the citizenship education programmes developed by voluntary women's societies during the inter-war period.[42]

John Field and Peter Weller have described the concept of citizenship advanced by the AEC as 'broadly social democratic'. It involved 'high-minded public service, tolerance of difference … and the beneficial exercise of rights'.[43] Throughout the 1930s and 1940s, the group published a series of pamphlets outlining a theory of citizenship and ways in which citizenship education could be incorporated into the national curriculum.[44] The AEC called for citizenship education in schools, universities and through adult education. History, politics and economics were singled out as the most important subjects for citizenship education. The AEC acknowledged, however, that it was difficult to stimulate an interest in public affairs, which many regarded as a 'dreary business'.[45] To overcome this problem, local study groups and the use of film, drama and discussion were recommended in order to arouse public interest.

It is significant that these were some of the methods already incorporated by the larger women's organisations in their efforts to educate members in citizenship. Indeed, the AEC recognised that voluntary societies, including the WI, Women's Citizens Associations and TG, had a significant contribution to make to education in citizenship. Although providing less formal education, these groups were judged capable of stimulating 'a sense of social responsibility and a more widespread, if somewhat superficial, study of social conditions, and are therefore all to the good'.[46] Following the outbreak of war in 1939, the AEC continued to highlight the dangers that fascism posed for the future of democratic societies. In 1942, Eva Hubback warned that if Britain was to avoid autocracy it was imperative 'to imbue our people with the belief in the democratic way of life and with pride in its achievement … to make active citizens of a democracy capable of building a fine civilisation'.[47]

Constance Braithwaite expressed similar concerns about the future of democratic citizenship in her book *The Voluntary Citizen: An Enquiry into the place of Philanthropy in the Community* (1938). Braithwaite suggested that the most urgent social problem facing Britain in the 1930s was the need to establish 'the right relationship' between the state and its citizens. She argued that liberal economic individualism 'no longer provides an adequate basis for ensuring the best possible conditions of a good life to all individuals'.[48] Braithwaite condemned totalitarianism, arguing that it sacrificed the freedom of development of its own citizens as well as the welfare of citizens in other countries.[49]

Drawing on the principle of 'high-minded public service', her concept of 'the voluntary citizen' referred to the involvement of citizens in charitable and philanthropic work. Braithwaite argued that the relief of poverty should be the responsibility of the state and not charitable organisations. She did acknowledge, however, that as long as poverty existed and was not adequately relieved by the state, charitable organisations were necessary.[50] The central argument in *The Voluntary Citizen* was that in order to improve the relationship between the state and its citizens, people must first of all be encouraged to become active in the administration of public social services.

For citizens to participate successfully in social welfare, it was necessary for them to be educated in citizenship. Braithwaite wrote that 'individuals do not become intelligent and public spirited citizens merely by keeping the law, paying taxes, and recording their votes at election. They require opportunities of insight into the lives of fellows and into the practical work of group administration.'[51] In order to benefit from such opportunities, Braithwaite recommended participation in organisations promoting recreational, educational and charitable activities. Organisations such as the WI and the MU were regarded as ideal for this purpose.[52] In common with the AEC, Braithwaite stressed the importance of informed public opinion for the survival of democracy during the inter-war period.

Contemporary discourses on the concept of citizenship reflect a number of similar themes. The value of voluntary philanthropic work is emphasised, as is the need for an educated populace. Participation in adult organisations, including women's societies, was regarded as an important aspect in the training of citizens. These groups not only provided opportunities for education in citizenship, they also inculcated democratic values amongst the membership through their management and administration. It was hoped that experiences of associational life would facilitate the smooth running of democratic government and protect against the threat of totalitarian regimes.

Voluntary women's organisations and education in citizenship

Following the extension of the parliamentary franchise to women in 1918 and 1928 a diverse range of women's organisations recognised the importance of educating their members in citizenship to ensure that women took full advantage of the power of the vote.[53] As Sue Innes has written, these groups included post-suffrage societies, feminist pressure groups, trade union and professional bodies, the three main political parties, the WCG as well as mainstream women's organisations.[54] Innes argues convincingly that 'the idea of citizenship' invigorated the women's movement at this time and 'enabled a synthesis of equality and social feminisms'.[55]

Anxious to ensure that women did not squander the new political powers they now possessed, post-suffrage and feminist societies, along with the established political parties, published articles in their journals and produced pamphlets and handbooks with the aim of instructing the new female voter in the art of democracy. *Time and Tide*, the well-known feminist journal, ran a series of articles in 1921 on 'The Common-Sense Citizen' to inform readers about the mechanics of parliamentary democracy. The paper also acknowledged that all women 'were preoccupied with the same issues: peace, children, homes, temperance, and equality' and that women needed to speak out and take action on these issues to ensure their voices and opinions were heard.[56] In the 1920s the NUSEC published pamphlets to advise first time female voters entitled

The New Privilege of Citizenship and *How Women Can Use the Vote*.[57] Similarly, in their attempts to encourage more women to support the Conservative Party, party organisers reminded female voters that 'the vote carries the gravest responsibility' and that the best way to learn how to use the vote was 'by joining the women's branch of the Unionist Association.'[58]

The post-suffrage period also saw the emergence of new organisations aimed at educating women about the importance of the vote and encouraging women to become more actively involved in local and national politics. In 1917 the NUWW had set up a committee to focus on citizenship education for women which in 1918 evolved into a new body, the National Women Citizens' Association (NWCA). Its principle aim was to encourage the study of 'political, social and economic questions and to secure adequate representation for women in local administration and in the affairs of the nation.'[59]

Local Women Citizens' Associations (WCAs) could affiliate to this national organisation and branches were established throughout England, Wales and Scotland.[60] Innes writes that the 'WCAs participated in a broad agenda centred on the perceived power of women's votes in forwarding gender equality and social reform, shaped by a view of why women's suffrage mattered and by developing ideas of social citizenship.'[61] These attempts to mobilise women, the vast majority of whom were housewives and mothers, required feminist and party political organisations to focus on the issues that mattered to women in their domestic roles and therefore to embrace a difference-based interpretation of women's citizenship. Innes illustrates this point when she writes that the Edinburgh WCA 'used a gendered construction of citizenship to articulate their [women's] role as political actors and to bridge divergent interests.'[62]

A gendered construction of citizenship, based on the role of women as housewives and mothers, was also clearly evident amongst voluntary women's organisations throughout the decades following enfranchisement. Unlike feminist societies such as the NUSEC, the MU, CWL, NCW, WI and TG did not experience the dilemma of having to choose between the merits of equality *versus* difference when debating women's citizenship. Instead for them citizenship for women was inextricably linked to their roles as wives and mothers and it was in this context that women should be educated as good and active citizens.

In common with other women's organisations at this time the MU acknowledged that the average woman might not embrace her new responsibility as a citizen and 'believes it makes little or no difference whether she uses her vote or not.'[63] In 1934 *The Mothers' Union Journal* proclaimed that it remains true for all time that our real job as mothers is making of citizens and not laws ... yet as thinking human beings we must see that laws good or bad, play a great part in helping or hindering us ... Let us do all in our power, through our rights of citizenship to make a new England, a new world 'safe for little children to live in.'[64]

The Union outlined ways to foster a sense of political and social responsibility amongst wives and mothers. Members were urged to 'take an intelligent interest in things, reading and thinking for ourselves, instead of taking our opinions ready-made from someone else'.[65]

In August 1934, an article entitled 'The Good Citizen' appeared in *The Mothers' Union Journal*, highlighting the attributes of active citizenship. The importance of the vote was emphasised to ensure that 'good men' were appointed to maintain and develop community life. These 'good men', once elected 'deserved the respect and willing co-operation of all citizens'.[66] This endorsement of the suitability of men for public office illustrates concerns within the MU during the 1930s that political office could distract women from their primary role as mothers.[67]

Despite having reservations about women taking up public positions, the MU had no such qualms when it came to women having a clear understanding of how the law could impact on family life. Taking an interest in public questions was therefore encouraged because 'good citizens, men and women alike, should think deeply about these matters and act according to the dictates of conscience'.[68] Central Council was particularly anxious that members would use their vote to protest against legislation conflicting with Christian teaching, for example divorce law reform during the 1920s and 1930s.[69]

As a society for Anglican women, the MU endorsed the concept of Christian citizenship, defined by the Conference on Christian Politics, Economics and Citizenship (COPEC). First convened in 1924 by William Temple, then Bishop of Manchester, the COPEC Report stated that 'the duties of citizenship are ... a sacred obligation for Christian people'.[70] The report recommended that the state should guarantee, to every family, decent housing, education and an adequate income.[71] The MU added to this list of social rights by including free healthcare for married women, family allowances paid to mothers and adequate maternity services. The following chapters will explore the way in which the MU actively campaigned to secure these social rights for women.

Not surprisingly, the Union saw the duties of women citizens closely allied to their role as wives and mothers. The second objective of the Union highlighted the responsibilities that mothers had in caring for their children, the fathers and mothers of the future. However, if mothers were to make the world a safer and more Christian place for their children, they had a duty to contribute to life beyond their homes. It was suggested that 'for a woman to give up all outside interests, to entirely merge her personality in that of another, is to help in producing husbands and fathers of a wrong type; the bully, the autocrat, the dictator. We have no use for that type [of mother] today.'[72]

It is difficult to ascertain just how successful the national organisation was in encouraging rank and file members to become active and well-informed citizens. However, in order to educate members in citizenship, speakers were supplied by the Central Council to address local meetings on subjects ranging from religious education to current affairs. In 1937, the list of lectures offered by central speakers included 'Citizenship and the Mothers' Union', 'The Right Use of Money' and 'Why Am I a Churchwoman?'.[73]

Despite these efforts on the part of the National Executive it is likely that many women who joined the MU were more interested in the social and recreational activities offered by local branches. In 1930, reports from the London branches revealed the popularity of social gatherings and fundraising events over all other activities. For example, the Twickenham branch held a winter festival and pageant while other branches raised money for church repairs and local charities.[74] It would be wrong, however, to dismiss the work of the national organisation because rank-and-file members were more interested in social activities. Like any large voluntary organisation, the MU had both active and passive members who took different things from the organisation depending on their personal interests and circumstances.

What is perhaps more significant is the fact that such an influential, respected and conservative organisation, representing over half a million women throughout the 1930s, believed that women had an important contribution to make to life outside the home and sought ways to encourage members to fulfil their duty as active citizens. The Union may have argued that a woman's first duty was to her family, but as intelligent and responsible citizens, women also had a duty to society. It was the Union's aim, therefore, to encourage its members to get involved in local and national affairs and to give Christian women a voice in public life.

The concept of Christian citizenship was also central to the work of the CWL. One of the League's primary objectives was 'to help women to become good citizens through being good Catholics ... [women have] an important role in safeguarding the laws of God and the rights of the family'.[75] In 1918, when the franchise was extended to women, the CWL published a series of leaflets on the rights and duties of citizenship.

Members were advised about the equal moral duties and moral rights of men and women in a democratic society. This meant that all citizens had the right to freedom of speech, education and a family wage.[76]

In these leaflets, the League made it clear that the family was the 'unit of human existence' and that 'the necessity for married women to work outside their homes during the infancy of their children should be regarded as an evil.'[77] Once again there was no doubt that the League, like the MU, firmly believed that a woman's first place was in the home caring for her husband and children. However, the CWL also recognised that women had responsibilities as citizens and that it was their duty to contribute to life beyond the home by participating in community work and taking an active interest in local and national affairs.

To facilitate these activities, the League set up a Social Service Bureau in 1928, to offer advice on careers for young women in professional and voluntary social work. The League hoped that this scheme would encourage more Catholic women to become social workers. Consequently, women would be better represented in voluntary and state sector welfare services, thereby incorporating the principles of Catholic social teaching into social policy.[78] The League also set up a Public Service Bureau to encourage and support members to get involved in a wide range of local activities, with the aim of raising the profile of Catholic women in the community. Members of the League were encouraged to stand as candidates for urban and district councils, join secular women's societies and set up local debating and study clubs.[79] Members of the CWL did join local branches of secular women's groups during this period. For example, in 1938 it was reported that the chairman of the Wolverhampton CWL was also the chairman of the local townswomen guild. The same year members of the League's West Riding branch were also affiliated to the local NCW and TG.[80]

Unlike the MU, the CWL was quick to deny that there was any conflict between public service and women's domestic duties within the home. In October 1932, Mrs Chambers, speaking on behalf of the League's Executive, made it clear that home life could not be separated from local and national affairs. In an article published in *The Catholic Women's League Magazine* she told readers that 'homes are very often built by the local authority, children attend schools built by the local authority ... if you want to live and work under decent conditions, you have got to be represented on that local authority.'[81] Mrs Chambers added that it was imperative to get Catholics elected to local government 'so that they are always there to deal with anything which affects Catholic interests'.[82]

In 1933, members of the Durham County branch were urged to 'record their vote at municipal elections' as this was considered to be the 'first step towards being good citizens'.[83] The importance of borough councils was emphasised because they were responsible for decisions regarding the 'education of our children, for health, housing and the safety of ourselves and our children'.[84] At this meeting, it was suggested that any Catholic woman who did not take an interest in local and national affairs was a 'shame to her religion'.[85] These views were reiterated at a meeting of the Northern Province Public Service Committee in October 1935. During an address on 'Catholic Women in the Home and Public Life', Mrs Kemball, chairman of the committee, told her audience that 'although women's work is and must always be mainly in the home', it should not end there. She stressed that women must also be encouraged to take part in national life 'to uphold and defend Catholic principles'.[86]

In spite of these appeals, the Church hierarchy remained concerned that Catholic women were not doing enough to make their voice heard in political life. In 1936, the Archbishop of Liverpool urged members of the CWL to make their views more widely known in the protest against moral dangers such as divorce and birth control. Speaking at the League's Annual Council Meeting, the archbishop warned that 'now women are emancipated and have the freedom they fought for … what is the result of this liberty? It is seen that sometimes women appear to be throwing away their influence and doing their best to wreck our social system'.[87]

The same year Mrs Kemball deplored the apparent apathy amongst the Catholic electorate. She claimed that 'if we are pulling our full weight as citizens and rendering real service to the communities in which we live, it is only reasonable to suppose that we shall be listened to when any matter affecting our principles is under discussion'.[88] To ensure that this objective was achieved, Dr Rewcastle, the President of the League, told members attending the 1936 Annual Conference that it was the 'manifest duty of Catholic women to take a share in civic responsibilities'.[89]

From these statements it is clear that the CWL saw citizenship for women as a way to uphold the teaching of the Catholic Church. However, this should not detract from the fact that as a women's organisation, the League was encouraging its members to use their vote and to take an active interest in life beyond their homes. At the same time, the CWL recognised that women as citizens were entitled to social and economic support from the state. As a result, the League was able to campaign throughout the 1930s and 1940s for social and welfare reforms it believed would improve the quality of life for all women working within the home.

Like many women's groups during this period, the NCW was concerned that newly enfranchised women should be made aware of their duties as citizens and encouraged to use their vote. In March 1918, the NUWW (renamed the NCW in October 1918) had facilitated the establishment of the NWCA. Maria Ogilvie Gordon was elected first President of the Association and over the years many women active in the NCW served on the NWCA Executive. However, with its narrow focus on citizenship education and local representation for women, the NWCA failed to attract a large membership and as a result many local WCAs decided to join the more established and influential NUSEC.[90]

In 1929 the NCW set up its own Women Citizens' Section, under the chairmanship of Mrs Ogilvie Gordon. The aim of this committee was to co-ordinate the work of the ten WCAs affiliated to the NCW and to promote active citizenship amongst these groups as well as local branches of the NCW.[91] Ogilvie Gordon highlighted the importance of this work when she remarked that 'it must be recognised that vast numbers of women, leading circumscribed lives, with little leisure for anything outside their home duties, take little interest in the wider problems of government.'[92]

In common with the NWCA, the NCW believed that involvement in local politics and community affairs 'soon develops into a sense of wider civic responsibility' which would lead to 'an interest in parliamentary legislation.'[93] The Council recognised the different viewpoint that women had on public issues and encouraged its members to participate in community work and social service, 'which by its very nature calls urgently for the particular experience of women … the domestic detail of which the nation is sorely in need.'[94] In January 1928, the Council's journal, NCW News, reminded women that it was their 'definite obligation as citizens to give their opinion on national questions by choosing as their representatives in parliament those who hold the same views as themselves on justice, freedom, honesty and peace.'[95]

Later that year, when the franchise was extended to women over the age of twenty-one, the president of the Council, Lady Emmott, suggested that 'our duty in the coming months is to encourage the younger members of the community to educate themselves in civic matters, so that they may take full advantage of their powers and responsibilities.'[96] She was particularly concerned that younger women were 'holding back from our particular kind of work' and added that 'the State has a real claim on us all to give service, either paid or unpaid, and I long for our young women to take their part just as their brothers did in the past.'[97]

To stimulate the interest of women in public affairs, the Birmingham branch of the NCW set up a Citizenship Committee to 'encourage the study and practice of citizenship'.[98] The aims of the committee included working for 'all such reforms to secure a real equality of liberties, status and opportunities between men and women' and to promote the 'election and appointment of women to local government'.[99] During the late 1920s, the subjects dealt with by this committee included the appointment of women police, the Equal Franchise Act and the provision of local health services.[100]

Persuading women to stand in local elections was a major preoccupation for both the local and national sections of the NCW. In February 1928, the Council had urged 'all women citizens to do all in their power … to combat the indifference and apathy which have been so appalling a feature of local government elections in past years'.[101] The fact that fifteen county councils (out of a total of sixty-two) had no female members was deplored, particularly in view of the fact that there were 6,000 more women local electors than men.[102] In spite of the Council's efforts, however, the Birmingham NCW reported in September 1929 that its efforts to recruit women candidates for local council elections had proved disappointing.[103] Undeterred, the Council continued to urge women to work together 'to promote the social, civil, moral and religious welfare of the community' and 'to remove all the disabilities of women, whether legal, economic, or social'.[104]

The importance of the franchise, the need for an informed public opinion, voluntary social work and women's engagement in life outside their homes were all themes evident in the work of the WI throughout the inter-war years. In her history of the WI, Inez Jenkins wrote that rural women were 'experiencing in the Institute movement a unique excursion from the preoccupations of home and family … and were becoming for the first time aware of their own potentialities'.[105] Like other voluntary women's organisations, the WI gave members the opportunity to contribute to life outside their homes, both as housewives and citizens.

When in 1918 the number of women local government electors increased from one million to over 8.5 million, the WI encouraged its members to use their vote to add to the number of female candidates elected to serve in local government. In May 1921, the West Suffolk Federation put forward a resolution urging that it should be 'the recognised duty of individual Institutes to educate their members in the powers of the Parish Councils, Rural District Councils, and County Council with a view to getting local women on all these bodies'.[106] It is difficult to confirm just how successful this scheme was as the Institute did not provide any detailed figures of members elected to local government. However, by the late 1920s the NUSEC had acknowledged that the increase in the number of women elected to Parish Councils owed much to the work of the WI movement.[107]

In 1928, the WI celebrated the passing of the Equal Franchise Act by sending a telegram to Prime Minister Baldwin, thanking him for introducing this long-awaited reform. Once the Act became law, the editor of *Home and Country* wrote that 'it now remains for women to show that they have sufficient political zeal and intelligence to justify the trust of the House of Commons'.[108] The August edition of *Home and Country* proclaimed that the WI was 'a remarkable mechanism for political, as distinct from party-political, education in rural districts'.[109] As an educational organisation, the WI acknowledged that it was the responsibility of each institute to ensure that every member was aware of 'her sense of obligation to the country in which she is a citizen, to help her develop her mental powers, to make her realize the importance of the intelligent use of the vote'.[110]

As well as offering classes in handicrafts, cookery and other domestic skills, the WI gave women the opportunity to discuss political and social issues. Throughout the 1920s and 1930s, weekly meetings often included talks on topical subjects ranging from the problem of maternal mortality to the international crisis. In 1928, the Gloucestershire Federation reported that lectures held in its 128 branches had included, 'Health', 'The Younger Generation' and 'Ideal Citizenship'.[111] At the same time, members were kept up to date on national affairs through the pages of *Home and Country*. Every month the journal reported on current events and followed the passage of legislation affecting the lives of rural women and children.

The National Federation regarded local institutes 'as a splendid training ground for public work and Institute representatives will be quite capable of putting Institute views before the local authority'.[112] Annual reports for the 1920s and 1930s show that the majority of WIs were involved in community work during this period. The Cheshire Federation's report for 1928 provides a typical example of some of the civic duties undertaken by members. In the course of the year parties had been organised for village children, eggs had been collected and donated to local hospitals and fund-raising schemes had been successful in providing relief to the families of unemployed men living in mining villages.[113]

The leadership of the WI hoped that this kind of charitable work, together with the greater participation of women in local government, would stimulate the interest of members in national questions affecting the lives of women and children. Women who avoided the responsibilities of citizenship were frowned upon. In July 1928, *Home and Country* criticised three women jurors who had refused to sit on a case involving the sexual assault of a young boy. The editor accused the three of being 'shirkers' and wrote that 'if women want the rights of citizenship they must carry out its duties … moreover what is women's work if it is not to protect and safeguard the children of the nation.'[114]

The democratic structure of the WI movement was itself regarded as a training ground for women citizens. Speaking in 1937, Lady Denman concluded that 'the greatest achievement of the Institutes is that we have learnt to govern ourselves. We do not believe in dictators; we believe that each member should be responsible for her Institute and should have a share in the work.'[115] This firm commitment to democracy and education in citizenship remained an important aspect of the WI's work throughout the 1930s and 1940s. In 1948 Lady Albemarle, President of the National Federation, told delegates attending the Annual General Meeting that 'we are traders in democracy. In a democracy public opinion is a sovereign factor and that lays on each single one of us a responsibility … we must seek knowledge and pursue it. The Institute should give to the citizen opportunities for studying the questions of her day.'[116]

When the TG was first established by the NUSEC in 1932, its principle objective was 'to encourage the education of women to enable them as citizens to make the best contribution towards the common good.'[117] However, it soon became clear that the activities most favoured by guild members were handicrafts, home-craft, dancing and drama. The 'dreary business' of citizenship education proved to be less popular amongst the rank and file membership.[118] A 1933 survey of guild activities revealed that there had been 230 lectures and demonstrations on handicraft skills in comparison to the 116 lectures on current affairs and citizenship. Nevertheless, the leadership of the TG remained committed to citizenship education, and like the MU, CWL, NCW and WI ,acknowledged that as a national organisation for housewives it had a duty to encourage women to become better informed on public questions. Moreover women needed to get more involved in local and national life because as wives and mothers they had an important contribution to make.

This view was reiterated in 1933 when the *Annual Report* of the TG claimed that a woman was the 'best citizen, who is not only able to appreciate her responsibilities as a voter, but also is able to contribute her share to the home life of the nation and is able to make a profitable use of her leisure'.[119] Through the work of its Civics Committee, the TG hoped not only to encourage members to use their vote, but to give them every opportunity of 'developing themselves as citizens, encouraging and enabling them to fit themselves for the duties and responsibilities'.[120]

During the 1930s Eva Hubback, a member of the TG leadership and joint founder of the AEC, advised the Civics Committee on its approach to citizenship education. She suggested that the Guild adopt a broad definition of citizenship encompassing 'any question affecting the lives of individuals as citizens, that is, as parts of communities, local, national and international'.[121] In 1942 the AEC had published a number of booklets on democracy, public housing and discussion groups and advised that local guilds should purchase these booklets as soon as possible.[122]

In the local guilds, citizenship education took the form of lectures and debates on current affairs, as well as on issues affecting the lives of women and children. In 1933, the reports of 120 guilds revealed that there had been twenty-three lectures on the work of local councils, twenty on local history, ten on the work of the League of Nations and five on the state and the child.[123] Typical lecture topics during the 1930s also included 'Disarmament', 'Maternal Mortality', 'Women Police' and 'Local Government'.[124]

Throughout this period, the TG remained mindful of its commitment to provide a common meeting ground for women and so was careful to avoid party political or sectarian issues. At the same time however, the TG sought to encourage members 'to equip themselves, as individuals, for service to the community, by the study of any subject; and so to develop their powers of discrimination and their ability to make decisions on questions affecting the common good'.[125] To overcome this apparent contradiction, special study groups were set up within local guilds, which could focus on important but potentially controversial questions. By 1945 most local guilds reported that they had formed special study groups to allow for more specialist debate on a range of subjects.[126]

Topics selected by these groups included the international situation and the programmes of the various political parties. By discussing party politics in this way, it was hoped that members would be able to make up their own minds on which way to vote, instead of depending on the advice of their husbands.[127] Women were also encouraged to join the established political parties, as well as feminist women's societies, so that they could participate in political activities within their own communities. So committed was the TG to this area of work, it announced in 1943 that its post-war priority would be to

> take in all urban women, especially those who are not yet politically conscious, so that they may have an opportunity of having their interest aroused in the well-being of the community, local, national and international, and of developing their powers of discrimination in preparation for joining political parties of their own choosing.[128]

Social service was another important aspect of the TG's citizenship work. In 1935, Margery Corbett Ashby told delegates attending the AGM that

> It is no longer a burning sense of injustice that unites us but a growing realisation of our civic responsibilities, a growing conviction that the greatness of our country has its roots in *our* homes, that our cities can only grow and flourish, if fed by the contribution of citizens.[129]

The civic activities undertaken by TG members during the 1930s were similar to those of other voluntary women's societies. In 1932 it was reported that sewing parties had donated clothes to the local poor and that soup kitchens had been set up for the unemployed.[130] Other projects included organising parties and outings for children, old people and the blind, as well as hospital visiting and fund-raising for charitable causes.[131] TG branches also got involved in local issues, including anti-litter protests, calls for efficient bus services and improved street lighting.[132]

Following on from these community campaigns, the leadership of the TG hoped that members would consider putting themselves forward as candidates in local government elections. In 1933, it was claimed that many members had been elected to urban district councils or co-opted onto local committees, although no exact figures were given. Membership of a local guild was thought to give women the confidence to stand for election as the business of the weekly meeting with its formal procedures, public speaking and debates on public issues ensured that women 'gained the poise and assurance needed to take up public work'.[133]

The TG has often been regarded as a conservative, middle-class organisation accused of having betrayed its feminist origins.[134] There is no doubt that the TG avoided discussing difficult issues such as birth control and divorce during the 1930s and clearly sought to distance itself from party politics and the feminist movement. At the local level, traditional activities such as handicrafts, cooking and dressmaking proved to be most popular amongst guild members. Nevertheless the TG, through its education programmes, study groups and local civic work, gave women important opportunities to step outside their homes and develop the confidence to participate in civil society. From the perspective of the national organisation, engagement in campaigns for women's social and welfare rights would not only enhance the lives of individuals but also raise awareness about the rights and duties of women's citizenship. This aspect of the TG's work should no longer be ignored.

It is now evident that voluntary women's organisations valued the role of women as citizens, sought to educate their members in citizenship and had no doubt about the importance of civil, political and social citizenship for women. Although women had been involved in philanthropic and political activities long before the extension of the parliamentary franchise, the fact that the 1918 Representation of the People Act and the 1928 Equal Franchise Act gave formal citizenship rights to women was of enormous significance.

Women's societies, whether they were feminist, political or mainstream, were immediately aware of the power of the vote and responded by educating and informing their members about the rights and duties of democratic citizens. Voluntary women's groups focused on the contribution that women, as wives and mothers, could make to society. Moreover they sought to encourage women to have the confidence to participate in public life. Their emphasis on a gendered citizenship, on the different and unique contribution that housewives could make, made sense because they represented hundreds of thousands of women who were full-time wives and mothers.

Feminist interpretations of citizenship, which recognise that men and women were granted the rights of citizenship at different times and which link individual rights, political participation and the power of female agency, help explain why women's organisations placed so much emphasis on citizenship in the decades following women's suffrage. When the involvement of all women's groups, feminist, political and voluntary, in this 'citizenship project' is taken into account, a much more unified women's movement begins to emerge.

This movement cannot be limited to feminist societies or to groups who shared a similar understanding of women's role in society. Instead the women's movement, like all social movements, embraced a wide diversity of opinion united by a common aim: to enhance the lives of women. The following chapters will explore how the MU, CWL, NCW, WI and TG contributed to this women's movement. What will become clear is how they used their influence, their popularity and their respectability to speak out on behalf of wives and mothers, so that they could secure the civil and social rights believed to be the entitlement of all citizens.

Notes

1 R. Lister, *Citizenship: Feminist Perspectives* (Basingstoke: Palgrave, 1997), p. 4.
2 K. Canning and S. O. Rose, 'Gender, Citizenship and Subjectivity: Some Historical and Theoretical Considerations', in K. Canning and S. O. Rose (eds), *Gender, Citizenship and Subjectivities* (Oxford: Blackwell, 2002), p. 5.
3 T. H. Marshall, *Citizenship and Social Class* (Cambridge: Cambridge University Press, 1950), pp. 28–29.

4 *Ibid.*, p. 10.
5 N. Yuval-Davis, 'Women, Citizenship and Difference', *Feminist Review*, 57 (1997), R. Lister, 'Citizenship: Towards a Feminist Synthesis', *Feminist Review*, 57 (1997), Lister, *Citizenship: Feminist Perspectives* and S. Walby, 'Is Citizenship Gendered?', *Sociology*, 28:2 (1994).
6 Walby, 'Is Citizenship Gendered?', p. 381.
7 See Hollis, *Ladies Elect* for an account of women's participation in local government during these years.
8 P. Thane, 'Women in the British Labour Party and the Construction of State Welfare, 1906–1939', in S. Koven and S. Michel, *Mothers of a New World: Maternalist Politics and the Origins of Welfare States* (London: Routledge, 1993), p. 334. See also Thane, 'Women and Political Participation'.
9 Walby, 'Is Citizenship Gendered?', p. 385.
10 Yuval-Davis, 'Women, Citizenship and Difference', p. 6.
11 Walby, 'Is Citizenship Gendered?', p. 385.
12 K. Hunt, 'Women as Citizens: Changing the Polity', in D. Simonton (ed.), *The Routledge History of Women in Europe Since 1700* (London: Routledge, 2006), p. 220.
13 B. S. Turner, 'Outline of a Theory of Citizenship', *Sociology*, 24:2 (1990).
14 Walby, 'Is Citizenship Gendered?', p. 383.
15 Lister cited in Canning and Rose, 'Gender, Citizenship and Subjectivity', p. 4.
16 Lister, 'Citizenship: Towards a Feminist Synthesis', p. 32.
17 *Ibid.*, p. 33.
18 *Ibid.*, p. 35.
19 In 1918 women were admitted to the women's sections of the Labour Party. By 1931 the women's sections had a membership of some 250,000 women. See P. Thane, 'Visions of Gender in the Making of the British Welfare State: The Case of Women in the British Labour Party and Social Policy, 1906–1945', in G. Bock and P. Thane, *Maternity and Gender Policies: Women and the Rise of the European Welfare States, 1880s to 1950s* (London: Routledge, 1991), p. 94. See also C. Rowan, 'Women in the Labour Party, 1906–1920', *Feminist Review*, 12 (1982) and K. Cowman, *Women in British Politics, c. 1689–1979* (Basingstoke: Palgrave Macmillan, 2010), pp. 101–112.
20 For a history of the Primrose League see M. Pugh, *The Tories and the People 1880–1935* (Oxford: Oxford University Press, 1985), B. Campbell, *The Iron Ladies: Why Do Women Vote Tory?* (London: Virago, 1987). Following the extension of the franchise, many Conservative women joined the Women's Unionist Organisations which by 1924 had over 4,000 branches. Cowman, *Women in British Politics*, p. 135.
21 *Ibid.*, p. 80.
22 S. Koven and S. Michel, 'Womanly Duties: Maternalist Politics and the Origins of Welfare States in France, Germany, Great Britain, and the United States, 1880–1920', *American Historical Review*, 95:11 (1990), p. 1099.
23 Hunt, 'Women as Citizens', p. 237.
24 Pugh, *Women and the Women's Movement*, pp. 230–234. See also G. Scott, '"A Trade Union For Married Women": The Women's Co-operative Guild 1914–1920', in S. Oldfield (ed.), *The Working Day World: Women's Lives and Culture(s) in Britain 1914–1945* (London: Taylor and Francis, 1994).
25 Walby, 'Is Citizenship Gendered?', p. 385.
26 Pugh, *Women and the Women's Movement*, pp. 107–111 and Thane, 'Women and

Political Participation', pp. 19–23.

27 E. Rathbone, 'Changes in Public Life', in Strachey (ed.), *Our Freedom and Its Results*, p. 16.

28 S. Pederson, 'Gender, Welfare and Citizenship in Britain during the Great War', *American Historical Review*, 95:4 (1990), pp. 983–1005.

29 C. Pateman, 'The Patriarchal Welfare State', in A. Gutmann (ed.), *Democracy and the Welfare State* (Princeton: Princeton University Press, 1988), p. 252. For a discussion of the concept of citizenship for women see also A. Phillips, 'Citizenship and Feminist Theory', in G. Andrews (ed.), *Citizenship* (London: Lawrence and Wishart, 1991) and C. Pateman, *The Disorder of Women* (Cambridge: Cambridge University Press, 1989).

30 C. Pateman 'Equality, Difference, Subordination: the Politics of Motherhood and Women's Citizenship', in G. Bock and S. James (eds), *Beyond Equality and Difference* (London: Routledge, 1992), p. 20. See also Offen, *European Feminisms*, pp. 1–26.

31 Hunt, 'Women as Citizens', p. 238. For a discussion of the British context see for example A. Davin, 'Imperialism and Motherhood', *History Workshop Journal*, 5 (1978).

32 Hunt, 'Women as Citizens', p. 238.

33 *Ibid.*, p. 249.

34 Pedersen, 'Gender, Welfare and Citizenship', pp. 1002–1005. See also H. Land, 'Eleanor Rathbone and the Economy of the Family', in Smith (ed.), *British Feminism in the Twentieth Century*.

35 Cited in Land, 'Eleanor Rathbone and the Economy of the Family', p. 115.

36 See for example J. Alberti, *Beyond Suffrage: Feminists in War and Peace, 1914–28* (Basingstoke: Palgrave Macmillan, 1989) and Caine, *English Feminism*, pp. 197–202.

37 Beaumont, 'The Women's Movement, Politics and Citizenship', p. 264.

38 Thane, 'Visions of Gender', p. 96.

39 E. Darling, '"Enriching and Enlarging the Whole Sphere of Human Activities": The Work of the Voluntary Sector in Housing Reform in Inter-war Britain', in C. Lawrence and A. Mayer (eds), *Regenerating England: Science, Medicine and Culture in Inter-war Britain* (Atlanta: Editions Rodopi B. V., 2000), p. 152. See also J. Harris, 'Political Thought and the Welfare State, 1870–1940', *Past and Present*, 135 (1992).

40 E. Hubback and E. Simon, *Education in Citizenship* (London: Association for Education in Citizenship, 1934), p. 12.

41 Cited in Harrison, *Prudent Revolutionaries*, p. 286.

42 Ernest Simon was a Liberal businessman and an expert on housing policy who in 1931 was appointed Parliamentary Secretary to the Ministry of Health.

43 J. Field and P. Weller, 'The Association for Education in Citizenship, 1935–1955', unpublished paper presented to 'The Left and Citizenship in the 1940s and After', workshop held at the University of Warwick, 7 November 1991, pp. 5, 12.

44 These included: *Education for Citizenship* (London: AEC, 1934), *Training in Citizenship* (London: AEC, 1935) and *The Making of Citizens* (London: AEC, 1942).

45 Hubback, *The Making of Citizens*, p. 2.

46 Hubback and Simon, *Training For Citizenship*, p. 43.

47 Hubback, *The Making of Citizens*, p. 2.

48 C. Braithwaite, *The Voluntary Citizen: An Enquiry into the Place of Philanthropy in the Community* (London: Methuen, 1938), p. 78.

49 *Ibid.*

50 *Ibid.*, p. 15.

51 *Ibid.*, p. 80.

52 *Ibid.*, p. 58.

53 A desire to educate voters in citizenship was not restricted to women's organisations or political parties. As Helen McCarthy has argued, the inter-war years witnessed an expansion in civic organisation 'strongly invested in a discourse of active citizenship'. H. McCarthy, 'Parties, Voluntary Associations and Democratic Politics in Interwar Britain', *Historical Journal*, 50 (2007), p. 892.

54 Innes, 'Constructing Women's Citizenship', p. 624. For a discussion on Conservative, Labour and Liberal parties' efforts to mobilise female voters see Cowman, *Women in British Politics*, pp. 131–138.

55 *Ibid.*, p. 639.

56 Caine, *English Feminism*, p. 199.

57 Thane, 'Women and Political Participation', p. 17.

58 Cited in Cowman, *Women in British Politics*, p. 136.

59 The Women's Library, London (hereafter WL), Pamphlet Collection, *The Constitution of the National Women Citizens' Association* (1918).

60 Eleanor Rathbone had set up the first WCA in Liverpool in 1913 to educate local women about the power of the vote and the importance of democratic citizenship. Pugh, *Women and the Women's Movement*, p. 50. See also Innes, 'Constructing Women's Citizenship' and Wright, 'Education for Active Citizenship'.

61 Innes, 'Constructing Women's Citizenship', p. 624.

62 *Ibid.*, p. 622.

63 *The Mothers' Union Journal*, 157 (August 1934), p. 20.

64 *Ibid.*

65 *Ibid.*

66 *Ibid.*, p. 19.

67 Cordelia Moyse writes that the MU did not officially support the campaign for women's suffrage, believing in 'the complementarity of the different duties and responsibilities of the sexes'. Moyse, *A History of the Mothers' Union*, pp. 65–66.

68 *Ibid.*, p. 20.

69 The Union's campaign against divorce is discussed in Chapter 3.

70 *The Mothers' Union Journal*, 157 (August 1934), p. 20.

71 Cited by John Kent in his unpublished paper 'The attitudes of the British Churches to citizenship and national identity 1920–1960, with special reference to the work of William Temple', presented at the conference 'The Right to Belong, Citizenship and National Identity', University College London, 7 May 1994.

72 *The Mothers' Union Journal*, 158 (September 1934), p. 11.

73 MSH, Central Council Minutes, Vol. 11 (1937–42), 'Minutes of the Mothers' Union Central Council', December 1937, p. 45.

74 *The Mothers' Union Journal* (London Cover), 90 (March 1930), p. 5.

75 *The Catholic Women's League Magazine*, 309 (July 1937), p. 14.

76 *The Catholic Women's League Magazine*, 90 (April 1919), p. 22.

77 *Ibid.*

78 *The Catholic Women's League Magazine*, 253 (November 1932), p. 13.

79 *The Catholic Women's League Magazine*, 246 (March 1932), p. 15.

80 *The Catholic Women's League Magazine*, 317 (March 1938), p. 12.

81 *The Catholic Women's League Magazine*, 252 (October 1932), p. 13.

82 *Ibid.*
83 *The Catholic Women's League Magazine*, 257 (March 1933), p. 10.
84 *Ibid.*
85 *Ibid.*
86 *The Catholic Women's League Magazine*, 290 (December 1935). p. 8.
87 *The Catholic Women's League Magazine*, 302 (December 1936), p. 16.
88 *Ibid.*
89 *Ibid.*
90 In 1924 the NUSEC merged with the WCAs and in 1947 the NWCA merged with the NCEC. Pugh, *Women and the Women's Movement*, p. 51.
91 *NCW Handbook 1929–1930* (1930), p. 59. WCAs affiliated to the NCW during this period included the Newport WCA, the Kingston, Malden and Surbiton and District WCA and the Sutton Coldfield WCA.
92 *Women in Council*, 5 (May 1931), p. 4.
93 *Ibid.*
94 *Ibid.*
95 *NCW News*, 158 (January 1928), p. 16.
96 *NCW News*, 167 (October 1928), p. 2.
97 *Ibid.*
98 BCL, MSS 841 B/4, NCW Birmingham Branch Records, *The National Council of Women: What Is It?* (1929).
99 *Ibid.*
100 BCL, MSS 841 B/31, NCW Birmingham Branch Records (May 1925–January 1931), 'Minutes of the Citizenship Sub-Committee', January–March 1928.
101 *NCW News*, 159 (February 1928), p. 45.
102 *Ibid.*, p. 44.
103 BCL, MSS 841 B/31, Birmingham Branch Records (May 1925–January 1931), 'Minutes of Branch Meeting', 19 September 1929.
104 *NCW Handbook 1931–32* (1932), p. 61.
105 Jenkins, *The History of the Women's Institute Movement*, p. 45.
106 National Federation of Women's Institutes, *Keeping Ourselves Informed: Our Concerns, Our Resolutions, Our Actions* (London: NFWI, 1981), p. 48.
107 *Home and Country*, 10:5 (May 1928), p. 67. Martin Pugh writes that there was a steady increase in the number of women elected to local government during the inter-war period. By the late 1930s women were represented on almost two in every three local authorities but the total number still remained small, with women representing only five to six per cent of councillors in 1937. Pugh, *Women and the Women's Movement*, pp. 56–61.
108 *Home and Country*, 10:5 (May 1928), p. 67.
109 *Home and Country*, 10:8 (August 1928), p. 136.
110 *Ibid.*
111 WL, Pamphlet Collection, *National Federation of Women's Institutes Annual Report, 1928* (1928), p. 39.
112 *Home and Country*, 10:4 (April 1928), p. 47.
113 WL, Pamphlet Collection, *National Federation of Women's Institutes Annual Report 1928* (1928), p. 39.
114 *Home and Country*, 10:7 (July 1928), p. 84.

115 *Home and Country*, 19 (July 1937), p. 111.

116 *Home and Country*, 30:6 (June 1948), p. 91.

117 WL, Pamphlet Collection, *The National Union of Townswomen's Guilds Annual Report 1932* (1932), p. 40.

118 WL, Pamphlet Collection, *National Union of Townswomen's Guilds Annual Report 1933* (1933), p. 13.

119 *Ibid.*, p. 7.

120 WL, Pamphlet Collection, *National Union of Townswomen's Guilds Annual Report, 1938* (1938), p. 8.

121 WL, Pamphlet Collection, *National Union of Townswomen's Guilds Annual Report, 1937* (1937), p. 7.

122 *The Townswoman*, 10:1 (September 1942), p. 7.

123 WL, Pamphlet Collection, *National Union of Townswomen's Guilds Annual Report, 1933* (1933), p. 13.

124 WL, Pamphlet Collection, *National Union of Townswomen's Guilds Annual Report, 1932* (1932), p. 41.

125 WL, Pamphlet Collection, *National Union of Townswomen's Guilds, Handbook 1938* (1938), p. 17.

126 WL, Pamphlet Collection, *National Union of Townswomen's Guilds Annual Report, 1945* (1945), p. 42.

127 *Ibid.*, p. 43.

128 *The Townswoman*, 11:7 (July 1943), p. 148.

129 *The Townswoman*, 3:1 (April 1935), p. 3.

130 WL, Pamphlet Collection, *National Union of Townswomen's Guilds Annual Report, 1932* (1932), p. 41.

131 WL, Pamphlet Collection, *National Union of Townswomen's Guilds Annual Report, 1934* (1934), p. 16.

132 *Ibid.*

133 WL, Pamphlet Collection, *National Union of Townswomen's Guilds Annual Report, 1945* (1945), p. 9.

134 See for example Pugh, 'Domesticity and the Decline of Feminism', p. 202.

3

Moral dilemmas: divorce, birth control and abortion

Significant changes in public attitudes towards divorce, birth control and abortion occurred during the inter-war period. Legislation was introduced which extended the grounds for divorce and for the first time information on birth control was made available to married mothers at local authority clinics, albeit on strict medical grounds. Concerns about the rise in the maternal mortality rate highlighted the prevalence, as well as the dangers, of illegal abortion. This led to a number of women's groups campaigning throughout the 1930s for the introduction of safe and legal abortion. Campaigns for reform in the law relating to these important social questions have been well documented by historians.[1]

Omitted from these studies, however, are the views and voices of voluntary women's organisations, representing hundreds of thousands of women, on key issues affecting the daily lives of housewives and mothers. This chapter will challenge such an oversight and demonstrate that throughout the inter-war years an important discourse emerged within the wider women's movement about the moral and social dilemmas related to marital and sexual behaviour.[2]

The MU and CWL's objection to reform of the law on divorce, birth control information and abortion, highlights their genuine concern that any change in the law would undermine the domestic role of women. In raising such objections conservative women's groups asked important questions about the level of state support for wives and mothers. It was argued that state support for women needed to be expanded in order to offer effective alternatives to divorce, birth control and abortion.

Voluntary women's organisations wishing to unite women from different social and religious backgrounds were reluctant to adopt a viewpoint on moral or sectarian issues. As a result the WI and the TG refused to discuss divorce, birth control and abortion throughout the inter-war period in order to protect the unanimity of the membership. It is clear that this decision was influenced by the belief of both groups that their members had conflicting views with regard to these moral questions. Conversely the NCW, working alongside a number of feminist societies, was outspoken in calling for reforms which would facilitate greater access to these social and civil rights. Although the views expressed by the MU and the CWL were very different from those held by the NCW, all three organisations claimed to represent the interests of women and placed women's welfare at the top of their agendas.

Divorce

The reaction of the MU and the CWL to the liberalisation of divorce legislation during the inter-war years was predictable. Both the Catholic Church and the Church of England endorsed the belief that marriage was a sacred indissoluble sacrament, not to be ended by divorce.[3] As church societies representing the views of devout women, it was hardly surprising that the MU and the CWL opposed any proposal to introduce new grounds for divorce.[4] By the early 1920s, divorce in England and Wales was only possible under the restrictive terms of the 1857 Divorce Act. This Act allowed men to divorce their wives for adultery while women had to prove additional grounds of cruelty and desertion.[5]

The *Report of the Royal Commission on Divorce* (1912), advised that reforms should be introduced to remove the discrimination against women and extend the grounds for divorce to include desertion, cruelty and insanity.[6] The MU, in evidence to the Commission, had made clear that its objection to divorce law reform was based on the belief that the marriage vow 'lasts till death breaks it'.[7] In contrast the WCG, representing 27,000 working-class wives, argued that cruelty, insanity and mutual consent should be accepted as grounds for divorce, demonstrating that not all women were satisfied with the existing divorce law. Much to the relief of the MU however, the recommendations of the Royal Commission were not acted upon because, as Roderick Phillips has suggested, they were 'out of line with the prevailing conservative attitudes' held at that time.[8]

Following the First World War, the number of marriages ending in divorce increased significantly. Between 1910 and 1913 an average of 701 divorces took place each year. However, partly due to wartime disruption, separation and infidelity, the yearly average rose to 1,407 divorces in 1918.[9] In that same year the franchise was extended to women over thirty and members of the MU and the CWL were urged to use their influence as electors to prevent any change in the divorce law. In 1918 the Archbishop of York, addressing the National Conference of the MU, told delegates that

> your adhesion to the fundamental principle of the Mothers' Union in regard to indissoluble marriage is something which concerns you closely as citizens, now that citizenship of this country is very specially committed to your care. A great responsibility has been laid upon you in the life of the Church and the Nation.[10]

Similarly, the Catholic Bishop of Northampton advised members of the CWL in June 1921, that the

> main reason for conferring citizenship upon women was that women might speak for women … many of the ablest speakers of the day are pledged to easier divorce. Were they [women] going to give such leaders their votes to impose that abomination of divorce on a Christian nation? The answer would be emphatically NO![11]

When two private members bills were introduced before the House of Lords in 1920 and 1921,[12] advocating desertion as a ground for divorce, both the MU and the CWL protested. As Cordelia Moyse writes, by the early 1920s the MU had 'gained recognition as a stakeholder in public discussions of marriage and divorce reform'.[13] The MU Central Council urged Diocesan Presidents and individual members to write to local MPs outlining their objections to divorce.[14] Equally opposed to any reform of the divorce law, the CWL drew up a petition against Lord Gorell's 1921 bill and a deputation led by the President of the League, Lady Sykes, visited Westminster and urged MPs to reject any new grounds for divorce.[15]

Neither bill won the support of the Conservative government and both failed to become law. It is important to note, however, that Lord Gorell's bill was passed in the House of Lords by a narrow majority, despite opposition from members of the Anglican hierarchy. Even more significant is the fact that the Bishop of Durham supported desertion as a ground for divorce, arguing that the marriage laws should adapt to 'modern conditions'.[16] The bishop's views reflected the concern of a small but influential group of churchmen who believed that the existing divorce law was in need of amendment.[17]

Evidence of a gap opening between the views of the MU and Church leaders became even more pronounced when in 1921 the Archbishop of Canterbury, Randall Davidson, expressed his support for the right of wives to have the same access to divorce as their husbands. To achieve this the existing law would have to be reformed to allow both men and women to sue for divorce on the grounds of adultery alone.[18] Explaining his action to the MU the Archbishop stated that he believed reform should be introduced where there was inequality between men and women. Based on these arguments the MU Executive decided that the Union would not publicly oppose any such reform but neither would it support such a measure.[19]

Following on-going pressure from women's groups, including the NUSEC and the WCG, limited divorce law reform was introduced in 1923 when wives were given the right to sue for divorce on the single ground of adultery. The extension of the franchise to women and the passing of the 1919 Sex Disqualification (Removal) Act had highlighted the fact that the continued discrimination against women under the divorce law was 'an anachronism and an indefensible anomaly'.[20] Although the Act did not include any new grounds, the number of divorce petitions filed by women immediately increased. As a result, between fifty and sixty per cent of divorce proceedings initiated each year, until the outbreak of the Second World War, were requested by women.[21]

Just as in 1921, the MU again adhered to the wishes of the Archbishop of Canterbury who instructed the Union not to oppose the legislation, which in his view did not conflict with Church teaching as no new grounds for divorce was being proposed.[22] Although the measure made the legal position of women more equitable, the fact that the Archbishop had to intervene to prevent the MU from protesting is significant. This episode reflected the uncompromising nature of the Union's attitude towards divorce, which by the early 1920s had already proved to be more conservative than the teaching of the wider Church.

In 1920 the MU had published its Fundamental Principles, outlining the Union's views on marriage and the family. With the rise in the number of divorces and the increasing likelihood of divorce law reform, the Union wanted to make its position on divorce clear. This document reaffirmed the Union's objective 'to uphold the sanctity of marriage' which was the 'lifelong and indissoluble union of one man with one woman to the exclusion of all others on either side'.[23] In 1923, a footnote was added to the Union's membership card explaining that 'in the words "to uphold the Sanctity of Marriage" the Mothers' Union affirms the Christian principle of the permanence of the relationship between husband and wife'.[24]

Having reaffirmed its official view on divorce, each member of the MU was now expected to uphold the first object 'by loving, helping and being faithful to her husband' as well as supporting 'every effort made to prevent any further weakening of our marriage laws'.[25] In 1926 the MU's new constitution went even further when for the first time the Union excluded women who married a divorcee with a living former spouse from membership.[26] This rule was added to membership restrictions on women who had been unfaithful to their husbands or who themselves had gone through a divorce. In addition, all those who did join were expected to protest against any further attempts to extend the grounds for divorce. This decision by the MU Central Council created some considerable controversy within the organisation throughout the 1930s.

In December 1931, Lady Maxse, President of the Army Division of the MU, argued that the Union could not expect members to 'pledge themselves in advance to oppose every bill or every clause in a bill which extends the grounds for divorce.'[27] Lady Maxse agreed that as an organisation for Anglican women, the MU was right to condemn divorce, but that each individual member had the right to make up her own mind about the law as it applied to those outside the Christian Church. A second prominent member of the MU, Dame Beatrix Lyall, endorsed this view. She argued that although all members of the Union stood firmly for the sanctity of marriage, in private life they should have the freedom to deal with people who did not accept the laws of the Church.[28] In response to these objections Mrs Boustead, the Central President, defended the Council's action explaining that 'if we are baptised communicant members of the Church and we pledge to believe and accept her laws and remember our marriage vows ... are we not bound to stand up and try to prevent further weakening of the married state?'[29]

However, the fact that the Union felt entitled to impose its own views on the rest of society did go beyond the official policy of the Anglican Church. In 1930, the Church of England had confirmed its belief in the indissolubility of marriage for all 'Christian people to maintain and bear witness' but declined to pass judgment on those who were not members of the Church.[30] This view was reiterated by the Archbishop of Canterbury in March 1932, when he advised Mrs Boustead that the MU should 'avoid any controversial statements as to the attitude which its workers and members may feel obliged to take on this difficult question ... relating to those outside its membership.'[31] With this warning the matter appeared to be resolved only to re-emerge four years later with the publication of A. P. Herbert's divorce reform bill.

In the meantime, the Union focused its attention on the importance of the marriage relationship and traditional family life. Throughout the 1930s, the Union published numerous pamphlets offering advice to members on questions relating to marriage and family life, such as *Happy Home Life* (1932), *To Those about to Be Married* (1935) and *Birth control: A Different Approach* (1935). The Union's journals also included articles on marital questions. The September 1936 edition of *The Mothers' Union*

Journal stressed that mutual compatibility, not mere physical attraction, formed the basis of a good relationship.[32] Engaged couples were advised about the importance of sex in marriage which 'like any other of God's good gifts ... needs to be carefully guarded. Modesty and self-control are guardian virtues of the marriage relationship together with mutual consideration and understanding.'[33]

Through its branch meetings and various publications, the MU promoted equal partnership and mutual respect between couples in the hope that this would reduce the likelihood of marriage breakdown. However, the Union did accept that some marriages would end in failure. In these cases it was made clear that judicial separation or nullity, and not divorce, was the Christian solution. In contrast to divorce, separation did not break the bond of marriage and 'sad through its necessity may be does still leave an "open door"'.[34]

During the 1930s, the CWL also emphasised the importance of Christian marriage. Members of the League and its sister organisation, the Union of Catholic Mothers, were urged to 'instil the ideals of marriage into the minds of their children.'[35] Upholding the teaching of the Catholic Church, the League believed that women were best suited for marriage and family life.[36] In 1936 the League's President, Dr Genevieve Rewcastle, reiterated this belief when she suggested that 'the successful home is where the father is looked up to as the head and breadwinner and the woman is the homemaker.'[37] Such a view was clearly influenced by Catholic social teaching on the role and status of women in society.

The papal encyclical *Rerum Novarum* (1891) outlined the 'natural' duty of woman, who is 'by her nature fitted for home work and it is this which is best adapted to preserve her modesty and promote the good upbringing of children and the well being of the family.'[38] In 1931 a new encyclical, *Quadregesimo Anno*, reinforced this view when it proclaimed that 'mothers will above all devote their work to the home and the things connected with it.'[39] In the view of the CWL and the Catholic Church, divorce would break up the traditional family and therefore threaten the role assigned to women within Catholic social teaching.

Although the divorce rate increased following the enactment of the 1923 Matrimonial Causes Act, the number of married couples who sought a divorce remained relatively small. For example, in 1936 only six per cent of all marriages ended in divorce. As Claire Langhamer has suggested, divorce before the Second World War was restricted to those who could afford it due to the lack of legal aid available to pursue divorce cases through the courts. Langhamer points out that 'working class access to divorce was severely circumscribed and recourse was made instead to summary separation orders awarded by the magistrates courts, which precluded remarriage.'[40]

Despite the small numbers of marriages ending in divorce throughout the 1930s there was growing concern about the inadequacies of the 1923 legislation as it granted a divorce only on the grounds of proven adultery. As a result, collusion between husbands and wives wishing to part was a distinct possibility. This usually occurred when one partner, invariably the husband, agreed to be caught in the act of adultery, so that his wife could sue for divorce.[41] If wives were found to be unfaithful, a husband could claim damages against a co-respondent involved with his wife in order to compensate for the break-up of the marriage. Wives were not afforded the same right. This ruling once again reflected the inequality embedded in divorce law, and the assumption that husbands would suffer the most financially as a result of a divorce.[42]

Limited grounds for divorce also encouraged the practice of cohabitation, as separated men and women began new relationships. In 1934, concern about the moral welfare of the community, as well as the plight of deserted wives left to support their children, prompted the NCW to address the sensitive issue of divorce. At its Annual Conference that year the Council passed a resolution calling on the government to reconsider the existing legislation, which it was argued 'encourages immorality and leads to much individual hardship'.[43] It is significant that the NCW couched its support for liberalisation of the divorce law in terms of moral purity and the vulnerability of deserted wives rather than on the legal right of women of all classes to obtain a divorce. What is clear is that, like the WI and the TG, the NCW was also aware of how divisive the issue of divorce could be and so framed its support in moral and welfare terms to ensure greater support from both its own membership and the wider public.

At the 1934 Annual Conference the NCW also urged that the grounds for divorce should be extended to include desertion, cruelty, drunkenness and incurable insanity, as recommended by the 1912 Royal Commission on Divorce. It should be noted that the MU immediately disassociated itself from this resolution whilst the CWL had allowed its membership of the NCW to lapse in 1930.[44] Although the WCG had advocated such reforms for many years, feminist societies such as the NUSEC had been somewhat reluctant to demand extended grounds for divorce. This was because its membership was divided on whether or not divorce should be made more easily available.

This fact once again highlights the level of controversy surrounding this moral issue and demonstrates that the difficulty in publicly advocating

liberalisation of the divorce law was not restricted to mainstream voluntary women's groups.[45] Despite these concerns however, by 1936 the
majority of feminist societies, as well as the NCW and the WCG, showed
no such qualms in supporting a new initiative to curtail the incidence of
collusion and cohabitation associated with marriage break-up. This new
proposal came in the shape of A. P. Herbert's divorce reform bill.

The bill, drawn up by the backbench MP Alan Herbert, proposed to
extend the grounds for divorce to include desertion after three years, cruelty,
insanity and habitual drunkenness.[46] It also recommended that divorce
proceedings should be initiated after two years of judicial separation, in
an effort to prevent cohabitation. Herbert hoped that extended grounds
for divorce would do away with the sense of scandal and immorality
surrounding divorce cases common during this period. Indeed, the scandal
surrounding the abdication of Edward VIII at the end of 1936 to marry a
twice-divorced woman, Wallis Simpson, highlighted the fact that divorce
was still regarded by many as a rather disreputable business.[47]

Although Herbert's bill introduced new grounds for divorce, it was
not his intention to allow 'quick and easy' divorces. The first clause of
the bill ensured that a divorce could not be granted within the first three
years of marriage.[48] Aware of the opposition to divorce amongst members
of the Anglican clergy, Herbert included a relief clause ensuring that no
clergyman could be compelled to marry a divorced person whose former
partner was still living.[49] Even though the Church of England still stood
firmly against divorce, Archbishop Lang welcomed the inclusion of this
proviso which he hoped would be 'retained and strengthened, otherwise
it would be necessary to organise strenuous opposition to the bill as a
whole'.[50]

When the bill came before the House of Lords with the relief clause
intact, Archbishop Lang abstained on the vote because 'as a statesman he
believed that the bill provided a "timely and valuable remedy" for many
abuses, yet as a clergyman he could not support any law in favour of
divorce'.[51] Explaining his action to Nina Woods, Central President of the
MU, Archbishop Lang assured her that the Church of England remained
committed to the principle of indissoluble marriage. He wrote that the
Union, as an independent society within the Church, was entitled to
oppose the 1936 bill without appearing in any way disloyal to the Church.
He went on to suggest however that there should be 'freedom of opinion
as to the various extra grounds for divorce ... [they] must be considered
one by one on their merits'.[52]

The idea that members of the MU would be free to make up their
own minds about new grounds for divorce remained a very contentious

issue. When Central Council came to debate the 1936 reform bill, it soon emerged that some members were not convinced that it should be rejected out of hand. The growing incidence of collusion and scandal in divorce cases had not gone unnoticed. The abdication crisis had demonstrated that even the Royal Family, much revered by the MU, could not avoid the moral dilemma of divorce and remarriage.

At the December 1936 meeting of Central Council, Beatrix Lyall outlined the beneficial aspects of Herbert's bill, which she believed would improve the existing divorce laws. The guarantee that divorce proceedings could not be initiated within the first three years of marriage would, she argued, safeguard against quick divorces. Dame Lyall also referred to the clause ruling that any application for divorce found to be based on false evidence would be rejected. She felt that this clause would do much to prevent the incidence of collusion and perjury in divorce cases.[53]

During the debate, Lyall made it clear that as a member of the MU she did not believe that divorce was a viable option either for herself or her fellow members. However, she felt that reform of the divorce law would 'be an attempt to make the law a little more decent and wholesome for the people outside [the MU] who do not acknowledge the Law of Christ'.[54] This view was supported by the Hon. Mrs Carfield, who argued that Herbert's bill had been drawn up 'with the earnest wish to raise the standards of morality in this country'.[55]

In spite of these appeals by high-ranking members, the Central President of the MU, Nina Woods, insisted that the Union could not support a bill proposing to extend the grounds for divorce. If this happened, the divorce rate would increase and the family life of the nation, which the MU had always fought to protect, would be put in jeopardy. Mrs Woods also rejected the new grounds proposed in Herbert's bill. She argued that the inclusion of desertion would encourage 'unworthy' husbands and wives to walk away from difficult marriages, whilst divorce on the grounds of insanity and drunkenness conflicted with the Christian marriage vow to remain faithful 'in sickness and in health'.[56]

When put to the vote, the majority of Central Council members agreed that the MU should campaign against the 1936 divorce reform bill. A statement was issued explaining that

> while there are some clauses in the Marriage bill that the Mothers' Union would not oppose, the Central Council feel compelled to record the opposition of the Mothers' Union to the bill as a whole because of the clauses … which would increase the grounds for divorce.[57]

Following this decision, the MU launched a major campaign to protest against any change in the divorce law. The Central Council and local branches, outlining the Union's objections to divorce, wrote letters to MPs and to national newspapers. Individual members were also encouraged to write to their MP and advised to 'get your husband to sign the letter as well which will add greatly to its value'.[58]

It is clear that the letter-writing campaign made some impact in parliament. In February 1937, Alan Herbert remarked that 'member after member [in the Commons] displays to me with glee, the latest fiery postcard or shocked resolution from the local [MU] branch'.[59] Following a meeting at Westminster with members of the MU to discuss the bill, Herbert expressed his dismay that an organisation representing married women did not support extended grounds for divorce. He asked

> will any member of the Mothers' Union tell me what 'sanctity of married life' remains and what precious thing we are destroying by permitting the deserted, the ill-treated, or the sane spouse to cast off a cruel mockery and marry again.[60]

In response to these criticisms the Central Secretary of the MU, Eva Remson Ward, defended the Union's desire to protect family life and the principle of indissoluble marriage. She warned that if the 1936 divorce bill became law it would 'bring disaster on the community as a whole'.[61] Remson Ward also argued that women opposed the bill because they would be the first to suffer if divorce became more widespread. Writing in *The Sunday Pictorial* (21 February 1937), she asked 'what about the women in the forties, no longer young or particularly attractive? A husband of that age, with looks and figure well preserved might easily fall for someone younger and more entertaining'.[62]

This statement underlined the Union's belief that deserted and divorced wives would be left without an income or home of their own. In a leaflet published by the Union on marriage and divorce, it had been suggested that more liberal divorce legislation would set aside 'the security not only of the home and family life, but of the married women of our nation'.[63] It is important to recall, however, that during the period 1931–35, women filed fifty-five per cent of divorce petitions. This trend of greater numbers of women seeking divorce continued throughout the late 1930s and well into the post-war period, with the exception of the years 1941–50.[64] The fact that on average more women than men wished to initiate divorce proceedings was never alluded to by the MU during this period, perhaps because it weakened their argument that women were less likely than men to want a divorce.

In spite of a well-organised protest campaign the MU failed to prevent the enactment of Herbert's bill and it passed into law at the end of 1937. The NCW welcomed the legislation, as it removed the need for collusion and cohabitation while allowing deserted and ill-treated wives the freedom to remarry. It should also be noted that despite the CWL's objection to divorce there is no evidence it campaigned against Alan Herbert's bill. Instead, the League concentrated on social welfare issues more likely to affect its own members, who as devout Catholics were unlikely to seek recourse in the divorce courts when experiencing marital difficulties.

The effects of the 1937 Matrimonial Causes Act were immediate, with the number of petitions for divorce almost doubling by the end of 1938.[65] The real increase came, however, in the aftermath of the Second World War when it was reported in 1947 that 48,501 divorce petitions had been lodged in that year alone, with the majority filed by husbands on the grounds of wartime adultery.[66] In the wake of the 1937 Act and the rise in the number of divorces, the MU continued to highlight the danger to traditional family life caused by divorce.

At the end of the war, the Union expressed its anxiety about the dramatic increase in the divorce rate by calling on the government to 'consider revising the law governing divorce, so as to include some provision for attempted reconciliation.'[67] This resolution was followed by a statement to the Royal Commission on Marriage and Divorce (1951), calling for 'a new and positive approach to matrimonial legislation which will give just consideration to the safeguarding of the institution of marriage and the integrity of the home.'[68]

It was clear, therefore, that the MU had lost none of its resolve to 'maintain and exemplify the full and uncompromised position of marriage' in a society slowly adapting to the idea of divorce and remarriage.[69] This hardline position on divorce also continued to cause tension and controversy within the organisation. Disagreement over the meaning of the first object remained and in 1939 the Muswell Hill branch was closed by the MU when its branch officials made statements to the press challenging the Union's rigid view on divorce law.[70]

In order to clarify the Union's position once and for all in December 1939, the Central Council voted in favour of the view that there was only one interpretation of the first object and that was that marriage was indissoluble and could not be ended in divorce. Furthermore it was agreed that any branch or individual that did not comply with this ruling 'should be asked if their consciences would allow them to remain as loyal members'.[71] Despite this unequivocal position some dissent remained and Moyse reports that the Archbishop of Canterbury, William Temple, felt compelled to intervene in the debate in early 1940. The Archbishop advised that all members of the MU should feel able to continue working within the Union and that personal views on divorce law reform should be a private matter of personal conscience. The Archbishop also recommended that there should be no further discussion of the controversial first object until after the war.[72]

There is no doubt that the attitude of the MU to divorce law reform during the 1930s and early 1940s was both conservative and unyielding. As a Church of England society, the Union saw divorce as an attack on the Christian principle of indissoluble marriage. For this reason, the MU was unwilling to accept any legislative reform enabling an increase in the number of marriages ending in divorce. The MU regarded divorce as a threat to traditional family life. Moreover divorce would cause great financial and emotional hardship to women and children. Any undermining of marriage would also threaten the status of women as wives and mothers, the very group which the Union sought to support and represent throughout the inter-war years.

The CWL also objected to divorce on religious grounds and it too wished to promote the status of married women. The idea that the law should be changed to help women escape bad marriages was unacceptable to both the MU and the CWL and neither group was willing to engage with the evidence that in many cases it was women themselves who initiated divorce proceedings. Both groups firmly believed that women were happiest within marriage and that extended grounds for divorce would deprive women of their right to marriage and motherhood. Conversely, the NCW supported reform of the divorce law in order to protect the moral and physical welfare of women and children. In spite of the religious dilemmas involved, the Council welcomed legislation to prevent the immoral acts of collusion and cohabitation. At the same time the Council believed that deserted and abused wives had the right to divorce their husbands and seek happiness in a second marriage.

Despite the fact that the MU and the CWL were inflexible in their stance against divorce law reform and the NCW accepted that women did have the right to end their marriages, each group was anxious to safeguard the security and status of married women. To do so was important at a time when the marriage rate was increasing, especially during the latter half of the 1930s.[73] It is significant, therefore, that the debate surrounding divorce reform revealed not only the conservative attitudes of the MU and the CWL, but the genuine desire of all three groups to protect the interests of married women in society.

Birth control

Moral dilemmas confronting women's organisations were not restricted to divorce legislation throughout the inter-war years. Birth control, like divorce, was a highly controversial and potentially divisive issue for women's societies. It was not until the early 1920s, when the provision of birth control information became more widely available and the use of contraceptives more respectable, that feminist and some voluntary women's organisations finally tackled this important issue.[74] Once again, however, the WI and the TG, mindful of the religious and moral sensibilities of their members, refused to discuss publicly the question of family limitation or lobby for greater access to such information. This refusal to comment on birth control was taken so seriously that Lady Denman, chairman of both the WI and the National Birth Control Association (NBCA), made it clear that in her work for the WI she could not discuss the principle of birth control because it was a 'sectarian matter'.[75]

Although many women's groups avoided this contentious issue, significant numbers of couples were already practising some form of birth control well before the outbreak of the First World War. Traditional methods included withdrawal (*coitus interruptus*), the sheath and the 'safe-period'.[76] Since the beginning of the century, the impact of family limitation and later marriages meant that the average Victorian family of seven or eight children had fallen to just one or two children by the early 1930s.[77] Yet in spite of the general decline in family size, many women, in particular working-class women, continued to give birth to large numbers of children, which often had a detrimental effect on their health and the economic stability of their family.[78]

In 1915 the WCG published *Maternity: Letters from Working Women* to highlight the detrimental physical and emotional effects frequent childbirth had on mothers. When Marie Stopes published *Married Love* in 1918 she received thousands of letters from men and women enquiring about all kinds of sexual problems, including the use of birth control.[79] Many of these letters detailed the suffering of women with large families who did not want to have any more children. For example, one thirty-seven-year-old woman, who wrote to Stopes in 1922, already had fourteen children and was anxious to avoid another pregnancy because of a weak heart and prolapsed womb. However, because her husband was 'not a careful man in that respect' she needed some urgent advice about contraception.[80]

Providing women with information on family planning was at the centre of the birth control debate during the 1920s and 1930s. In 1921, Marie Stopes opened her first birth control clinic in London where married women could go for advice about contraception and be fitted with a 'Pro-Race' cervical cap. Although Stopes was a member of the Eugenics Society,[81] her work in the clinics focused primarily on the health and welfare of mothers and less on the economic and eugenic advantages of birth control.[82] She argued that parents who planned and spaced their children would not only produce healthier babies but also give mothers time to recover from childbirth.

The impact of Stopes's work in birth control and her emphasis on the health of mothers was far-reaching. During the 1920s a number of societies and clinics were established which advocated the use of birth control for married women.[83] These voluntary organisations could only provide a limited service and campaigners urged the government to sanction the provision of birth control information at local authority maternity and child welfare clinics. In 1930 the NBCA was set up by the leading birth control societies to bring pressure to bear on the government to introduce this important service for married women.

The establishment of birth control clinics and the association between family limitation and women's health succeeded in drawing women's societies into the debate. By the end of the 1920s, the WCG, the Labour Party Women's Sections, the Women's National Liberal Association and the NUSEC had all voted in favour of the provision of birth control information at local authority clinics.[84] As well as campaigning for the wider availability of such information to all married women, these groups also recognised that working-class women were less likely to have access to this type of advice as many would be unable to afford private medical treatment. Nevertheless, concern about the falling birth rate[85] and the moral implications of family limitation meant that throughout the 1920s both the Labour and Conservative administrations refused to yield to the demand for free birth control advice to be made available to married women.

In 1929 the NCW added its voice to those calling on the Ministry of Health and local authorities to provide birth control information at publicly funded clinics. The Council recommended that contraceptive advice should be given 'in cases in which either a married mother asks for such information, or in which, in the opinion of the medical officer, the health of the parents renders it desirable.'[86] Like other women's societies, the NCW was concerned about the welfare of married women whose health was put in danger by repeated pregnancies and childbirth.

Predictably, the MU and the CWL dissociated themselves from this resolution. In 1919, the Central Council of the MU had agreed that 'all artificial checks to conception are against the laws of nature.'[87] The Union disapproved of the voluntary birth control clinics and was outraged when in 1927 Marie Stopes converted two horse-drawn caravans into mobile clinics, which travelled to towns and cities in the northeast of England.[88] When a Catholic woman in Bradford destroyed one of the caravans by setting it on fire,[89] the Central Council of the MU did not condemn the action and warned members 'to be ready for the caravan' when it came to their city'.[90]

The Union's objection to artificial methods of birth control was based on the teaching of the Church of England. At the Lambeth Conference of 1908 and again in 1920, the Church had refused to condone the use of contraceptives, even in cases of medical or economic necessity.[91] However, as it became clear that many couples were using birth control as a way of limiting their families, the Church came under increasing pressure to modernise its views.[92] It is worth noting that on average the number of children in the families of Anglican clergymen during this period was actually smaller than the national average. This indicated that many clergymen, whose wives were likely to be members of the local MU, were themselves using some form of family limitation.[93] Even more significant were the letters to Marie Stopes from members of the clergy revealing the hardship caused by abstinence (in one case for over twenty-nine years) and the desire for more information about birth control methods.[94]

It is perhaps not surprising therefore that at the 1930 Lambeth Conference, the Church of England conceded that in certain circumstances there may be 'a moral obligation to limit or avoid parenthood'.[95] In these instances abstinence was recommended, but the Church accepted that where 'a morally sound reason for avoiding complete abstinence existed other methods may be used'.[96] Couples were warned, however, that 'the use of any methods of conception-control from motives of selfishness, luxury, or mere convenience' was unacceptable and must always be condemned.[97]

The Church's new ruling on birth control created some difficulties for the MU. Having declared that artificial birth control was unchristian, the Union was forced to rethink its attitude towards family limitation. The Archbishop of Canterbury William Temple advised the Union's President, Mrs Boustead, to 'face the fact' that the use of contraceptives in certain circumstances was, as he put it 'not wrong'.[98] As a result, the Central Council of the MU acknowledged that family limitation was a private matter for married couples and did not make the rejection of birth control a condition of membership. In December 1930 the Central Council confirmed that the Union 'did not dictate to members on the subject of birth control'.[99]

Nonetheless, the MU advised that 'all young couples should be willing to have at least one or two children to complete their marriage' and urged members to 'strive to restore a public opinion which will rate the possession of children higher than owning a motor-car or a comfortably furnished house'.[100] While the risk to the health of mothers who had large families was acknowledged, the Union claimed that 'much of the nervous strain and consequent ill-health accompanying child-birth to-day was unknown to earlier generations who rejoiced whole-heartedly in the prospect of motherhood.'[101]

Here the Union would appear to be criticising women themselves for not embracing motherhood in the way their own mothers had and suggesting perhaps that modern women were not as committed to motherhood as they should be. This view would also imply that birth control was being used by women to avoid the wider responsibility they had to society as mothers, a view in keeping with concerns at this time regarding the population question and the need for young women to be encouraged to have children.

In contrast to the MU, the CWL was not prepared to compromise in any way on the question of birth control. As with divorce, the League's objection to the use of contraceptive devices was based firmly on Catholic social teaching. The papal encyclical *Casti Connubii* (1930) reaffirmed the Church's opposition to the 'grave sin' of contraception. Catholic couples were advised that total abstinence and the 'safe-period' were the only acceptable and Christian methods of family limitation.[102] It was not surprising, therefore, that the Catholic Church became one of the most outspoken critics of Marie Stopes and the birth control movement.[103] As a result, the CWL mounted a national campaign to protest against the provision of birth control information at voluntary and local authority clinics.

Following continued lobbying from women's groups, the Women's Sections of the Labour Party and from birth control societies during the late 1920s, the Labour Minister of Health, Arthur Greenwood, reluctantly agreed to tackle the question of birth control information being made available at publicly funded clinics. In 1930 he issued a memorandum allowing maternity and child welfare clinics to advise married women about birth control in 'cases where further pregnancy would be detrimental to health'.[104] This was a limited measure and local authorities were not compelled to offer the service, but it was an important step in the provision of free contraceptive advice to married women.[105]

The CWL objected to the fact that public welfare clinics could now provide women with birth control information. In 1935, the League issued a statement highlighting its opposition to 'any policy of the Government or its departments which allows information on artificial birth control to be given at centres and clinics maintained out of public funds.[106] By this time, local League members had already demonstrated their willingness to protest against the establishment of family planning clinics. In 1932, the Birmingham branch passed a resolution calling on its members to 'protest against the public recognition of the immoral and pagan practice of birth control ... it [the CWL] will oppose strenuously the establishment of clinics for such teaching and also all persons who advocate their establishment.'[107]

CWL members regularly disrupted meetings held by birth control campaigners in an effort to highlight their opposition to birth control clinics. It was hoped that any hint of controversy would dissuade local authorities from providing information on contraception at maternity and child welfare centres. This tactic proved successful in April 1932, when members of the League and the Union of Catholic Mothers attended a meeting of birth control campaigners in Bolton. The meeting had been called to urge the local authority to sanction the provision of information at welfare clinics. However, following the objections raised by the Catholic women, the local council rejected the proposal.[108]

The CWL also disrupted the 1936 Conference of the NBCA held in Birmingham. During a discussion on the work of voluntary birth control clinics, a League member who was in the audience attempted to have a resolution accepted from the floor. The local press reported that Mrs Morton, representing the League, moved that 'this meeting holds that birth prevention is the wrong method of attacking social evils, and that everyone should rather support such remedies as better housing for the working-classes and some form of family allowances.'[109] Although the resolution was ruled out of order, *The Catholic Women's League Magazine* described the 'attack as successful' having surprised the NBCA by its 'energetic and well argued opposition.'[110]

It is difficult to ascertain the exact impact that the protests launched by the CWL had on the provision of birth control information at local clinics. What is clear however is that by 1937 only 95 out of 423 maternal and child welfare clinics were providing information on contraception.[111] The unwillingness of local authorities to provide such a free service to married women was the result of a number of factors including lack of resources during a time of economic depression, local opposition and growing national concern about the falling birth rate. As Martin Pugh reports, fears about the ability of the population to replicate itself during the 1930s resulted in advice from official sources in 1933 that 'each woman should bear an average of three children.'[112]

The increasing panic about falling population levels highlights the difficulties that women's organisations faced when campaigning for greater access to birth control. Such opposition however did not deter the NCW from attempting to refocus the debate surrounding the use and availability of birth control firmly on the health and welfare of mothers. Taking a radical stance, in 1938 the Council urged the public health authorities not only to provide information on birth control at local clinics but to remove the medical restrictions on birth control advice and provide 'contraceptive information to all married women who desire it.'[113]

One member of the Council, Mrs Bryant (Sutton Coldfield, WCA), supported the resolution, arguing that birth control 'is a question of woman's freedom as an individual and a responsible citizen.'[114] This resolution reflected the Council's concerns about the welfare of women, equal access to contraceptive advice for all women as well as the right of women as citizens to decide when and how many children they would have. Despite this attempt to highlight the health implications of repeated and unwanted pregnancies it was not until the 1960s that contraceptive advice was provided free of charge to all married women.

Although the NCW advocated the right of married women to birth control information, the unregulated sale and advertisement of contraceptives was strongly condemned. This opposition stemmed from the fear that young unmarried men and women would regard contraceptives as a licence for illicit sexual activity. Speaking in 1936, Lady Nunburnholme, President of the Council, described 'the indiscriminate use of contraceptives' as a social evil 'damaging the moral health and self-control of the nation.'[115] Working closely with the Public Morality Council,[116] the NCW campaigned to have the public display and advertisement of birth control devices banned.

In 1936 the Council passed a resolution urging the government to support a contraceptives bill drawn up by the Public Morality Council. The bill proposed to outlaw the display and advertisement of birth control devices 'in, upon or outside any shop so as to be visible to persons outside the shop.'[117] Selling contraceptives in public places, either by individuals or automatic vending machines, would also be prohibited. Finally, anyone found to have mailed birth control information to unmarried persons under eighteen would face prosecution if the bill were enacted.[118]

Lady Nunburnholme saw the bill as an excellent opportunity to prevent the 'indiscriminate display of these goods which undoubtedly leads to promiscuous use by all and sundry.'[119] Another member of the Council, Mrs Charles Ramsden, argued that it was a good way to control the supply to women of contraceptive devices which 'needed to be skilfully fitted' at a birth control clinic and not sold over the counter without proper instruction. Representing the MU, Mrs Michael Sadler said she believed the proposed legislation would do much to 'stop such displays and that thing [birth control] which was destroying the moral sense of young people'.[120]

Not surprisingly, the CWL also supported the Public Morality Council's contraceptive bill. In March 1936, Dr Rewcastle had advised her members 'to report to the nearest police station any case they know of contraceptives being advertised and sold through the post'.[121] It is significant that the NCW was united with the MU and the CWL in calling for the control of contraceptive information. In keeping with the social mores of the day, all three groups, along with feminist societies including the NUSEC, firmly believed that sex outside marriage was wrong and that birth control should never be made available to unmarried men and women.

Despite this consensus, which demonstrated the ability of religious and secular women's organisations to work together on issues of joint concern, the NCW, CWL and MU remained divided on the question of family planning for married women. This fact was reflected in the evidence each group gave to the Royal Commission on Population. The Commission, set up in 1944 in response to on-going concerns about the population level, sought to investigate the low birth rate of the 1930s and 'to consider what measures, if any, should be taken in the national interest to influence the future trend of population'.[122] In evidence to the commission the NCW reiterated its belief that all married women should have access to free birth control information.[123] Representing the CWL, Stella Given Wilson told the commission that people had made a mistake in thinking that birth control was 'right and legitimate'. She argued that 'the wholesale use of contraceptives and the planned family were not compatible with healthy national life'.[124]

Speaking on behalf of the MU, its Central President Rosamond Fisher confirmed the Union's acceptance that birth control was a private matter for 'every couple to decide for themselves'.[125] She also acknowledged that the majority of married couples now used some form of family limitation. However, as late as 1949, the Union continued to believe that it was 'improper for the State to use public funds for instruction in birth control, as many objected to their use'.[126] That same year the Royal Commission on Population reported that 'there was nothing inherently wrong in the use of mechanical methods of contraception'.[127] This decision was based on health grounds and the need to provide women with the freedom to 'engage in activities outside the home as well as within it'.[128] The views of the commission also reflected the radical change in public opinion regarding the use of birth control for family limitation by the end of the decade.

There is no doubt that the attitude of the MU and the CWL to birth control was both conservative and conventional. Their views appeared to place religious and moral principles before the health and welfare needs of mothers and, it could be argued, the civil rights of women citizens. Whilst a number of women's societies, including the NCW, campaigned for greater access to contraceptive information, the CWL and the MU objected even to the limited instruction provided at welfare clinics. However, it would be wrong to suggest that these two groups ignored the difficulties encountered by mothers during this period.

Throughout the 1930s and 1940s, both the CWL and the MU urged the government to introduce measures to improve the quality of life for wives and mothers. Family allowances, better housing, improved health and maternity services were amongst the reforms demanded to support women in the home. The NCW also recognised the need for these important social welfare benefits, considered to be the entitlement of all women. The part played by these three organisations in campaigns relating to social policy will be assessed in the following chapters.

Abortion

As the changing attitude of both the Church of England and the MU suggests, by the end of the 1930s it was generally accepted that birth control was a private matter for married couples, the majority of whom did practice some form of family limitation. Abortion, however, remained a criminal act and as such attracted a great deal of public condemnation. At the 1930 Lambeth Conference, Anglican bishops who had advocated the limited use of contraceptives, recorded their 'abhorrence of the sinful practice of abortion'.[129] This was in spite of the fact that the incidence of abortion, like the use of birth control, was on the increase throughout the inter-war period.[130]

Despite the fact that abortion was prohibited under the Offences Against the Person Act 1861 and the Infant Life (Preservation) Act 1929, it continued to be regarded as a legitimate method of family limitation. As late as 1938, the Birkett Committee inquiry into abortion found that 'many mothers seemed not to understand that self-induced abortion was illegal'.[131] Jane Lewis has written that working-class women in particular regarded abortion as a 'natural and permissible' solution to unwanted pregnancies.[132] Indeed abortion, which could be carried out within the privacy of one's own home, was often considered more respectable than the use of internal contraceptives, which had to be fitted at birth control clinics.[133] Kate Fisher, in her study of birth control and marriage following the First World War, highlights the prevalence of self-induced abortion in the early months of pregnancy, which women believed was 'a valid method of limiting family size'.[134]

Traditional remedies reputed to bring on miscarriage were also more widely available than artificial methods of birth control. They included pills, tonics and douches for 'female ailments' as well as homemade abortifacients, for example pennyroyal tea.[135] If these methods failed, a visit to a professional abortionist was the only other option. This increased the risk of death or injury to the woman if the practitioner was unqualified or failed to take the precautions necessary to avoid infection.

During the inter-war years, concern about the rise in the maternal death rate focused greater public attention on the incidence of criminal abortion.[136] Ministry of Health investigations, set up to explore the causes of maternal mortality, revealed that the number of women dying from septic abortion was on the increase.[137] In 1934 alone it was estimated that some 68,000 illegal abortions had taken place, despite the fact that only seventy-three cases had been reported to the authorities.[138] In these circumstances, women's societies became increasingly concerned about the incidence of abortion and the associated deaths.

In 1934 the WCG urged that in view of the persistently high maternal death rate the government ought to revise the abortion laws of 1861.[139] The following year the NUSEC voted in favour of reform to help combat the problem of criminal abortion and maternal mortality.[140] The NCW added its voice to these expressions of concern about the increasing number of fatalities attributed to abortion. In 1935 the Council called on the government to set up a committee to

> enquire into the incidence of abortion and as to the law dealing with criminal abortion and attempted abortion and its administration, and to consider what measures, if any, medical, legal, social or administrative, are advisable to improve the existing position.[141]

Speaking in favour of this resolution, Miss E. Kelly of the Council's Executive Committee informed members attending the Annual Conference that the 'taking of drugs of various kinds, noxious and otherwise, and the employment of domestic measures to procure abortion have increased beyond all knowledge'.[142] She highlighted the fact that it was the older married mother, not the unmarried woman, who turned to abortion when they feared that the family's income could not support another child.

The concern here about the welfare of older women resorting to abortion after repeated pregnancies and for economic reasons is very significant. It would suggest that contrary to public perceptions regarding the loosening of sexual morals amongst the young, the NCW was convinced that those seeking an illegal abortion were more likely to be a 'respectable' working-class wife than a young single pregnant woman. Such fears were well founded as eighty-five per cent of the women who died after an abortion during the period 1926 and 1930 were married.[143] The high incidence of abortion amongst married women confirms the view of historians, for example Jeffrey Weeks and Judy Giles, that the move towards more liberalised sexual relations outside marriage occurred only gradually throughout these years.[144]

Speaking at the 1935 Conference of the NCW, Lady Ruth Balfour emphasised the damage done to women's health from illegal abortion. She told the conference that women who survived abortion attempts often suffered from 'permanent inflammation and subsequent abortions, even when they did not wish to have them.'[145] What emerged from this meeting was the very genuine concerns amongst members of the NCW for the health of mothers and pregnant women. Women who resorted to abortion were not condemned. Instead, it was argued that the government should consider social, legal and economic reforms that would deter women from seeking an abortion in the first instance. Free birth control information, the introduction of family allowances and an increase in the number of prosecutions against 'back-street' abortionists were amongst the reforms recommended by the Council during this period.

As part of this campaign, the NCW sent a deputation to the Minister of Health, Sir Kingsley Wood, in February 1936 again urging him to set up a Committee of Inquiry into abortion. It was also requested that Medical Officers of Health should issue their reports 'showing deaths due to abortion, and deaths due to criminal abortion, separately from returns regarding other maternal deaths.'[146] It was hoped this measure would allow the true facts about abortion to emerge so that the problem would be given the attention it deserved. The Minister assured the Council that the matter would be given careful consideration although it was made clear that no action could be taken until the latest government inquiry into maternal mortality had been completed.[147] When the Ministry of Health's *Report on an Investigation into Maternal Mortality* was published in 1937 it concurred with the NCW's recommendation that a separate study of abortion was required to discover the 'influence it may exert on maternal mortality and morbidity and future childbearing.'[148]

As an affiliated member of the NCW, the MU welcomed the Council's efforts to highlight the incidence of abortion and supported the Council's resolutions in this regard. However, as a religious organisation the Union made it clear that abortion was wrong as 'human life is sacred because it belongs to God; therefore it is a grave sin deliberately to destroy innocent life.'[149] In order to uphold this belief, the Union was determined to ensure that its members realised that self-induced abortion, even before the quickening (the third month), was not only a sin but also illegal.[150]

In its publication, *The Christian Attitude towards Birth Control and Abortion* (1936), the Union confirmed that 'procuring an abortion at any time during pregnancy involves the deliberate destruction of life.'[151] The Union did accept that therapeutic abortion, where 'an operation in which the death of the foetus is an indirect result and not the primary purpose of the operation' was acceptable.[152] When pregnancy occurred following a rape or sexual assault, it was acknowledged that 'a well-nigh intolerable burden has been placed upon the victims of the sins of others.'[153] Nonetheless abortion in these cases could never be condoned, as to do so would go against the teaching of the Christian Church.

As the NCW and the MU urged the government to investigate the incidence of abortion, seven feminists came together in 1936 to set up the Abortion Law Reform Association (ALRA).[154] They included Stella Browne, Dora Russell and Frida Laski, all of whom were active supporters of birth control and were involved in the labour movement.[155] This new association called for safe legal abortion to be made available to all women when other methods of birth control had failed.[156] It was argued that this measure would do much to reduce the maternal death rate attributed to illegal abortions.

Following pressure on the government from organisations such as the NCW, and on the basis of recommendations made by the 1937 Ministry of Health's report on maternal mortality, an inter-departmental committee on abortion was finally established. The committee, chaired by Norman Birkett and known as the Birkett Committee, was instructed to

> inquire into the prevalence of abortion and the present law relating thereto, and to consider what steps can be taken by more effective enforcement of the law or otherwise, to secure a reduction of maternal mortality and morbidity arising from this cause.[157]

This investigation provided women's groups with an important opportunity to present their views on abortion as well as making suggestions on how the problem could be solved. Lady Ruth Balfour of the NCW was appointed to serve on the new committee, demonstrating that the

NCW was now an acknowledged authority on the question of abortion and women's welfare.

In November 1937, the MU submitted a memorandum to the Birkett Committee outlining its principal objections to abortion. The fact that abortion was the destruction of an innocent life was reiterated and the Union expressed its fear that the desire to reduce maternal mortality could result in the legalisation of abortion.[158] Although the Union accepted that the intention of such a reform was to help women, it argued that

> should abortion be legally recognised there would arise a quite undue pressure, well meant but on the materialistic plane, making it difficult for women to maintain that utterly vital recognition of their motherhood as the core and centre of both their spiritual and physical life, without which they are robbed of the fullest meaning of their womanhood.[159]

As an alternative to abortion, the MU recommended social and economic reforms, as well as adequate housing, to remove the financial burdens on larger families and restore 'a healthy attitude towards childbearing'.[160]

In keeping with the teaching of the Catholic Church, the CWL also rejected abortion as a sin against God and nature. Like the MU, the League went further, however, than just arguing that abortion was a sin. In evidence to the Birkett Committee it highlighted the fact that abortion would allow women to shirk the responsibility of motherhood.[161] Artificial birth control and abortion, it was argued, militated against 'the spirit of self sacrifice crucial for the practice of good citizenship'.[162] The use of the rhetoric of good citizenship here is interesting as it becomes clear that the League associated the definition of a woman's citizenship with her duties as a wife and mother and this was the role for women that the League wished to protect and promote.

This reminder that it was the duty of women to be wives and mothers in many ways reflects the anxiety that the League had of women being able, through the provision of birth control and abortion, to avoid motherhood and thereby gain independence from the family. For the League such 'freedom' was not to be celebrated but to be feared as women's identity and influence as mothers would be undermined. Stephen Brooke has highlighted this linking of abortion rights with female autonomy during the 1930s. He writes that the campaign for abortion reform not only acknowledged the need for women to be supported in their roles as mothers but 'also expanded the idea of maternity to include a public recognition of women's right to reproductive control and autonomy … of which the most fundamental quality was freedom from motherhood itself'.[163]

To counteract any challenge to the domestic role of women, the CWL, like the MU, hoped to convince the Birkett Committee that what mothers needed most was better social and economic support for their work as mothers and not easier access to abortion, which would render their domestic role obsolete. Moreover the League reminded the committee about public concerns with regard to falling population levels and advised that the provision of legal abortion at a time when the birth rate was declining would be disastrous. Instead, it was suggested that social welfare reforms including family allowance for all mothers, home-helps and improved maternity services were required in order to allow women to have children without the fear of economic hardship.[164]

In contrast to the views expressed by the MU and CWL, the NCW recognised that legal and safe abortion would not only protect and enhance the experience of motherhood for some women, in particular working-class women, but also reduce the number of deaths from criminal abortion. In its evidence to the Birkett Committee, the Council repeated its demand that the law in relation to abortion should be reviewed in order to protect the health and welfare of women.[165] By this time, the Council had become increasingly concerned about the number of maternal deaths attributed to criminal abortion. Accepting that some women, in particular married women, would always regard abortion as a way of preventing unwanted pregnancy, the Council took the controversial step of urging the government to consider 'the need for the legalisation of abortion under adequate safeguards'.[166]

This radical resolution was passed by the Council in October 1938 and carried by 236 votes to 12. Not surprisingly the MU and the CWL were quick to register their opposition. The MU immediately dissociated itself from the resolution on abortion and in December 1938 announced that it was withdrawing its 597,412 members from the organisation. Nina Woods explained that this action had been taken as a result of the NCW policy on divorce, birth control and abortion, all of which conflicted with 'the chief principles for which the MU stands'.[167] Similarly the CWL made public its 'complete dissent' from the Council's resolution.[168] Nevertheless, the League acknowledged that the Council had undertaken important work for the protection of women and children and encouraged its members 'to join the local branches of the NCW in order to keep in touch with women's public work, and to put forward the Catholic point of view when desirable'.[169]

Despite the fact that a diverse range of women's groups supported safe and legal abortion in limited circumstances, including the ALRA, the WCG and the NCW, the Birkett Committee did not advocate any change in the law.[170] When the committee published its Majority Report in 1939,[171] it was clear that concern about the falling birth rate and the medical view that 'abortion may entail danger to life and health' had outweighed all demands for reform.[172] Although the Majority Report confirmed that therapeutic abortion on health grounds was acceptable, it advised that legal abortion for any other reason would only contribute to the population problem and 'prove an added temptation to loose and immoral conduct'.[173] The Committee's recommendation on therapeutic abortion was influenced by the findings of the 1938 Bourne case, which set legal precedence in ruling that an abortion carried out following the rape of an underage girl, in order to 'preserve the life the mother', was not unlawful.[174]

The Majority Report shared the fears of the CWL and the MU that legal abortion would undermine the role of women as mothers. The report suggested that women's role within the family would change as 'women have entered into competition with men in numerous spheres of activity … the child may be, or may be thought to be, a hindrance to her progress in the career she has chosen.'[175] As Brooke suggests such fears were exaggerated as on the eve of the Second World War the majority of married women were not forging out new careers or in competition with men. Instead working-class wives were engaged in paid work out of necessity to compensate for the unemployment of their husbands following years of economic depression.[176] It is clear therefore that the Birkett Committee regarded legalised abortion as a step too far towards female autonomy and too great a challenge to traditional notions of motherhood and domesticity.

The outbreak of war in September 1939 quickly overtook events and the recommendations of the Birkett Committee were never adopted. By 1945, the dramatic recovery in the national birth rate, coupled with a decline in the number of maternal deaths, diverted public attention away from the difficult subject of abortion. This was in spite of the fact that the incidence of abortion appears to have increased during the war years as a result of casual sexual encounters and marital infidelity.[177] By the early 1950s the ALRA had rejuvenated its campaign for abortion law reform by targeting parliamentary channels. This new campaign encouraged other women's groups, including the NCW and later the TG, to raise the issue of abortion law reform amongst their own members and to campaign actively for the introduction of legalised abortion.

The MU and the CWL objected to divorce, abortion and birth control on religious and moral grounds but also on the basis that easier access to all three would challenge traditional domesticity and undermine the role of women as wives and mothers. It was argued that legal abortion, like divorce and birth control, would do nothing to enhance the quality of women's lives and 'would be the heaviest blow possible to their highest expression of womanhood'.[178] Conversely, the NCW supported the extension of grounds for divorce, the introduction of free birth control advice and legal abortion in order to protect the health and welfare of women, in particular wives and mothers, and allow them greater security in their domestic role. The Council, in common with a number of other women's societies and feminist groups, accepted that a significant number of women would always utilise divorce, birth control and abortion in order to alleviate the difficulties of their everyday lives and so such services should be made available and affordable to all.

The conservative view that groups such as the MU and CWL held with regard to divorce, birth control and abortion has often resulted in their activities and achievements being omitted from the history of the women's movement. What emerges, however, from an exploration of the objections of both groups and the contrasting viewpoint of the NCW is that mainstream voluntary women's groups were at the heart of an important discourse on the role, welfare and status of women within the home throughout the inter-war years. Crucially all three groups were successful, in their different ways, in highlighting the very real difficulties and dilemmas faced daily by housewives and mothers. By drawing public attention to the reality of women's lives and debating the difficult choices that wives and mothers had to make, these groups were successful in giving a public voice to 'ordinary housewives' and ensuring that their views on private and personal matters were made known.

Notes

1 For example L. Stone, *The Road to Divorce, England 1530–1987* (Oxford: Oxford University Press, 1990), J. Lewis, 'The Ideology and Politics of Birth Control in Inter-war England', *Women's Studies International Quarterly*, 2 (1979), B. Brookes, *Abortion in England 1900–1967* (London: Croom Helm, 1988) and S. Brooke, 'The Sphere of Sexual Politics: The Abortion Law Reform Association, 1930s to 1960s', in Crowson, Hilton and McKay (eds), *NGOs in Contemporary Society*.
2 See also C. Beaumont, 'Moral Dilemmas and Women's Rights: The Attitude of the Mothers' Union and Catholic Women's League to Divorce, Birth Control and Abortion in England 1928–1939', *Women's History Review*, 16:4 (2007).
3 For a detailed account of the history of divorce in England and the attitudes of the Anglican and Catholic Churches to divorce see R. Phillips, *Putting Asunder: A History of Divorce in Western Society* (Cambridge: Cambridge University Press, 1988) and Stone, *The Road to Divorce*.
4 See also Moyse, *A History of the Mothers' Union*, pp. 116–126.
5 Phillips, *Putting Asunder*, p. 525.
6 *Ibid.*, p. 514. See also O. Banks, *Faces of Feminism* (Oxford: Blackwell, 1981), p. 196.

7   Moyse, *A History of the Mothers' Union*, p. 118.

8   Phillips, *Putting Asunder*, p. 525.

9   In 1920, 2,985 marriages ended in divorce increasing to 3,956 the following year. *Ibid.*, p. 517.

10 Lambeth Palace Library, London (hereafter LPL), Archbishop Temple Papers, Vol. 35, No. 55, 'Typed document outlining the history of the Mothers' Union's policy on divorce', 1930.

11 *The Tablet* (19 June 1921), p. 830.

12 The two Law Lords were concerned about the increasing number of marriage breakdowns and the inability of existing legislation to deal with grounds other than adultery. Stone, *Road to Divorce*, pp. 393–395.

13 Moyse, *A History of the Mothers' Union*, p. 120.

14 LPL, Archbishop Lang Papers, Vol. 107, No. 212, 'Typed document on the machinery for mobilisation against Bills for increasing facilities for divorce', 1930.

15 *The Catholic Women's League Magazine*, 253 (November 1932), p. 12.

16 Cited in Stone, *Road to Divorce*, p. 395.

17 Dean Inge of St Paul's and the Bishop of Salisbury also expressed the view that desertion should be included as a ground for divorce. *Ibid.*

18 Moyse, *A History of the Mothers' Union*, p. 120.

19 *Ibid.*, p. 122.

20 These were the words of Major Entwhistle who sponsored the bill, quoted in Phillips, *Putting Asunder*, p. 525.

21 *Ibid.*, p. 526.

22 LPL, Archbishop Temple Papers, Vol. 35, No. 55, 'Mothers' Union's policy on divorce', 1930.

23 LPL, Archbishop Temple Papers, Vol. 35, No. 47, 'Typed document reiterating the fundamental principles of the Mothers' Union', 9 October 1930.

24 Parker, *For the Family's Sake*, p. 51.

25 LPL, Archbishop Lang Papers, Vol. 107, No. 216, leaflet on the 'Beliefs of the Mothers' Union', 1931.

26 Moyse, *A History of the Mothers' Union*, p. 123.

27 LPL, Archbishop Temple Papers, Vol. 35, No. 82, 'A statement by the Army Division on divorce', November 1931.

28 MSH, Central Council Minutes, Vol. 9 (1930–32), 'Minutes of the Mothers' Union Central Council', December 1931, p. 157.

29 LPL, Archbishop Lang Papers, Vol. 107, No. 209, 'Central President's speech to the Annual Conference of the Mothers' Union', Exeter, 1931.

30 LPL, Encyclical Letter from the Bishops, *Resolutions and Reports of the Lambeth Conference 1930* (1930), p. 42.

31 LPL, Archbishop Lang Papers, Vol. 133, No. 25, 'Letter from the Archbishop of Canterbury to Mrs Boustead, Central President of the Mothers' Union', 16 March 1932.

32 *The Mothers' Union Journal*, 166 (September 1936), p. 19.

33 *Ibid.*

34 *The Mothers' Union Journal*, 138 (September 1929), p. 23.

35 *The Catholic Women's League Magazine*, 243 (January 1932), p. 5.

36 See Pope Pius XI, *Quadragesimo Anno: The Social Order – Its Reconstruction and Perfection* (Encyclical, 1931), p. 32.

37 *The Catholic Women's League Magazine*, 292 (February 1936), p. 24.

38 Pope Leo XIII, *Rerum Novarum: The Condition of the Working Classes* (Encyclical, 1891), p. 38.

39 Pope Pius XI, *Quadragesimo Anno*, p. 32.

40 C. Langhamer, 'Adultery in Post-War England', *History Workshop Journal*, 62 (2006), p. 94.

41 Lewis, *Women in England 1870–1950*, p. 130. See also A. P. Herbert, *Holy Deadlock* (London: Methuen & Co., 1934).

42 Langhamer, 'Adultery in Post-War England', p. 94.

43 *NCW Handbook 1934–1935* (1935), p. 78.

44 *Ibid.* All of the other 135 member societies, including the YWCA, the NCEC and the WFL supported the resolution.

45 See H. Smith, 'British Feminism in the 1920s', in Smith (ed.), *British Feminism in the Twentieth Century*, p. 54.

46 Under the terms of the bill women were also able to file for divorce on the grounds of rape, sodomy and bestiality. Phillips, *Putting Asunder*, p. 526.

47 *Ibid.*, p. 529.

48 A. P. Herbert, *The Ayes Have It: The Story of the Marriage Bill* (London: Methuen & Co., 1937), p. 212.

49 *Ibid.*, p. 223.

50 LPL, Archbishop Lang Papers, Vol. 152, No. 293, 'Letter to Nina Woods, Central President of the Mothers' Union, from the Archbishop of Canterbury', 1 December 1936.

51 Stone, *The Road to Divorce*, p. 398.

52 LPL, Archbishop Lang Papers, Vol. 152, No. 293, 'Letter to Nina Woods, Central President of the Mothers' Union, from the Archbishop of Canterbury', 1 December 1936.

53 MSH, Central Council Minutes, Vol. 10 (1932–37), 'Minutes of the Mothers' Union Central Council, December 1936', p. 400.

54 *Ibid.*, p. 399.

55 *Ibid.*, p. 402.

56 *The Mothers' Union Workers' Paper*, 277 (January 1937), p. 6.

57 MSH, Central Council Minutes, Vol. 10 (1932–37), 'Minutes of the Mothers' Union Central Council', December 1936, p. 405.

58 LPL, Archbishop Lang Papers, Vol. 152, No. 317, 'Open letter advising all members of the Mothers' Union to protest against the 1936 divorce bill', December 1936.

59 *Sunday Pictorial*, 14 February 1937.

60 *Ibid.*

61 *Ibid.*

62 *Ibid.*

63 MSH, Pamphlet Collection, E. Noel Barclay, *Marriage and Divorce* (1936), p. 1,

64 Pugh, *Women and the Women's Movement*, p. 217.

65 The 5,903 divorce petitions filed in 1937 had increased to 10,233 in 1938. Phillips, *Putting Asunder*, p. 529.

66 *Ibid.*, p. 558.

67 MSH, Central Council Minutes, Vol. 12 (1943–47), 'Minutes of the Mothers' Union Central Council', December 1945.

68 MSH, Pamphlet Collection, 'Memorandum submitted by the Mothers' Union to the Royal Commission on Marriage and Divorce, 1951–55', 1955, p. 14.

69 LPL, Archbishop Fisher Papers, Vol. 105, No. 315, 'Archbishop Fisher's address to the Mothers' Union', 10 June 1952.
70 For a full account of this episode see Moyse, *A History of the Mothers' Union*, p. 125.
71 *Ibid.*
72 *Ibid.*, p. 126.
73 Pugh, *Women and the Women's Movement*, p. 223.
74 Richard Soloway writes that the suffrage societies did not address the divisive issue of birth control because to do so would have weakened the suffrage campaign. R. Soloway, *Birth-Control and the Population Question in England 1877–1930* (Chapel Hill: University of North Carolina, 1982), p. 134.
75 *Home and Country*, 18:3 (April 1936), p. 199.
76 Lewis, *Women in England 1870–1950*, p. 18. The use of diaphragms, for example the Dutch cap, grew increasingly popular during the 1920s as they became made more widely available at birth control clinics. See also K. Fisher, *Birth Control, Sex and Marriage in Britain, 1918–1960* (Oxford: Oxford University Press, 2006).
77 There were, however, were significant regional and local variations to family size throughout this period. See D. Gittins, *Fair Sex: Family Size and Structure* (London: Hutchinson, 1982).
78 Lewis, 'The Ideology and Politics of Birth Control', pp. 33–40.
79 See R. Hall (ed.), *Dear Dr. Stopes: Sex in the 1920s* (London: Deutsch, 1978).
80 *Ibid.*, p. 19.
81 The Eugenics Society was set up in 1908 to enhance the 'quality of the race' and advocated birth control for the 'unfit', which usually referred to members of the working-class and the disabled.
82 D. Cohen, 'Private Lives and Public Spaces: Marie Stopes, the Mothers' Clinics and the Practice of Contraception', *History Workshop*, 35 (1993), p. 101.
83 In 1921 the Malthusian League (1877) opened a family planning clinic in London. This group advocated the use of birth control amongst the working-classes to reduce economic hardship and poverty. The Workers' Birth Control Group was set up in 1924 and campaigned for the right of working-class women to have access to information on family planning.
84 Despite support amongst men and women within the Labour Party for the provision of free birth control information at public clinics, the 1924 Labour government refused to act, mainly because of pressure from the Catholic Church. See Thane, 'The Women of the British Labour Party and Feminism', p. 137.
85 During the inter-war period the crude birth rate (per thousand of population) in England and Wales fell from 18.6 in 1924–25 to 15.8 in 1931 and reached a record low of 14.8 during the years 1932–40. Pugh, *Women and the Women's Movement*, pp. 87–90.
86 *National Council of Women Handbook 1929–1930* (1930), p. 81.
87 Parker, *For the Family's Sake*, p. 91.
88 Ruth Hall writes that the caravans were not very successful because women were embarrassed to be seen visiting the clinic and 'one of the nurses, as well as being incompetent, was nearly always drunk.' R. Hall, *Marie Stopes: A Biography* (London: Virago Ltd, 1978), p. 265.
89 The woman, Elizabeth Ellis, justified her action in court by claiming that the caravan was 'a source of immorality and venereal disease'. She was sentenced to two months in prison. *Ibid.*

90 MSH, Central Council Minutes, Vol. 8 (1927-29), 'Minutes of the Mothers' Union Central Council', June 1929, p. 252. There is no evidence that the Union took further action against the birth control caravans.

91 Soloway, *Birth Control and the Population Question*, p. 237.

92 *Ibid.*, pp. 233-254.

93 Hall, *Marie Stopes*, p. 156.

94 Hall, *Dear Dr. Stopes*, pp. 59-80.

95 In cases where the health of the mother was at risk or where the mother was exhausted and unable to care for any additional children, a moral obligation existed to limit family size. LPL, Encyclical Letter from the Bishops, *Resolutions and Reports of the Lambeth Conference 1930* (1930), p. 44.

96 *Ibid.*

97 *Ibid.*

98 LPL, Archbishop Temple Papers, Vol. 35, No. 49, 'Letter to Mrs Boustead, President of the Mothers' Union, from Archbishop Temple', 10 November 1930.

99 MSH, Central Council Minutes, Vol. 9 (1930-32), 'Minutes of the Mothers' Union Central Council', December 1930, p. 45. See also Moyse, *A History of the Mothers' Union*, pp. 126-130.

100 MSH, Pamphlet Collection, D. Ward, *The Christian Attitude towards Birth Control and Abortion* (1937), pp. 11, 15.

101 *Ibid.*, p. 15.

102 Soloway, *Birth Control and the Population Question*, p. 254.

103 For an account of the Catholic Church's opposition to Marie Stopes during the 1920s see Hall, *Marie Stopes*, pp. 197-212.

104 E. F. Griffith, *Modern Marriage and Birth Control* (London: Gollancz, 1935), p. 182.

105 In May 1934 the Ministry of Health issued a second circular to local authorities advising that birth control information should also be made available to women suffering from illnesses such as TB, heart disease and diabetes.

106 *The Catholic Women's League Magazine*, 290 (December 1935), p. 11.

107 *The Catholic Women's League Magazine*, 249 (July 1932), p. 6.

108 *The Catholic Women's League Magazine*, 252 (October 1932), p. 15.

109 *The Catholic Women's League Magazine*, 295 (May 1936), p. 8.

110 *Ibid.*

111 Seventy voluntary birth control clinics had also been set up by this time. Pugh, *Women and the Women's Movement in Britain*, p. 257.

112 *Ibid.*, p. 89.

113 *NCW Handbook 1939-40* (1940), p. 116. Once again the MU dissociated itself from the resolution.

114 WL, Pamphlet Collection, *Report of the NCW Council Meeting and Conference, October 1938* (1938), p. 61.

115 WL, Pamphlet Collection, *Report of NCW Council Meeting and Conference, June 1936* (1936), p. 88.

116 The Public Morality Council, founded in the late nineteenth century, was part of the social purity movement and had campaigned against the advertisement of contraceptives since 1889. See E. Bristow, *Vice and Vigilance: Purity Movements in Britain since 1700* (Dublin: Gill and Macmillan, 1977), pp. 165-205.

117 WL, Pamphlet Collection, *Report of NCW Council Meeting and Conference, June 1936* (1936), p. 87.

118 *Ibid.*

119 *Ibid.*

120 *Ibid.*, p. 90. The Public Morality Council's contraceptive bill reached a second reading in the Commons in December 1938 but was talked out and failed to become law.

121 *The Catholic Women's League Magazine*, 293 (March 1936), p. 3.

122 *The Report of the Royal Commission on Population* (London: HMSO, 1949), p. 1.

123 BL, Royal Commission on Population, 1944–49, 'NCW oral evidence to the Royal Commission on Population', 29 March 1944.

124 *Ibid.*

125 BL, Royal Commission on Population, 1944–49, 'Mothers' Union oral evidence to the Royal Commission on Population', 13 October 1944.

126 *The Mothers' Union Workers' Paper*, September 1949, p. 134.

127 *The Report of the Royal Commission on Population*, p. 159.

128 J. Lewis, *Women in Britain Since 1945: Women, Family, Work and the State in the Post-war Years* (Oxford: Blackwell, 1992), p. 17. Lewis writes that this official endorsement of birth control was possible in 1949 because of the dramatic increase in the post-war birth rate and the fact that 'public sanction had been given to women's work' outside the home. See Lewis, 'The Ideology and Politics of Birth Control', p. 44.

129 LPL, Encyclical Letter from the Bishops, *Resolutions and Reports of the Lambeth Conference 1930* (1930), p. 44.

130 For a detailed history of abortion in England during the twentieth century see Brookes, *Abortion in England*.

131 Cited in Lewis, *Women in England 1870–1950*, p. 18.

132 For working-class women, poverty and the need to remain in work were strong incentives for resorting to abortion when other methods of birth control failed. *Ibid.*, p. 17.

133 Brookes, *Abortion in England*, p. 4. See also Fisher, *Birth Control, Sex and Marriage*, pp. 158–160.

134 Fisher, *Birth Control, Sex and Marriage*, p. 158.

135 Lewis, *Women in England 1870–1950*, p. 17.

136 In 1923 the maternal mortality rate for England and Wales was 5.15 per thousand births. This figure had risen to 5.59 in 1930 and peaked at 5.94 in 1933. See I. Loudon, *Death in Childbirth: An International Study of Maternal Care and Maternal Mortality, 1800–1950* (Oxford: Clarendon Press, 1992), p. 252.

137 In 1930, 10.5 per cent of all maternal deaths were attributed to abortion. By 1934, this figure had risen to 20.0 per cent. Brookes, *Abortion in England*, p. 43.

138 *Ibid.*, p. 27.

139 *Ibid.*, p. 93.

140 *Ibid.*

141 WL, Pamphlet Collection, *Report of the NCW Council Meeting and Conference, June 1935* (1935), p. 33.

142 *Ibid.*, p. 34.

143 Loudon, *Death in Childbirth*, p. 110.

144 J. Weeks, *Sex, Politics and Society: The Regulation of Sexuality since 1800* (London: Longman, 1981) and J. Giles, '"Playing Hard to Get": Working Class Women, Sexuality and Respectability in Britain, 1918–40', *Women's History Review*, 1 (1992).

145 WL, Pamphlet Collection, *Report of the NCW Council Meeting and Conference, June 1935* (1935), p. 36.

146 *NCW Handbook 1937–38* (1938), p. 105.

147 WL, Pamphlet Collection, *Report of the NCW Council Meeting and Conference, June 1936* (1936), p. 82.

148 Brookes, *Abortion in England*, p. 80.

149 Ward, *The Christian Attitude towards Birth Control and Abortion*, p. 18.

150 There was a common belief at this time that self-induced abortion during the first three months of pregnancy was acceptable. In 1921 Marie Stopes revealed she had received '20,000 requests for criminal abortion for women who did not apparently even know that it was criminal'. See Beddoe, *Back to Home and Duty*, p. 108.

151 Ward, *The Christian Attitude towards Birth Control and Abortion*, p. 18.

152 *Ibid.*

153 *Ibid.*

154 Brooke, 'The Sphere of Sexual Politics'.

155 Lewis, *Women in England 1870–1950*, p. 33.

156 Brookes, *Abortion in England*, p. 80.

157 *Ibid.*

158 *The Mothers' Union Workers' Paper*, 298 (January 1938), p. 18.

159 *Ibid.*, p. 19.

160 *Ibid.*

161 Brookes, *Abortion in England*, p. 110.

162 *The Catholic Women's League Magazine*, 326 (December 1938), p 22.

163 S. Brooke, '"A New World for Women?" Abortion Law Reform in Britain during the 1930s', *American Historical Review*, 106 (2001), pp. 442–443.

164 *The Catholic Women's League Magazine*, 326 (December 1938), p 22.

165 *NCW Handbook 1938–39* (1939), p. 56.

166 *NCW Handbook 1939–40* (1940), p. 116.

167 *The Mothers' Union Workers' Paper*, 304 (April 1939), p. 98. It should be noted that members of the Union were free to work with the NCW in a private capacity and it was hoped the two societies would co-operate on issues of mutual concern. In 1944 the MU reaffiliated to the NCW.

168 *The Catholic Women's League Magazine*, 326 (December 1938), p. 22.

169 *Ibid.*

170 For a detailed account of the evidence submitted by ALRA to the Birkett Committee see Brooke, '"A New World for Women?"', pp. 451–459.

171 A Minority Report published by Dorothy Thurtle, a member of the NBCA, supported the ALRA demands for abortion law reform and was welcomed by women's groups including the NCEC.

172 In addition, Barbara Brookes writes that members of the medical profession had no desire to carry out legal abortions due to moral and ethical concerns. Brookes, *Abortion in England*, p. 125.

173 *Ibid.*

174 For a full account of the Bourne Case see Brooke, '"A New World for Women?"', pp. 450–451.

175 Cited in Brooke, '"A New World for Women?"', p. 458.

176 *Ibid.*

177 See Loudon, *Death in Childbirth*, p. 266.

178 *The Mothers' Union Workers' Paper*, 289 (January 1938), p. 19.

4

Welfare rights for women: maternity care, social welfare benefits and family allowances

Although the MU, the CWL and NCW devoted considerable time and energy dealing with the contentious issues of divorce, birth control and abortion throughout the 1920s and 1930s, they never lost sight of the importance of other areas of social policy which had the potential to enhance the lives of women. Along with the WI and TG, these societies played an important and active role in highlighting the welfare needs of women, in particular wives and mothers. Campaigning for the social rights of women citizens during the 1930s and 1940s was of particular importance as it was at this time that the provision of state welfare rapidly expanded, culminating in 1946 with the introduction of the welfare state.

Women's access and entitlement to state welfare was a salient point as unlike men the majority of women did not work outside the home after marriage but instead became full-time housewives. As a result, women did not have the same rights to social citizenship as men because, as Sylvia Walby has argued, social citizenship 'usually depends on being a worker with access to such rights.'[1] Although the campaign for the extension of social and welfare rights to women by feminist and political women's organisations throughout the inter-war years has been well documented, the participation of mainstream voluntary women's groups in these campaigns remains less well known.[2] This chapter will focus on three major areas of social policy of particular significance to wives and mothers: maternity services and maternal welfare, social welfare rights for women and the campaign for family allowances.

Maternity services and maternal welfare

Anxiety about the health and welfare of women in pregnancy and child-birth was a major concern for women's organisations during the late 1920s and throughout the 1930s. The maternal mortality rate averaged 4.03 per thousand births during 1911–15 and 3.90 during 1921–25. In 1925 the figure began to rise and in 1933 peaked at 5.94 deaths per thousand births.[3] That such an increase should occur in the wake of the 1918 Maternity and Child Welfare Act, and at a time when infant mortality rates were falling, caused alarm and drew public and political attention to the whole question of maternal welfare and how death in childbirth could be prevented.[4]

Whilst the main cause of maternal mortality during this period was puerperal fever and haemorrhage, the rising death rate focused attention on the wider questions of maternal health and the provision of maternity care within local communities. In 1935 the leadership of the TG expressed anxiety about the issue and members were asked 'to give earnest consideration to the question of maternal mortality … and to take steps to investigate local conditions'. Moreover, members were urged 'to pledge themselves to assist in every way possible to combat this high rate of mortality'.[5] The fact that the TG was willing to speak out publicly on this question in the 1930s signifies that the issue of maternal mortality was regarded as a 'neutral' topic and not one which could be linked to either a political or a feminist agenda.

As an organisation representing wives and mothers, the TG had no qualms about joining the Women's Maternal Mortality Committee established in December 1927 to investigate and draw attention to death in childbirth. This voluntary committee, set up by the trade unionist and activist Gertrude Tuckwell, met regularly throughout the early 1930s. Concerned with the health and welfare of pregnant women, the committee's primary aim was to bring pressure to bear on the government and local authorities, in its quest to improve the standard of healthcare available for mothers.

Representatives from the MU, the WI, the TG and the NCW all attended the inaugural meeting of the Committee and were joined by a range of women's organisations including the YWCA and the WCG. At this first meeting, held at Westminster, participants were urged to familiarise themselves with 'what powers local authorities already possess and … find out why so many mothers do not avail themselves of help offered'.[6] Throughout the 1930s and 1940s, voluntary women's organisations took up this challenge and set out to improve the standard of maternity health care available to their members.

The need for a co-ordinated and comprehensive maternity service to overcome the high rate of maternal mortality became evident during the 1930s. At a time when unemployment and poverty were rife in many districts, particularly in the north and west, contemporary studies showed that areas suffering from high unemployment and poverty did not always experience an excessive number of maternal deaths. A study carried out in Rochdale during the 1930s revealed that when maternity and child welfare services were dramatically improved, there was a significant decrease in the number of maternal fatalities. This was in spite of the fact that high levels of unemployment and economic hardship in Rochdale continued unabated.[7] The realisation that poverty and economic factors were not the only causes explaining an increased risk of death in childbirth resulted in the quality of medical care given to pregnant and labouring women coming under increased scrutiny.

Research carried out in Leeds in the 1920s showed that the maternal mortality rate was lower in working-class areas than in middle-class districts.[8] One explanation offered for this disparity was the fact that middle-class women could afford to pay a doctor to attend the birth whereas working-class women were reliant on the help of a midwife, whose services were cheaper and at times paid for by the local authority. Throughout the inter-war period, trained midwives attending births were less likely to use instruments during labour and as a result experienced a lower rate of maternal mortality than many doctors.[9] Writing on the history of maternity mortality, Irvine Loudon has argued that one of the most significant causes of maternal mortality during the 1930s was the poor standard of obstetric care.[10]

Inadequate maternity services and poor standard of care were compounded by the general ill health of women during the 1920s and 1930s. Under the 1911 National Health Insurance Act, married women working within the home were not entitled to free healthcare insurance. This meant that many women were unable to afford the services of a private doctor when ill. Women in full-time paid employment, who were eligible for free healthcare, showed a higher propensity for sickness than the majority of their male counterparts.

In addition, statistics revealed that during the period 1931–32 married women experienced 140 per cent more sickness and sixty per cent more disablement than anticipated by the government.[11] Poverty, unemployment and poor nutrition, combined with inadequate health care and poor working conditions in the home, all contributed to the appalling state of women's health. This was particularly the case amongst working-class women and a problem the WCG had highlighted since the beginning of the century.[12]

Members of the Women's Maternal Mortality Committee, and the organisations they represented, were united in demanding that the government take some action to improve conditions for mothers. At a time when both Labour and Conservative parties endorsed traditional gender roles through the public service marriage bar and their support for the family wage, the reality of rising maternal mortality proved to be a major embarrassment. Well aware of this fact, voluntary women's organisations took the opportunity to engage in a public campaign to improve maternity services for women.

This situation was exacerbated further by the dramatic decline in the national birth rate during the inter-war period. If women were to be encouraged to have more children it was imperative that they should not be afraid of childbirth. As the previous chapter has demonstrated, this was a critical issue for the MU and CWL in particular. Both groups believed that pregnancy and childbirth had to be made more attractive to women, with adequate financial and medical aid provided by the state, to ensure that women would have larger and healthier families. Consecutive governments also shared these concerns and during the period 1924 to 1937 the Ministry of Health carried out five separate investigations into maternal mortality.

This research confirmed that maternal mortality rates were increasing and a number of recommendations were made in an attempt to curb further escalation. Dr Janet Campbell, author of the 1927 report, *The Protection of Motherhood*, concluded that up to half of all maternal deaths could be prevented by 'better ante-natal care, better training of midwives, improved obstetrical techniques and antiseptic methods'.[13] Later reports supported the idea of hospital births and advised that maternity hospitals should have a minimum of seventy beds, which would ensure the services of a consultant.[14]

Official investigations into the problem of maternal mortality were welcomed by voluntary women's organisations. The WI acknowledged the publication of *The Protection for Motherhood* as a sign that the Ministry of Health was at least aware of the maternal mortality problem.[15] Likewise, the NCW welcomed the report but went on to urge that 'the Ministry of Health shall be given every facility for the promotion of research work, and for the carrying out of preventive and remedial measures'.[16] In spite of the official enquiries into maternal mortality, the number of women dying in childbirth continued to rise throughout the early 1930s. The MU, CWL, NCW, WI and TG viewed this with growing alarm and their leaders called on both the government and their own members to take appropriate preventative action.

When the *Interim Report on Maternal Mortality* was published in 1930, the NCW passed a resolution appealing to all local authorities to 'put into force the powers they already possess with regard to the provision of maternity services'.[17] Under the terms of the 1918 Maternity and Child Welfare Act, local authorities were responsible for providing maternity services in their own area. Amongst the services the authority could provide were maternity and child welfare clinics, maternity hospitals, free or cheap food for pregnant and nursing women, day nurseries and home-helps for women in the weeks before and after confinement.[18]

The 1918 Act did not, however, make the provision of any of these services compulsory. It was left to the individual authority to decide which maternity services were to be offered and who was eligible to receive free care. This meant that the quality and range of maternity services in any given locality was dependent on the availability of resources and the commitment of each individual authority. As a result the standard of maternity care in different regions varied considerably.[19]

The CWL expressed the view of many when it blamed the high level of maternal mortality and morbidity on the 'outstanding failure of the maternity and child welfare movement'.[20] Figures released by the NCW in 1935 showed that thirty-three out of sixty-two County Councils and 141 out of 185 County Boroughs provided less than half of the services recommended by the government.[21] That same year the NCW passed a resolution urging all local authorities to provide 'easily accessible ante-natal and post-natal clinics, staffed by competent obstetricians [as well as] gynaecological clinics staffed by competent gynaecologists'.[22] The resolution was endorsed by affiliated societies, including the MU and the CWL, and was sent to hospitals, medical schools and local authorities.

By 1938, the provision of maternity services had improved somewhat with most local authorities in England providing ante-natal and post-natal clinics for women. If the council itself did not run a clinic, it ensured that there were equivalent voluntary clinics operating in the locality grant-aided by the council. This commitment to extending maternity services was meaningless, however, if women did not attend the clinics. In 1937, Ministry of Health statistics showed that only ten per cent of women visited post-natal clinics.[23] The CWL highlighted the difficulties faced by pregnant women wishing to attend their local clinic. Mothers had to ensure that their other children were cared for in order to allow them to attend. If no relative or neighbour was available, the mother would have to pay someone to watch over her children while she was away and not all mothers could afford this extra expense.

The cost of travel to and from the clinic was another potential obstacle. In 1936, the CWL suggested that women should be able to reclaim the bus and train fares they incurred when visiting the clinic. It was argued that women who needed free maternity care would find it difficult to meet such travel expenses and would therefore be reluctant to seek the medical attention they required.[24] The Ministry of Health however did not adopt this practical proposal by the CWL, most likely on the grounds of limited funds. The proposal did however illustrate the CWL's belief that if the state sought to encourage women to have more children, then it was beholden upon it to provide medical, practical and financial support to allow women to fulfil their maternal role.

Increasingly aware of the importance of good maternity care both before and after birth, housewives' organisations realised that they themselves had an important role in encouraging members to avail themselves of the free treatment available at maternity and child welfare clinics. Despite the fact that the CWL objected to the dissemination of birth control information at publicly funded clinics, the organisation showed no hesitation in recommending maternity services to Catholic women. In opposing birth control and abortion, the CWL recognised that it had a particular responsibility to speak out for the rights of women, married or unmarried, who became mothers and to ensure that they received the care they required.

The MU also encouraged its members to seek medical advice during pregnancy. In 1936, readers of *The Mothers' Union Journal* were advised that expectant mothers 'can be greatly helped by all that modern science has taught us about infant and child welfare and she will no doubt gladly avail herself of the advice and encouragement which is easily found nowadays in clinics and welfare centres.'[25] Similarly the TG advised its members to visit local maternity centres and ante-natal clinics and report any shortcomings in the service provided to the national organisation.[26] In 1933 the NCW passed a resolution calling on all branches and affiliated societies

> to persuade expectant mothers to avail themselves of the facilities for ante-natal treatment, and, later, of post-natal medical advice, where provided by their local authorities or otherwise, and to report to the Ministry of Health and to the local authority where facilities for either ante-natal or post-natal care are not available in their areas.[27]

In urging their members to take advantage of the maternity services made available to them, voluntary women's organisations were clearly asserting the right of women citizens to public healthcare, particularly during pregnancy.

Having recommended that members take up the offer of free medical attention, women's organisations were anxious that the care they received was of the highest quality. Throughout the 1930s questions were raised about the training and standards of care provided by midwives and doctors attending maternity cases. These concerns were raised in the report *The Protection of Motherhood*, which concluded that better training of midwives and improved obstetrical techniques would bring about a reduction in the number of maternal deaths. During the 1920s, a midwife attended fifty to sixty per cent of births. Under the terms of the 1918 Maternity and Child Welfare Act, local authorities were authorised but not required to provide subsidised midwifery services for all eligible women.

Women's organisations such as the NCW were eager for every local authority to employ qualified and well-trained midwives to oversee normal home deliveries. Although training requirements had been improved in 1926, the high rate of maternal mortality and morbidity continued to focus attention on the experience and qualifications of midwives and doctors.[28] In 1934, the NCW passed a resolution arguing that

> in view of the serious rate of maternal mortality and morbidity, it is desirable that more practical experience should be required of medical students and pupil midwives during their training in midwifery and that additional post-graduate courses should be arranged.[29]

One way to regulate the employment and training of midwives was to compel local authorities to provide a salaried and domiciliary midwifery service. The NCW backed this scheme whereby women unable to afford the services of a doctor or an independent midwife would be seen by a trained midwife employed by the local authority. This egalitarian reform would ensure that even the poorest women would receive professional care. It was hoped that salaried midwives would dissuade women from employing unqualified local 'handy-women' during their confinements.[30]

The Midwives Act 1936 went some way to ensuring that expectant mothers received the standard of maternity care to which all women citizens were entitled. This new legislation introduced a national midwifery service with private midwives becoming salaried employees of their local authority.[31] Janet Campbell strongly supported the Midwives Act and wrote a series of articles on the new legislation in *The Townswoman* and *Home and Country*.[32] The TG and the WI gave their full support to the new legislation, as did the NCW and the CWL. Significantly the MU had refused officially to support amendments to the 1936 bill on the grounds that to do so was to engage in party politics and therefore outside the scope of the Union's work.

Although the 1936 Midwives Act improved the training of midwives by placing it under the control of the local authority, the performance of doctors attending births remained a matter of grave concern. Very aware of this problem, the NCW urged all teaching hospitals 'to provide for their medical students a longer course in midwifery, with personal delivery of a larger number of cases and ... to encourage those students wishing to become general practitioners to undergo post-graduate training in midwifery and gynaecology'.[33]

As the numbers of women giving birth in hospital gradually increased throughout the 1930s, the demand for better-trained doctors took on even greater significance.[34] Women's organisations were initially cautious about recommending hospital births for normal deliveries. There was a general feeling that the family home was the best and safest place for women to give birth. Hospital wards could prove a source of infection resulting in puerperal fever and death. In evidence to the Royal Commission on Population, the NCW expressed its belief that maternal mortality occurred more often in hospitals than in the home. Jane Lewis has written that it is difficult to prove these claims. Hospitals tended to treat abnormal cases and so recorded a higher mortality rate. Lewis does suggest, however, that the standard of hospital care varied considerably and that middle-class nursing homes were dangerous places in which to give birth during this period.[35]

The NCW did concede however that 'for the abnormal case or the woman whose home conditions are unsuitable, the certainty of a [hospital] bed ought to be assured.'[36] Midwives' accounts of cramped, dilapidated living conditions, infestation and the lack of running water were common in areas of acute social deprivation such as the East End of London.[37] In these extreme cases, the middle-class leadership of the NCW and the MU concurred with the WCG that a hospital birth was the best option.

The availability of anaesthesia was another reason why housewives organisations favoured hospital births for some women. During the 1930s it was more likely, though by no means a certainty, that women giving birth in hospital would receive some form of pain relief. It was much less likely that women having their babies at home would receive any relief from the pain of labour. In 1936, the Royal College of Obstetricians and Gynaecologists prohibited midwives from giving chloroform capsules to women in their care. Midwives were only permitted to administer gas and air, but many lacked the training and equipment needed and could not afford to employ the assistance necessary to perform this procedure.[38]

A number of women's organisations supported calls by the National Birthday Trust Fund to allow midwives to administer new forms of pain relief during home births.[39] Members of the WI, at their annual general meeting in 1938, urged their Executive Committee 'to take all possible steps to get the new methods of analgesia made available for all countrywomen in childbirth in their own homes provided there are adequate safeguards'.[40] The issue of pain relief for women giving birth at home was of particular importance to rural women, many of whom lived great distances from the nearest hospital and who were therefore much more likely to give birth at home without pain relief. In 1946 the WI welcomed the decision to allow gas and air to be administered by one person. There still remained the practical difficulty of transporting the heavy equipment and in 1949 the Institute called on local authorities to provide rural midwives with a car allowance.[41]

Upper- and middle-class women who could afford the services of a private doctor benefited from pain-relieving drugs such as chloroform. The fact that midwives could not provide this service meant that working-class women more often than not had to endure the full pain of childbirth. The NCW highlighted this injustice when it called on local authorities to train midwives in gas and air techniques so that all women could benefit from pain relief during labour. Despite the Council's efforts to draw attention to this problem an official report published in 1946 revealed that over 60 per cent of women gave birth without the aid of pain relief.[42]

With the outbreak of war, maternity services in England underwent a number of crucial changes. In 1939, an emergency maternity service was established to meet the needs of expectant and nursing mothers during wartime. Pregnant women were evacuated from areas at risk from bombing to be accommodated in nursing homes and hospitals for the birth of their babies. As a result the number of hospital beds made available for maternity cases increased during the war.[43] The demand for hospital births was firmly established during the war years when many women came to expect that they would give birth in hospital.

This growing normalisation of hospital births was further emphasised in May 1943 when the MU campaigned for an increase in the number of maternity beds in urban and rural districts. Representatives from the Union visited the Ministry of Health and produced detailed accounts of maternity bed shortages in London and other areas of the country. Following a sympathetic hearing, Ministry of Health officials guaranteed that staffing levels in maternity hospitals all over the country would be increased as soon as possible. Dr Pursley, representing the Ministry, assured the MU representatives that 'all that can be done will be done to meet the needs of mothers and babies.'[44]

The Union's efforts to increase the allocation of maternity beds signified its approval of hospital maternity wards. For an organisation representing over 500,000 mothers, such an endorsement was extremely influential. The Union, most often associated with traditional images of home and family, now accepted that hospitals were a safe and appropriate place for women to give birth. In 1950 the Union's enthusiasm for hospital births was illustrated when the organisation took credit for the increase in the number of maternity beds available in London. This development, which occurred in 1946, was singled out as one of the Union's major achievements in the post-war years.[45]

By 1950, the number of women dying as a result of childbirth had declined dramatically.[46] Improvements in the training of midwives and doctors had contributed to this recovery. Other significant factors were wartime medical advancements, particularly the treatment with penicillin of puerperal fever and the use of blood transfusions to reduce the numbers of deaths resulting from haemorrhage.[47] The general health of women also improved during these years with expectant and nursing mothers benefiting from free milk and vitamin supply schemes for pregnant and nursing women, both of which had become more widespread and accessible during wartime.

The right of all pregnant women to a nutritious diet, including free or cheap supplies of milk, was a cause championed by voluntary women's organisations throughout the 1930s. The importance of diet in pregnancy was recognised by the NCW, who, in 1935, called upon all local authorities to give careful consideration 'to the results obtained from recent research on the value of diet to the expectant nursing [sic] mother, and the advisability of providing meals at convenient centres for those mothers who do not appear to be satisfactorily nourished at home.'[48] In the winter of 1934, the Sheffield branch of the NCW set up a day-care centre for disadvantaged women providing them with a hot midday meal five days a week. Twenty women, recommended by local health workers, benefited from the scheme. A doctor's report at the end of nine months concluded that twenty healthy babies had been born following 'uniformly satisfactory confinements.'[49]

Whilst the provision of nutritious meals for pregnant and nursing women went beyond the financial resources of many local authorities, voluntary women's groups concentrated on the campaign for the less costly objective of free or subsidised milk supplies. The WI took a leading role in this campaign when in 1936 it passed a resolution calling on the government to reduce the retail price of milk on the grounds that it was essential for the health of the nation. Representatives from the WI met with Mr Walter Elliot, the Minister of Agriculture, in July 1936 to discuss this issue and he reassured them that he would take the views of the WI into consideration.[50]

With the overall supply of milk increasing during the 1930s, the government introduced a system of quotas to maintain milk prices. This resulted in milk being made available to mothers at two shillings per gallon while milk sold to the manufacturing industries fetched the lower price of five pence per gallon.[51] In these circumstances, it is understandable that women's organisations protested that a mother's right to cheap milk was greater than that of industry. In 1937 another WI delegation visited the Minister of Health, Sir Kingsley Wood, to lobby for a reduction in the price of milk for mothers and young children. The delegation based its demands on a survey of local institutes which revealed that many local authority milk schemes were either ineffective or had not yet been introduced.

Later that year the WI expressed its intention to continue campaigning for cheaper milk at its AGM. The meeting expressed its regret that the government had not taken adequate steps to ensure that the price of milk was reduced for 'all needy parents of children under school age'.[52] A copy of this resolution was sent to the ministries of Health and Agriculture as well as to the Milk Marketing Board and the Maternity and Child Welfare Council. Individual members of the organisation were called upon to write to their local MPs requesting them to support the introduction of cheaper milk for every mother and children under the age of five.[53]

On the eve of the Second World War, it was reported that subsidised milk schemes had been introduced by all the 409 welfare authorities in the country.[54] In spite of this positive outcome, the availability of low-cost milk for mothers and children aged five and under remained dependent on the commitment of individual local councils. Subsidising milk prices was a costly practice and some local authorities were unwilling to extend the service beyond a very limited number of women believed to be suffering from extreme hardship. Elizabeth Peretz has written of the wide variations in practice between local councils when it came to deciding which women were eligible for free or reduced priced milk. Local authorities acted independently on this issue and each had its own complicated qualification procedure.[55] Voluntary women's organisations were anxious that women who qualified for the scheme might not be aware of their right to apply. For example the CWL, through its own maternity and child welfare centre on the Old Kent Road, ensured that women attending the clinic were informed about the milk scheme. Staff at the clinic explained the application procedure to mothers so that all those eligible would receive the milk from the local borough council.[56]

Despite years of campaigning, it was not until the outbreak of war that the WI's proposal for a universal subsidised milk scheme was adopted. In July 1940, wartime food shortages led the government to set up a National Milk Scheme. Under the scheme all expectant and nursing mothers and children under five were entitled to one pint of milk a day at the reduced price of two pence.[57] If a family's income was below forty shillings a week, eligible women and children were given the milk free of charge. Official statistics showed that by September 1940, seventy per cent of those eligible for the National Milk Scheme had received subsidised milk with thirty per cent of them benefiting from free milk.[58]

Maternal health improved during the war years as a result of free-milk schemes, the availability of vitamin and iron supplements and food rationing, which gave poorer women access to a balanced and affordable diet.[59] Mothers did have to contend, however, with the difficulties of caring for their children during wartime. This situation was made even more arduous when mothers were deprived of the support of their husbands and relatives, many of whom were serving in the forces or engaged in paid war work. In addition many middle-class women who would normally have employed domestic servants were unable to do so during wartime as working-class women were conscripted into industry.[60]

The National Service (Number Two) Act 1941 ordered the compulsory registration of women between the ages of nineteen and forty at employment exchanges. Married women were not conscripted on account of their responsibilities within the home but were encouraged to volunteer for war work.[61] In 1943, the continuing labour shortage resulted in the government widening the eligibility for compulsory national service. Married women with children over fourteen years of age were now called upon to register for part-time work. Once again women with young children were encouraged, though not required, to engage in part-time work in their local community. By 1943, an estimated 7,750,000 women were in paid employment, forty-three per cent of whom were married.[62]

As the war progressed, voluntary women's organisations, including the MU and NCW, became increasingly concerned about the welfare of pregnant and nursing mothers, as well as mothers with young children, during wartime. In 1942, the MU began a campaign to increase the number of home-help schemes available to mothers. The employment of home-helps by local authorities had been one of the demands made by the WCG and Women's Sections of the Labour Party throughout the inter-war years.[63] The 1918 Maternity and Child Welfare Act had given local authorities the right to employ home-helps as part of their maternity welfare programme. By 1928, however, it emerged that authorities were spending only 0.1 per cent of their maternal and child welfare budgets on home-helps.[64] Ten years later only an estimated 190 out of 305 local authorities were providing home-helps for mothers in their areas.[65]

As has been suggested, war conditions created new difficulties for young mothers. Without the traditional support of husbands and family, women coping with young children as well as a new baby required the assistance of a home-help more than ever before. During the early 1940s, the MU began to focus more on the needs of young mothers. This was part of 'the young wives campaign', a concerted effort to attract greater numbers of young women into the organisation.[66] Highlighting issues such as maternity care and home-helps were obvious ways of appealing to this constituency of women.

In February 1943, a delegation of 'young wives' from the MU visited the MP Margaret Keir. Three major difficulties facing mothers in wartime were addressed at this meeting: the lack of home-helps available to mothers, the shortage of maternity beds and the scarcity of adequate housing for mothers with young children.[67] Keir agreed to assist the MU in its campaign and did so by raising the subject of home-helps in the House of Commons and bringing the matter to the attention of Ernest Bevin, the Minister of Labour and National Service. The following May, the MU was invited to appear before the Parliamentary Woman Power Committee where the need for more home-helps, maternity beds and suitable housing for young mothers was discussed.[68] The Union's representatives were given a sympathetic hearing by the members of the all-party Committee who acknowledged that the Union was 'the most influential body of women in the country … it has tremendous weight'.[69]

The ability of the MU to bring the government's attention to the problems facing young mothers during wartime was impressive, if not surprising. The MU was seen as a highly respected national women's organisation representing conservative middle-class values. Affiliated to the Church of England, the Union was itself very much part of the establishment. When such an organisation became openly critical of the government and suggested that the state was failing mothers, the authorities were quick to react.

Following their meeting with the Woman Power Committee, representatives of the MU met with officials from the Ministry of Labour and the Ministry of Health to discuss their grievances. At the Ministry of Labour, Union members warned of the risk of miscarriage and ill-health to pregnant women who received no help with housework and child-care in the weeks before and after giving birth. The Union urged that all pregnant women, but particularly those with young children, should be provided with a home-help and managed to persuade the Ministry of Labour that the shortage of home-helps for mothers was a matter of national importance.[70]

Throughout 1942, the Ministry had encouraged 'immobile' women, usually married women with older children, to volunteer as home-helps in their local area. These efforts had proved largely unsuccessful. Many older women regarded domestic work as a menial task and the low rates of pay offered did not persuade them otherwise. When the MU suggested that women aged between forty and forty-five should be directed into work as home-helps, the Ministry rejected the idea on the grounds that older women would not do the work.

The Ministry favoured proposals that County Councils and voluntary organisations should provide professional part-time help for pregnant and nursing women.[71] One such scheme was set up in Oxford in 1944 by the local Women's Voluntary Services (WVS) branch, who assisted the local council in recruiting and overseeing the employment of twenty-three home-helps who visited fifty-five households each week.[72] However, despite the Ministry of Labour's enthusiasm for home-helps, the number of women actually benefiting from the scheme remained relatively small. In 1945, only 13,605 pregnant women had been assisted in this way.[73] Home-helps for mothers remained a key issue for women's organisations throughout the later years of the war.

In evidence to the Royal Commission on Population, both the NCW and the CWL insisted that home-helps were essential if women were to be encouraged to have more children. Interestingly, they argued that home-helps were important not only for the physical well-being of pregnant and nursing women but also to ensure that women had time to be 'a companion to their husbands'.[74] Continued pressure by women's organisations for the provision of home-helps proved successful when in 1946, under the terms of the Health Service Act, home-helps became a regular part of local authority welfare services.[75]

It is clear therefore that throughout the 1930s and 1940s, housewives' associations became increasingly active in their efforts to improve the standard of maternity care and maternity services for women. Reacting first of all to the increasing number of maternal deaths and then to the consequences of war, voluntary women's groups called into question the government's commitment to mothers. On the one hand, they put pressure on both the government and local authorities to provide all of the maternity services recommended under the Maternity and Child Welfare Act 1918. On the other, these groups encouraged their members to use whatever services were available to them as this was imperative if the health and welfare of expectant and nursing mothers was to be improved.

Women were informed of their right as housewives, mothers and citizens to an efficient, high-quality and freely available maternity service and the MU, CWL, NCW, WI and TG repeatedly demonstrated their willingness to lobby and campaign for the extension of these services to women. In this way, housewives' organisations played an important part in establishing the right of women to state-funded healthcare, particularly during pregnancy, at a crucial time in the development of state welfare provision.

Social welfare rights for women

As part of their campaign to reduce the maternal mortality rate, voluntary women's organisations became increasingly critical of the status of women under the existing social welfare system. Women's organisations condemned the fact that women working within the home, revered by the state as the centre of family life, were not entitled to free healthcare under the National Health Insurance Act 1911. Not only were women working full-time within the home deprived of free medical attention, but also insured women who missed work because of pregnancy were not considered eligible for sick pay.

The majority of approved societies responsible for paying out sickness benefits did not accept that pregnancy was an illness. The approved societies' view was that 'if a woman is disabled by pregnancy alone, if such an expression is permissible, she cannot thereby be entitled to sickness benefit.'[76] This meant that women who missed work because of morning sickness or other illnesses relating specifically to pregnancy were disqualified from receiving sick pay.

Housewives' organisations were indignant that women should be discriminated against in this way. Once again it was clear to them that the ideology of domesticity, promoted by the state, would not translate into financial benefits for wives and mothers. In an effort to rectify this situation, pressure was exerted on the government by the larger women's societies to include uninsured housewives and pregnant working women in the National Health Insurance Scheme. In 1936, the WI proposed that women insured before marriage should be entitled to medical expenses after marriage, so long as a payment of six pence per week, or whatever sum was considered necessary, was maintained.[77]

Throughout the 1930s, the government refused to accept any financial responsibility for the general medical expenses of housewives or pregnant women beyond the one-off payment of maternity benefit. As official statistics revealed, it was married women who were most likely to suffer from ill health during this period. Not surprisingly, therefore, the government was reluctant to include married women working at home in any national healthcare scheme as this would prove an expensive addition to social welfare bills. Married women, like children, were regarded as dependents and as such were to be looked after by their husbands. This meant that husbands were expected to pay for their wives' medical expenses regardless of the family's ability to afford private medical care.

Despite the government's unwillingness to accept responsibility for married women's health, the provision of health care for housewives and extended benefits for pregnant women workers remained important issues for the WI. An article which appeared in *Home and Country* in 1942, under the heading 'The Nation's Cinderella', bemoaned the fact that married women working within the home were expected to perform 'unpaid domestic labour'. That these women were not even allowed to contribute to or benefit from national health insurance meant that women either resorted to medical treatment only when they were already very ill, or not at all. The hope was expressed that new laws would be introduced in peacetime which would make the position of women within the home more equitable.[78]

As the war continued and the numbers of married women entering the workforce rose significantly, the MU campaigned for the provision of an adequate period of paid maternity leave for mothers. It is important to note here however that it was only when married middle-class women began to work in significant numbers outside the home that organisations such as the MU began to campaign on their behalf. The WCG and the Women's Sections of the Labour Party had for many years highlighted the difficulties faced by working-class wives and mothers who worked outside the home in order to supplement their family's income.[79]

In July 1942, 'A Charter for Motherhood' appeared in *The Mothers' Union Workers' Paper* condemning the fact that pregnant women were not eligible for cash benefits under the National Health Insurance Scheme. The author argued that 'it is true that a mother receives maternity benefit, but this is to cover the cost of confinement. For a month thereafter she is prevented by law from working in a factory; during this period, whatever her state of health, she is legally debarred from drawing national health benefit.[80] The charter went on to highlight the fact that working women who decided not to return to work following the birth of their child, thereby failing to pay insurance contributions, lost their right to full cash benefits for up to two-and-a-half years. It concluded that

> such conditions as this strike at the root of our national health, for they present a bonus to the mother who ignores her own well-being and her baby's health. Childbirth makes lifelong partial casualties of

many working women, but it is not necessary and should not happen if only health insurance were extended to cover the unborn baby and the nursing mother.[81]

These were strong words from an organisation often dismissed as conservative and traditional. Rather than condemn women for going out to work the MU directed its anger instead at the government for not providing adequate support to wives and mothers.

The MU and the CWL publicly denounced the meagre maternity benefit paid to nursing mothers under the terms of the National Insurance Act 1911.[82] As the 'Charter for Motherhood' emphasised, the benefit fell drastically short of providing financial support to mothers for the four-week period they were prohibited from paid work. In addition the benefit was limited to women workers who were themselves insured or the wives of insured men. These women were entitled to a one-off payment of two pounds (plus an additional two pounds if the woman herself was insured) to cover the medical and other expenses incurred by the birth. Unmarried women who were not insured or women whose husbands were unable to afford regular insurance payments were not entitled to the benefit. These women usually represented the poorest members of society, those in need of greatest support.

Outlining its demands for better maternity care, the CWL asserted the right of all mothers to maternity benefit, even when their husbands were unemployed. The League looked favourably on the French system, where expectant and nursing mothers were entitled to weekly cash payments during their period of maternity leave, eight weeks before and after the birth of their babies.[83] The organisation believed that if such a system were introduced in England it would greatly improve the quality of mothers' lives. It would also give parents the incentive to have more children, an important consideration when the decline in the birth rate was a matter for national concern.

In response to the growing disquiet of women's societies, the NCW set up a special subcommittee to investigate the problems encountered by women employees before and after childbirth. The committee, which first met in 1942, recommended that women workers should be paid maternity benefit during the weeks before and after the birth of their baby. The committee advised that 'normal pregnancy should entitle a woman to an adequate maternity benefit to be paid weekly to the woman in cash, to begin eight weeks before the expected birth of the child, and that such benefit should preclude a woman from employment.'[84]

The proposal that expectant and nursing mothers should be prevented from engaging in paid work for sixteen weeks was greeted with caution by some of the groups affiliated to the NCW. Dr Janet Aitkin, representing the Medical Women's Federation, argued that there was no need for a woman to stop work so early if she were in good health.[85] The SJCIWO and the WCG, along with egalitarian feminist groups, expressed concern that many less well-off women would be financially disadvantaged if excluded from paid work for such a long period.[86]

It was for this reason that the NCW's subcommittee stressed the importance of cash payments covering the entire sixteen weeks of maternity leave. This measure would ensure that women could take advantage of their extended period of leave without suffering undue financial hardship. As the MU 'Charter for Motherhood' had explained 'it is highly advisable that she [the mother] should stay at home for the first eight weeks, both for her own sake and the child's, but the present regulations encourage her to start work directly after lying-in, and break the law to do so.'[87]

The establishment of the Inter-Departmental Committee on Social Insurance and Allied Services in June 1941 gave women's organisations the perfect opportunity to present their proposals for reform of the social welfare system directly to government. The committee, under the chairmanship of Sir William Beveridge, had been set up by the government to review existing social welfare services and make recommendations for reform.[88] As it transpired, the committee's final report, known as the Beveridge Report and published in 1942, represented the blueprint for the modern British welfare state.

From the outset, women's organisations were aware of how crucial it was for them to make representations on behalf of women to the committee. To this end the NCW submitted a memorandum to the committee in February 1942. In this document the NCW outlined in detail the changes it wished to see in the existing social welfare system. The Council strongly criticised the National Health Insurance Scheme for being too narrow and not providing adequate cash benefits for workers entitled to health insurance.[89] The fact that insured women paid fewer contributions and received lower rates of sickness and unemployment benefit than men was condemned, as was the 'inadequate provision … made for the maintenance of the income of women, married or unmarried, during pregnancy, confinement and the early infancy of the baby'.[90]

The Council's memorandum also referred to the status of women under the various pension schemes and their eligibility for unemployment insurance. Any differentiation between the eligibility of men and women, whether for pensions or unemployment benefit, was unacceptable to the NCW. Married women in particular had suffered as a result of discrimination in the arrangements for unemployment assistance and pensions. The assumption that the majority of women would cease to be gainfully employed on marriage resulted in married women workers being treated as a separate category under National Insurance regulations.

Inequalities experienced by women applying for unemployment assistance or qualifying for pension schemes persisted throughout the 1930s.[91] As a result, women's organisations were anxious that any proposals for the reform of the social welfare system would eliminate the disparity between male and female workers. Traditional assumptions that married women did not need to work after marriage, backed up by the public service marriage bar, meant that many married women were unable to secure work during the 1930s. When these women applied for unemployment assistance they found that under the terms of the Anomalies Act 1931 they faced the double burden of having to prove that they were genuinely seeking work and that they had a realistic chance of securing employment in their local area.[92]

Variances in relation to the pension schemes available for men and women also existed during the inter-war years. The Widows, Orphans and Old Age Contributory Pensions Act 1929 gave widows of insured men a pension at the age of fifty-five. Old age pensions were granted to insured women at the age of sixty-five. In its submission to the Beveridge Committee, the NCW argued that it was unfair for an able-bodied widow to be given a pension earlier than a single woman on the sole ground that she had been the dependent of an insured man. The Council claimed that widows' pensions, which took no account of a widow's ability to find work, undercut the wages of other women workers and kept the wages of women at a minimum.[93]

In 1937, the NCW had welcomed the inclusion of married women in the Widows, Orphans and Old Age Contributory Pensions (Voluntary Contributions) Act. Married women working at home were now entitled to make voluntary contributions which would entitle them to a pension at the age of sixty-five.[94] The Act, however, excluded women whose income exceeded £250 a year while men were allowed an annual income limit of up to £400. The Council argued that this anomaly would 'not only seriously damage individual women, but introduces for the first time a new discrimination against women by making a difference of income level for admission into insurance based on the sex of the contributor.'[95]

The TG shared the NCW's concern on this issue and its National Executive undertook to inform members of any further attempts to exclude dependent women from the National Pensions Scheme.[96] It was this underlying discrimination encountered by women applying for welfare benefits that prompted the NCW's submission to the Committee on Social Insurance and Allied Services. As the ODC representative to the NCW explained, 'it is finally as a matter of principle, a denial to women of the full status and responsibility which is accorded to men ... we ought to stir up women to be vocal in their own interests.'[97]

The Beveridge Report was published in November 1942 and was initially welcomed by voluntary women's organisations. The WI greeted the report with a resolution recording its appreciation of 'Sir William Beveridge's great work for social security and particularly of his recognition that health insurance for housewives and children's allowances are essential if family life is to be free from want'.[98] This view was endorsed in *Home and Country*, which stated enthusiastically that 'housewives have come into their own at last! The Beveridge Plan for social security ... puts in its own words "a premium on marriage instead of penalising it".'[99]

The TG acknowledged the report's recognition of the work performed by the housewife as 'an improvement on the hitherto accepted view of those whose profession is described as "unpaid domestic duties".'[100] As these comments suggest, official recognition of the unpaid work undertaken by women in the home was regarded as an important victory by housewives' associations who had argued this point for many years. The Beveridge Report made it clear that in 'any measure of social policy in which regard is had to the facts, the great majority of married women must be regarded as occupied on work which is vital though unpaid, without which their husbands could not do their paid work and without which the nation could not continue.'[101]

Yet in spite of this long awaited recognition of women's unpaid work there was an inherent danger in assuming that the majority of women would not be engaged in paid work. As Carole Pateman has argued, Marshall's theory of social citizenship assumed that paid employment would entitle citizens to social welfare benefits 'just at a time when the architects of the welfare state were constructing men as breadwinner-worker and women as dependent-wife'.[102] Just how housewives and mothers were going to be able to claim their right to social citizenship within the new welfare state would remain an issue of contention for women's organisations in the decades that followed.

There was much, however, in Beveridge's recommendations to satisfy groups representing women at this time. The report did address many of the grievances raised by the NCW and went some way towards rectifying the discrimination and hardship faced by women under the social welfare system. Adequate provision of maternity benefit and maternity leave was considered a question of 'national interest'. The expectant mother 'should be under no economic pressure to continue work as long as she can, and to return to it as soon as she can.'[103]

The plan recommended that all mothers should receive a maternity grant of £4 on the birth of their baby. Women engaged in paid employment should be provided with a further cash benefit of thirty-six shillings per week to cover a period of thirteen weeks maternity leave.[104] This was a significant improvement on existing arrangements for expectant and nursing mothers, even if it did not extend the period of maternity leave to sixteen weeks as recommended by the NCW and the MU. Neither group protested against the shorter period of maternity leave and Beveridge's proposals were adopted in the National Insurance Act 1946.[105]

The establishment of a National Health and Rehabilitation Service (NHS) was another aspect of the Beveridge Plan widely acclaimed by both voluntary women's organisations and the general public. Free healthcare made available to 'one hundred per cent of the population' meant that uninsured housewives and mothers would be entitled to free medical attention at all times and not just during pregnancy and after childbirth. The introduction of this reform satisfied the demands made by women's groups, including the WI and the CWL, that married women must be included in any national health insurance scheme. The NHS was described by the WI as an important 'tightening up of the services offered' and a way to ensure that local health authorities maintained an adequate service 'for the care of expectant mothers'.[106]

Other reforms advocated by the Beveridge Committee included a revision of widows' pensions preventing able-bodied women receiving a full pension and earning an income at the same time. This meant that widows' pensions could not be used to undercut the wages of other women in paid work.[107] As a result of all these reforms the Beveridge Report successfully tackled three of the social insurance demands made by the NCW. But this still left the important issue of a married woman's right to unemployment assistance and the right of women workers to equal unemployment and sickness benefits. In dealing with these questions, Beveridge ignored the NCW's request that married women should not be treated as dependent citizens within the family. Because of this the report attracted criticism not only from egalitarian feminist groups but also from the larger mainstream women's organisations.

In his report, Beveridge made it clear that his plan for social security 'treats married women as a special insurance class of occupied persons and treats man and wife as a team'.[108] This meant that although the work done by housewives was recognised and marriage was considered a 'team effort', under the social welfare system married women would continue to be classified as their husband's dependent. Working women who paid national insurance lost their right to unemployment and disability benefit on marriage on the basis that their husbands were now responsible for their welfare. Married men received additional unemployment and disability benefit to cover the additional cost of supporting their dependent wives and children.

Women who continued to work outside the home after marriage were regarded as an oddity and were not treated in the same way as single female employees. Married women workers would not be required to pay insurance contributions after their marriage and so were not entitled to unemployment or disability benefit. Those who did opt to continue paying insurance contributions would receive lower benefits than their male colleagues. Beveridge took it for granted that married women would have children and would then be entitled to maternity benefit. This payment would compensate for the fact that women workers received lower sickness and unemployment benefits. So it was clear that Beveridge presumed that, after the war, women would choose between marriage and a career. He wrote that 'the attitude of the housewife to gainful employment outside the home is not and should not be the same as that of the single woman. She has other duties.'[109]

The NCW rejected Beveridge's proposals for the separate insurance arrangements made for married women workers. Following a special meeting of the NCW's Executive in December 1943, a list of objections was forwarded to the government. The Council called for the direct insurance of the married woman, who, like any other citizen, had the right to cash benefits when she was disabled by sickness or accident. Married women who had contributed towards their pension should also have the right to a retirement pension at sixty instead of being included in their husband's pension when he retired at the age of sixty-five. For married women workers, the Council argued that it was wrong for them to lose their insurance rights on marriage. All women workers, whether they were married or not, should have to pay compulsory contributions at the same rate as male workers. This would then entitle them to the same level of benefit as men. By voicing these objections the NCW, and its affiliated societies, was demanding nothing less than complete equality for men and women under any new scheme for National Insurance.

The Council's objections were modelled on the recommendations drawn up by two feminist activists, Elizabeth Abbott and Katherine Bompass, and published in the pamphlet *The Woman Citizen and Social Security* (1943).[110] Both women argued that the Beveridge Report was responsible for perpetuating the 'denial of any personal status to a woman because she is married, the denial of her independent personality within marriage … far from putting a premium on marriage, as it purports to do, the Plan penalises both the married woman and marriage itself.'[111] Often referred to as the 'feminist' reaction to the Beveridge Report, it is significant that the NCW, representing both feminist and mainstream middle-class women's groups, reproduced almost word for word the criticisms made by Abbott and Bompass. Voluntary women's organisations were delighted that women's work within the home had been recognised but were unwilling to tolerate any discrimination against women on the grounds that they were wives and mothers. This was a view they shared with feminist women's groups at this time.

The continued 'special treatment' of married women within the social welfare system prompted one high-ranking member of the WI to criticise Beveridge publicly. In an article published in the August 1944 edition of *Home and Country*, Cicely McCall, the Federation's Educational Organiser, objected to the government's White Paper on Social Security which incorporated many of Beveridge's recommendations.[112] In her article, McCall argued that it was wrong to exclude housewives from paying national insurance. She wished to make it clear to readers that this would prevent married women from claiming sickness and disability benefits. She also questioned the provision of a £20 death grant when the maternity grant was worth only £4 and the fact that working mothers were to receive a higher rate of maternity benefit than mothers who worked at home.[113] McCall urged that members should consider these anomalies, which if passed into law would mark the continuation of discrimination against women within the social welfare system.

This critique of Beveridge did make some impact on the general membership of the WI. In 1945, the organisation passed a resolution calling on the government to 'include in their National Insurance Scheme some cash sickness benefit for all non-gainfully employed married women and non-gainfully employed widows.'[114] Following up on this resolution, members of the WI Education and Public Questions Committee met with officials of the Ministry of National Insurance. They argued that married women should be classified as self-employed workers entitled to sickness benefit under the proposed National Insurance Act. The Ministry rejected these claims, insisting that insurance payments were intended to cover loss of earnings. This stipulation excluded housewives who 'must regard themselves as dependent on and insurable through their husbands.'[115]

By the late 1940s, it had become clear that the Beveridge Report was a mixed blessing for married women. The report did acknowledge the work done by women both in the home and the workplace. It promoted the ideal of the 'companionate marriage' in which husband and wife were to be considered equal partners. Yet when it came to actually catering for the needs of women, the report reaffirmed the dependent position of married women and denied married women workers the same rights to insurance as their male colleagues.

Nevertheless, by the end of the 1940s, women did have access to much improved maternity services, paid maternity leave and pension provision. Added to this, the general health of all women was to be greatly enhanced by the introduction of free healthcare under the NHS. There is no doubt that these reforms did much to improve the quality of hundreds of thousands of women's lives. Voluntary women's organisations, representing the interests of large numbers of housewives and mothers, had played a crucial part in the fight for these services. As Sylvia Walby has argued 'women played a more significant role in the struggle for this [the welfare state] than is sometimes suggested.'[116]

The campaign for family allowances

The Beveridge Report on *Social Security and Allied Services* included one other recommendation long fought for by women's organisations. This was the payment of family allowances. For over twenty-five years women had participated in the campaign for the introduction of family allowances to provide mothers with a degree of economic independence and their children with greater economic security.[117] Whilst Beveridge's scheme provided an allowance for each child after the first to be paid to 'those responsible for the care of children', it was not perceived as a wage for mothers and was set firmly in the context of a payment towards the upkeep of children. Indeed, Beveridge suggested that children's allowances 'can help to restore the birth rate' and benefit mothers and housewives who 'have vital work to do in ensuring the adequate continuance of the British race and of British ideals in the world'.[118]

Eleanor Rathbone, who spearheaded the campaign for family allowances throughout the inter-war years, viewed this reform as the ideal way to end the financial dependency of women in marriage. In her influential book *The Disinherited Family*, published in 1924, she warned of the dangers of economic dependency, which gave men the opportunity to dominate their wives and spend the family income on 'breeding pigeons or racing dogs or for some other form of personal gratification'.[119] Having witnessed at first hand the beneficial effects of separation allowances paid to the wives of servicemen during the First World War, Rathbone was convinced that a universal system of state payments to mothers should be introduced.[120]

From the early 1920s, however, Rathbone recognised that in mounting an effective campaign for family allowances, it would prove detrimental to focus exclusively on the question of economic independence for women. To do so would have linked the campaign too closely with what would have been regarded as a feminist issue and one which could be perceived as seeking to undermine the traditional role of the father as the breadwinner of the family. This would not have proved a popular or convincing argument during the 1920s and 1930s. Instead the campaign for family allowances was linked to key issues such as child poverty, the equal pay debate and the population question.

Indeed, it was in evidence to the Beveridge Committee that Rathbone explained her decision to focus on factors other than female economic independence. She explained that the argument for family allowances 'is really stronger if you leave out the wife'.[121] Focusing therefore on the less controversial benefits of family allowances, Rathbone campaigned for reform throughout the inter-war years with the support of the Family Endowment Society and its president William Beveridge.[122]

The principle of family allowances was supported by a wide range of women's organisations representing both working-class and middle-class women. The WCG and women within the Labour Party had been amongst the earliest advocates for the 'state endowment of motherhood'.[123] As the campaign for a scheme of allowances gathered pace throughout the 1920s and 1930s, mainstream voluntary women's organisations agreed to offer their support to the Family Endowment Society's campaign. These groups, with memberships consisting largely of wives and mothers, were in favour of payments to mothers as this acknowledged their domestic work and contributed towards the upkeep of their children.

The WI argued that 'women doing their own traditional and specific job of running a household and bringing up a family should be considered as important, as responsible and as much worthy of respect as women doing the kind of job ... done equally well by either sex ... their work is just as vital if not more so'.[124] The TG urged its members to study the question of family allowances and where possible to invite local MPs to speak at guild meetings so that members had a better understanding of what the measure entailed. Members were advised that family allowances were a matter 'on which members should be encouraged to make their own decision, and having reached that decision to take individual action by direct approach to their MP'.[125]

The MU was keen to emphasise the importance of a woman receiving an equal share of her husband's income in return for her work within the home. In September 1936 it was argued in *The Mothers' Union Journal* that 'it is not for a girl to have to ask her husband for money as a favour; this is specially intolerable to the women of to-day who have most probably earned an income of their own before marriage.'[126] It was however the CWL which was most outspoken in its support for family allowances during the 1930s. It suggested that the introduction of family allowances would curtail the use of birth control by making it easier for mothers to afford larger families. The League also hoped that the prospect of family allowances would help prevent women from resorting to abortion, an even greater sin in the eyes of the Church. To this end, the League envisaged allowances as a 'living wage' paid to married and unmarried mothers to assist them in the rearing of their children. To include unmarried mothers in the scheme for family allowances was a radical proposal and one notably absent from the agenda of the Family Endowment Society. The motive of the CWL was to encourage women to have children but the fact that the payment was to be made to the mother whether she was married or single is significant. In many ways the League's view echoed Rathbone's original feminist claim for the state endowment of mother-hood with women entitled to a 'wage' from the state in return for their service as mothers.

It was unlikely that a system of family allowances would have been introduced by either the Conservative or Labour administrations of the 1920s and 1930s. With the Labour Party divided over the relationship between family allowances and wage rates and the Conservatives reluctant to finance expensive public welfare schemes, the campaign for family allowances had little chance of success.[127] However, with the outbreak of war in 1939, this situation altered dramatically. The evacuation of children, particularly from inner-city areas, increased public awareness about the extent of child poverty. Accounts of malnourished and stunted children arriving in reception areas brought to light the devastating effects of unemployment and privation on the nation's children.

Voluntary women's groups, increasingly concerned about the welfare of women and children during wartime, put pressure on the government to introduce the legislation necessary for the introduction of family allowances. In October 1941, the NCW sent a declaration to the government urging that to 'preserve the welfare of the children of the nation the National Council of Women calls upon the Government to introduce a universal scheme of Family Allowances, paid by the State at the rate of six shillings per child, to be paid to the mother.'[128] Significantly, the Council's resolution emphasised the needs of children, not mothers. However, the demand that allowances be paid directly to the mother was a crucial issue for the NCW. In evidence to the Royal Commission on Population, representatives of the NCW took the opportunity to reiterate their belief that payment of family allowances must be made to the mother as 'a gesture of recognition to the mother by the state'.[129]

The MU became actively involved in the Family Endowment Society's campaign in 1941 when representatives attended two conferences on the subject held that year. The Union, always anxious to promote family life and the welfare of women and children, saw family allowances as an ideal way of protecting families from economic hardship. An article in *The Mothers' Union Workers' Paper* in September 1942 pointed out that 'the State is making real efforts to promote family life through better housing and the proposed schemes for family allowances'.[130] The Union's support for family allowances was made clear in its evidence to the Royal Commission on Population, submitted in March 1944. Its memorandum listed family allowances as one way to increase the birth rate, as the benefit would provide young couples with the financial security to start a family. Like the NCW, the MU representatives insisted that the allowance must be paid to the mother.

There is evidence to suggest however that not all MU members were in agreement that mothers should receive the allowance. A questionnaire sent to diocesan officials indicated that the majority of members supported the proposal that allowances be paid to mothers, yet it had been brought to the attention of the Central President, Rosamond Fisher, that some younger members were in favour of fathers being paid the money. Mrs Fisher admitted that she found this very odd and could not understand it. In an attempt to explain this view it was suggested that after five years of war some mothers were tired of shouldering all the responsibility for the family and hoped their husbands would take over when they returned home.[131] This difference of opinion within the MU is very interesting and it was surprising that it was younger members who were identified as objecting to mothers receiving the allowance. It may have been that older mothers, who had the benefit of experience, were themselves aware of how important it was for wives and mothers to have direct access to this cash benefit, as the allowance might be their only form of independent income.

Despite this lack of consensus, Rosamund Fisher endorsed the majority view and explained to the Commission on Population that 'we think it ought to be paid to the mother because she is the person really responsible for the child and for the spending of the money'.[132] On a more personal note, she suggested that family allowances paid to the mother would smooth the way for mothers returning to their homes after the war. She felt it unfair to expect women who earned their own income during the war to 'relinquish that bit of independence they get from money they earn for themselves'.[133]

In June 1944 the government set out its proposals for family allowances with the publication of the Family Allowances Bill. The principal reason for introducing the bill at this time was to curb inflationary wage levels with cash benefits for children. Family allowances were seen as a way of achieving this goal whilst at the same time addressing the problem of child poverty and the low birth rate.[134] Much to the consternation of stalwart campaigner Eleanor Rathbone and numerous women's groups, it quickly became clear that the government intended to pay the allowance to the father.

This decision sparked an immediate response from women's organisations. Members were urged to write to their local MP and to the national press demanding that the allowance be paid to the mother. This action was deemed essential if the government and the country were to be left in no doubt about 'the strength of women's opinion'.[135] A deputation of representatives from women's organisations, including the WFL, the NCW and ODC, visited Westminster to protest against the proposal to pay the allowance to fathers.[136] In addition, Eleanor Rathbone wrote to the WI appealing to members to voice their discontent. In a letter published in *Home and Country,* she explained that the payment to the mother has a symbolic value 'as a sign that the nation thinks of her not just as a "dependent" which literally means a hanger on, but as standing on her own two feet as the children's natural guardian'.[137]

The MU was also quick to take action and, following a request from the Family Endowment Society, the Union wrote to the Minister, Lord Woolton, in June 1944, impressing upon him the importance of paying the allowance to mothers and insisting that this proviso be included in the bill.[138] This decision to lobby the government once again demonstrates the willingness of the MU to engage in political action when the welfare of mothers and children was at stake. It is also of significance that Rathbone actively sought out the support of the WI and MU. This would suggest that she was well aware of the advantages of having such influential women's organisations on her side when confronting the government on this key question.

The efforts of Eleanor Rathbone and the Family Endowment Society, supported by women's societies, including the MU, the NCW and the WI, to ensure payment to mothers, ended in a resounding triumph. Faced with an onslaught of criticism from such influential women's organisations, the government was forced to capitulate. When the Family Allowances Act was passed into law in 1945 it was stipulated that payments would be made in cash to the mother. This was an important victory for the women's movement at this time and one which should not be underestimated. Disappointment was expressed, however, that the weekly payment of five shillings to all children after the first was lower than the eight shillings proposed by Beveridge and the MU and the six shillings suggested by the NCW. Women's organisations were also unhappy that the first child was not entitled to a weekly allowance.

By the end of the 1940s, voluntary women's groups, along with other women's groups including the WCG and the Labour Party Women's Sections, had contributed towards a number of far-reaching advances in the struggle to secure social welfare benefits for women. Family allowances paid to mothers, improved maternity services and free healthcare provided women, and in particular mothers, with some of the basic rights of social citizenship. It is true that the government introduced these reforms with other considerations in mind and that reform was limited due to the economic circumstances of the time. The introduction of family allowances had more to do with controlling wage levels and reducing child poverty than acknowledging women's work within the home. Likewise, improvements in maternity services were motivated by the high incidence of maternal deaths and falling population levels, rather than an acceptance that the state should support women in return for their services as wives and mothers.

Nevertheless it is clear that the impact of these reforms did make a difference to the quality of women's lives. Whatever the motive, family allowances did provide women with an independent source of income within the family. At the same time, maternity services and paid maternity leave gave women the support they needed as mothers and in doing so acknowledged their service to society in caring for children, the citizens of the future. Greater access to social welfare benefits and the introduction of the NHS were also particularly beneficial to women. The significance of these reforms was first recognised by working-class and feminist women's groups, including the WCG, the Fabian Women's Group and various individuals active in both the feminist and Labour movement. However, the participation of conservative middle-class women's organisations in calling for change must also be acknowledged as it did play a part in adding not only 'respectability' to these demands but also the sheer mass of numbers needed to launch successful national campaigns.

Notes

1 Walby, 'Is Citizenship Gendered?', p. 386.
2 See for example Pugh, *Women and the Women's Movement* and Thane, 'Visions of Gender'.
3 Loudon, *Death in Childbirth*, pp. 240–246.
4 The infant mortality rate declined from over 150 per thousand births in the 1890s to a figure of 51 in 1939. It should be noted, however, that there were significant regional and social variations. Pugh, *Women and the Women's Movement*, p. 250.
5 *The Townswoman*, 3:5 (May 1935), p. 25.
6 MSH, Central Council Minutes, Vol. 8 (1927–29), 'Minutes of the Mothers' Union Central Council', December 1927, p. 89.
7 Loudon, *Death in Childbirth*, p. 245.
8 *Ibid.*, p. 244.
9 *Ibid.*, p. 241. See also L. Marks, 'Mothers, Babies and Hospitals: "The London" and Provision of Maternity Cases in East London 1870-1939', in V. Fildes, L. Marks and H. Marland (eds), *Women and Children First: International Maternal and Infant Welfare 1870-1945* (London: Routledge, 1992).
10 Loudon, *Death in Childbirth*, p. 251.
11 See Lewis, 'In Search of a Real Equality', pp. 222–225.
12 In 1915, the Guild published graphic and disturbing first-hand accounts of the pain and misery caused by difficult and mismanaged labour. See M. Llewellyn Davies (ed.), *Maternity: Letters from Working Women* (London: Bell, 1915).
13 C. Mowat, *Britain between the Wars 1918-1940* (London: Methuen, 1955), p. 516.
14 Lewis, 'In Search of a Real Equality', p. 220.
15 *Home and Country*, 10:5 (May 1928), p. 98.
16 *NCW Handbook 1928-1929* (1929), p. 79.
17 *NCW Handbook 1929-1930* (1930), p. 82.
18 Thane, 'Visions of Gender', p. 106.
19 See for example E. Peretz, 'A Maternity Service for England and Wales: Local Authority Maternity Care in the Inter-war Period in Oxfordshire and Tottenham', in J. Garcia, R. Kilpatrick and M. Richards (eds), *The Politics of Maternity Care: Services for Childbearing Women in Twentieth Century Britain* (London: Clarendon Paperbacks, 1990).
20 *The Catholic Women's League Magazine*, 302 (December 1936).
21 WL, Pamphlet Collection, *Report of the National Council of Women Council Meeting and Conference, Southport June 29-July 2 1935* (1935), p. 111.
22 *NCW Handbook 1936-1937* (1937), p. 103.
23 Lewis, 'In Search of a Real Equality', p. 221.
24 *The Catholic Women's League Magazine*, 302 (December 1936), p. 34.
25 *The Mothers' Union Journal*, 166 (September 1936), p. 20.
26 *The Townswoman*, 3:7 (October 1935), p. 78.
27 *NCW Handbook 1933-34* (1934), p. 80.
28 See S. Robinson, 'Maintaining the Independence of the Midwifery Profession: A Continuing Struggle', in Garcia, Kilpatrick and Richards (eds), *The Politics of Maternity Care*, p. 68.
29 *NCW Handbook 1934-35* (1935), p. 82.

30   E. Roberts, *A Women's Place: An Oral History of Working-Class women, 1890–1940* (Oxford, Blackwell, 1984) and M. Sutton, *'We Didn't Know Aught': A Study of Sexuality, Superstition and Death in Women's Lives in Lincolnshire during the 1930s, '40s and '50s* (Stamford: Paul Watkins, 1992).

31   The Act legislated for the employment of midwives by local authorities or by welfare and voluntary groups approved of by the local authority. See Robinson, 'Maintaining the Independence of the Midwifery Profession', p. 71.

32   *The Townswoman* (March 1936); *Home and Country* (May 1936).

33   *NCW Handbook 1936–1937* (1937), p. 103.

34   In 1927 fifteen per cent of births took place in hospital. This rose to twenty five per cent in 1937 and forty five per cent in 1945.

35   J. Lewis, 'Mothers and Maternity Policies in the Twentieth Century', in Garcia, Kilpatrick and Richards (eds), *The Politics of Maternity Care*, p. 22.

36   WL, Pamphlet Collection, *Report of the National Council of Women Council Meeting and Conference, Leicester, 14–18 October, 1935* (1935), p. 112.

37   See Marks, 'Mothers, Babies and Hospitals'.

38   See J. Beinart, 'Obstetric Analgesia and the Control of Childbirth in Twentieth-Century Britain', in Garcia, Kilpatrick and Richards (eds), *The Politics of Maternity Care*.

39   The National Birthday Trust Fund was founded in 1928 in response to the increasing number of maternal fatalities.

40   National Federation of Women's Institutes, *22nd Annual Report 1938* (1938), p. 36.

41   *Home and Country*, 31:1 (January 1949), p. 49.

42   Beinart, 'Obstetric Analgesia and the Control of Childbirth', pp. 123–125.

43   In 1938 there were 10,000 maternity beds in England and Wales. By 1945 this figure had been increased to over 15,000.

44   MSH, Central Council Minutes, Vol. 12 (1943–47), 'Minutes of the Mothers' Union Central Council', June 1943, p. 68.

45   *The Mothers' Union Workers' Paper* (July 1950), p. 86.

46   The maternal mortality rate in 1950 was only one-fifth of the 1935 figure.

47   Loudon, *Death in Childbirth*, p. 254.

48   *NCW Handbook 1935–1936* (1936), p. 103.

49   The National Birthday Trust and the People's League of Health carried out two similar projects during this period, both of which resulted in a significant decline in the maternal mortality rate. See Lewis, 'In Search of a Real Equality', p. 225.

50   *National Federation of Women's Institutes Annual Report, 1936* (1936), p. 14.

51   Mowat, *Britain between the Wars*, p. 439.

52   *National Federation of Women's Institutes Annual Report, 1937* (1937), p. 17.

53   *Ibid.*

54   Thane, 'Visions of Gender', p. 106.

55   These inconsistencies meant that a woman entitled to free milk in Tottenham would have been excluded from the scheme if she moved to Oxford. E. Peretz, 'The Costs of Modern Motherhood to Low Income Families in Inter-war Britain', in Fildes, Marks and Marland (eds), *Women and Children First*, p. 272.

56   *The Catholic Women's League Magazine*, 306 (April 1937), p. 27.

57   The retail price of one pint of milk was four and a half pence.

58   S. Ferguson and H. Fitzgerald, *Studies in the Social Services* (London: HMSO, 1954), p. 157.

59 Loudon, *Death in Childbirth*, p. 263.

60 Official reports estimated that the number of domestic servants available for work fell by seventy-five per cent during the war. See Ferguson and Fitzgerald, *Studies in the Social Services*, p. 6.

61 See G. Braybon and P. Summerfield, *Out of the Cage: Women's Experiences in Two World Wars* (London: Pandora, 1987).

62 *Ibid.*, p. 167.

63 In 1922, the Labour Party voted to include the provision of home-helps to mothers as part of its official policy. See Thane, 'Visions of Gender', p. 105.

64 Lewis, 'In Search of a Real Equality', p. 220.

65 Ferguson and Fitzgerald, *Studies in the Social Services*, p. 10.

66 Moyse, *A History of the Mothers' Union*, p. 136

67 MSH, Central Council Minutes, Vol. 12 (1943–47), 'Minutes of the Mothers' Union Central Council', June 1943, p. 68.

68 The Parliamentary Woman Power Committee was set up in 1940 by women MPs from all parties. Its principal objective was to protect the welfare of women, in particular women workers, during wartime.

69 MSH, Central Council Minutes, Vol. 12 (1943–47), 'Minutes of the Mothers' Union Central Council', June 1943, p. 68.

70 Ferguson and Fitzgerald, *Studies in the Social Services*, p. 10.

71 MSH, Central Council Minutes, Vol. 12 (1943–47), 'Minutes of the Mothers' Union Central Council', June 1943, p. 72.

72 Hinton, *Women, Social Leadership and the Second World War*, pp. 202–203. The WVS was set up in 1938 to oversee the voluntary work of women during wartime. For a discussion of the WVS involvement in the provision of home-help services after the war see Hinton, pp. 198–212.

73 This was in comparison to a figure of 12,316 women attended by home-helps in 1938.

74 BL, Royal Commission on Population (1944–1949), Evidence No. 12, 'National Council of Women, written evidence to the Royal Commission on Population', June 1944.

75 Hinton, *Women, Social Leadership and the Second World War*, p. 201.

76 J. Lewis, 'Dealing with Dependency: State Practices and Social Realities, 1870–1945', in J. Lewis (ed.), *Women's Welfare/Women's Rights* (London: Croom Helm, 1983), p. 28.

77 National Federation of Women's Institutes, *Keeping Ourselves Informed*, p. 148.

78 Kitchen, *For Home and Country*, p. 27.

79 See Thane, 'The Women of the British Labour Party and Feminism', p. 124.

80 *The Mothers' Union Workers Paper*, 343 (July 1942), p. 159.

81 *Ibid.*, p. 161.

82 The WCG had led the campaign for the inclusion of maternity benefits in the 1911 National Health Insurance Act. Following strong protests from the Guild, the maternity benefit, which was at first made payable to the husbands of pregnant women, was in 1913 paid to the mother.

83 *The Catholic Women's League Magazine*, 302 (December 1936), p. 54.

84 Modern Record Centre, University of Warwick (hereafter MRC), MSS. 821.5 (1), TUC Archive, typed report of the NCW Executive Committee, 20 March 1942.

85 BL, Royal Commission on Population, 1944–1947, Evidence No. 4, 'National Council of Women, oral evidence to the Royal Commission on Population', 29 September 1944.

86 Smith, 'British Feminism in the 1920s', p. 60.

87 *The Mothers' Union Workers' Paper*, 343 (July 1942), p. 159.

88 See D. Vincent, *Poor Citizens* (London: Longman, 1991), pp. 117–125.

89 Male workers were entitled to a sickness benefit of 15 shillings while female workers received the lesser sum of 12 shillings on the grounds that women had fewer dependents than men.

90 MRC, MSS. 821.5(1), TUC Archive, 'NCW memorandum for submission to the Inter-Departmental Committee on Social Insurance and Allied Services', February 1942.

91 See Lewis, 'Dealing with Dependency', pp. 26–30.

92 Between 13 October 1931 and 3 December 1931, forty-eight per cent of women's claims were disallowed compared with four per cent of claims lodged by men. See Lewis, 'Dealing with Dependency', p. 27.

93 MRC, MSS. 821.5(1), TUC Archive, 'NCW memorandum for submission to the Inter-Departmental Committee on Social Insurance and Allied Services', February 1942.

94 In 1940 the Old Age and Widows Pension Act lowered the pensionable age of women to sixty.

95 *NCW Handbook 1937–1938* (1938), p. 109.

96 *The Townswoman*, 3:10 (January 1936), p. 2.

97 WL, Pamphlet Collection, *Report of the Council Meeting and Conference of the National Council of Women, Bournemouth, October 11–14 1937* (1937), p. 62.

98 The National Federation of Women's Institutes, *Keeping Ourselves Informed*, p. 148.

99 *Home and Country* (February 1943), p. 36.

100 *The Townswoman*, 10:7 (March 1943), p. 17.

101 W. Beveridge, *Social Insurance and Allied Services*, Cmd 6404 (London: HMSO, 1942), p. 49.

102 Yuval-Davis, 'Women, Citizenship and Difference', p. 21.

103 Beveridge, *Social Insurance and Allied Services*, p. 49.

104 *Ibid.*

105 Under the new legislation, women in paid employment were entitled to a maternity allowance for a period of thirteen weeks, beginning six weeks before the expected delivery date. Women working within the home whose husbands were insured qualified for maternity benefit covering a period of four weeks following the birth of their baby. The National Insurance Act, 1946 (London: HMSO, 1946), pp. 15–16.

106 *Home and Country*, 30:1 (January 1948), p. 2.

107 The Beveridge Report advised that widows under the age of sixty should be entitled to a pension of thirty-six shillings per week for thirteen weeks. Widows with children of school age were entitled to an additional guardian's benefit of twenty-four shillings, subject to a deduction for any earnings.

108 Beveridge, *Social Insurance and Allied Services*, p. 51.

109 *Ibid.*

110 Elizabeth Abbott was a founder member of the ODC and Katherine Bompass was an active member of the egalitarian feminist society the WFL. See Smith, 'British Feminism in the 1920s', pp. 49, 59.

111 WL, Pamphlet Collection, E. Abbott and K. Bompass, *The Woman Citizen and Social Security: A Criticism of the Proposals Made in the Beveridge Report as They Affect Women* (1943), p. 4.

112 Cicely McCall, a journalist and social worker, was also editor of *Women in Council* during this period. In 1945 she resigned from the WI to stand as a Labour Party candidate.

113 *Home and Country*, 28:8 (August 1944), p. 161.

114 WL, 5/FWI/A/2/3/06, Box 46, NFWI Archive, *AGM Reports*, 1945.

115 *National Federation of Women's Institutes 30th Annual Report, 1946* (1946), p. 37.

116 Walby, 'Is Citizenship Gendered?', p. 385.

117 For a detailed account of the campaign for family allowances see J. Macnicol, *The Movement for Family Allowances* (London: Heinemann, 1980).

118 Beveridge, *Social Security and Allied Services*, pp. 53, 154.

119 E. Rathbone, *The Disinherited Family* (London: Edward Arnold and Co., 1924), p. viii.

120 The payment of separation allowances during the war years contributed to an increase in the living standards of the wives and children of servicemen. See J. Lewis, 'Models of Equality for Women: The Case of State Support for Children in Twentieth-Century Britain', in Bock and Thane (eds), *Maternity and Gender Policies* p. 82. See also Pedersen, 'Gender, Welfare, and Citizenship'.

121 Land, 'Eleanor Rathbone and the Economy of the Family', p. 111.

122 Rathbone set up the Family Endowment Committee in 1917, renamed the Family Endowment Society in 1925.

123 During the 1930s, efforts by Labour women to have family allowances adopted as party policy were repeatedly frustrated. This was linked to the belief held by many within the party that family allowances would undermine the principle of the 'family wage' and so weaken the wage-bargaining ability of male workers. Thane, 'Visions of Gender', pp. 107–114.

124 *Home and Country*, 14:6 (June 1942), p. 147.

125 *The Townswoman*, 10:1 (September 1942), p. 7.

126 *The Mothers' Union Journal*, 166 (September 1936), p. 19.

127 See Thane, 'Visions of Gender', p. 110.

128 *NCW Handbook 1941–1942* (1942), p. 64.

129 BL, The Royal Commission on Population 1944–49, Evidence No. 4, 29 September 1944.

130 *The Mothers' Union Workers' Paper*, 345 (September 1942), p. 126.

131 BL, The Royal Commission on Population 1944–49, Evidence No. 5, 'The Mothers' Union', 13 October 1944.

132 *Ibid.*

133 *Ibid.*

134 Lewis, 'Models of Equality for Women', p. 86.

135 *Home and Country*, 26:10 (October 1944), p. 168.

136 Clements, 'Feminism, citizenship and social activity', p. 177.

137 *Home and Country*, 26:8 (August 1944), p. 126.

138 MSH, Central Council Minutes, Vol. 12 (1944–50), 'Minutes of the Mothers' Union Central Council', June 1944.

5

Active citizenship for women:
war and protest

The involvement of the MU, CWL, NCW, WI and TG in highlighting the welfare needs of housewives and mothers throughout the 1930s and 1940s has shown that these organisations were able to influence social policy and did so through their effective mobilisation of women as active citizens. The five did not limit themselves, however, to issues relating to social welfare. They also envisaged a role for women in a number of other key campaigns that came to public attention during these years. Three campaigns will be discussed in this chapter: the contribution made by each group to the war effort, the campaign for equal pay and the appointment of women police.

The involvement of voluntary women's organisations in each campaign was underpinned by their understanding of women's role in society as housewives, mothers and citizens. As such, women had a responsibility to be engaged in local and national affairs. Furthermore, women as citizens had a right to demand that the state implement legislation and adopt policies that would enhance women's lives and ensure that women were guaranteed fair treatment, whether it be in the home, the workplace or within the criminal justice system.

The war campaign: voluntary women's organisations in wartime

On 3 September 1939 Britain declared war on Germany. Members of women's organisations, like the rest of the nation, braced themselves for the forthcoming conflict. The WI reassured its members that the movement would 'strive to maintain tolerance and broad-mindedness and to continue as a unifying force by continuing our ordinary activities to foster a spirit of steadiness, self-discipline, and friendliness which will be of inestimable value whatever the future may bring forth.'[1] Similarly, *The Mothers' Union Workers' Paper* urged all members to 'prove by the steadfastness of our characters and the joyfulness of our lives that the Faith we practice will not fizzle out in the face of adversity'.[2]

The wartime experiences of women have been well documented by historians. However as Samantha Clements has argued, much of this work has tended to focus on the daily lives of women during wartime, on whether or not there was a revival in the feminist movement and on the longer-term impact of war on the status of women.[3] Less attention has been paid to the activities of women's organisations during wartime, although Clements's work on local women's groups in Nottingham and James Hinton's study of the WVS are notable exceptions.[4] Focusing on voluntary women's organisations and their activities during wartime not only draws attention to their contribution to the war effort but also raises interesting questions about the meaning of women's citizenship during wartime.

As Sonya Rose has suggested, women's citizenship during the Second World War 'had complex and often contradictory meanings and consequences' and this is apparent in the way in which mainstream women's groups grappled with the new demands made on women during the war.[5] Women were expected to engage in wartime work but at the same time had to maintain their domestic responsibilities to home and family. Women also had to become more independent in the absence of husbands and fathers, often living on their own for the first time, but any transgression with regard to their moral behaviour left them vulnerable to public censure and accusations of 'not being good citizens'.[6]

All of these demands and the ensuing conflicts they created for women were evident in the work of the MU, CWL, NCW, WI and TG during the war. These were articulated in numerous and at times contradictory ways. For example, housewives' associations encouraged women to engage in war work but requested only limited working hours for mothers with young children. Concerns about mothers taking on paid work were accompanied by campaigns to improve working conditions for women workers, including the demand for equal pay. The desire to uphold moral standards led to campaigns for the appointment of women police which in turn resulted in greater numbers of women engaging in paid work. The war years therefore represented a challenge for voluntary women's groups but also an opportunity to channel their activism and agency into protecting the rights of housewives and mothers, whilst at the same time making a significant contribution towards the common good.

The first months of war were a period of major readjustment for women's societies. Fearing that German air attacks on London were imminent, staffing levels at the national headquarters were reduced and plans made for the safe storage of files and records outside London. Restrictions on public meetings and the appropriation of halls and meeting places by the army created difficulties for all voluntary societies, who suddenly found themselves without a space to meet. In October 1939, branch closures were announced although the majority reopened when alternative arrangements for meetings had been made.

For example in November 1939, the Blackpool branch of the CWL reported that its weekly evening meetings had been switched to the afternoon due to the blackout and the demands of ARP (Air Raid Precaution) duty. Following the outbreak of war, MU branches were given permission to hold their meetings in local churches.[7] Branches also reported that fewer members were attending meetings as women volunteered for work with the WVS or the armed services.[8] The evacuation of 166,300 mothers with their children in September 1939 had some impact on branch membership in the larger cities, despite the fact that 88 per cent of mothers had returned home by the following January.[9]

During the war, membership of the MU, NCW, WI and TG declined as a result of the disruption of war and the recruitment of women into the workforce, armed services and WVS. The notable exception was the CWL, whose membership remained relatively static with 20,000 members in 1943. This may be explained by the fact that the League attracted new members through its wartime work setting up clubs and canteens for women serving in the Armed Forces. Membership of the WI fell from 331,600 in 1940 to 288,000 in December 1944. The MU's membership of 597,412 in 1937 had fallen to 484,869 by 1942. The NCW recorded a decline in individual membership from 12,421 women in 1939 to 8,699 in 1941 although it should be noted that its wartime figures are incomplete. Finally, the number of local guilds in the TG fell from 511 in 1938 to 448 in 1941. Although these losses were significant they were not disastrous and all five organisations remained active throughout the war years.

In addition to this decline in membership, women's groups also had to deal with the impact on their national organisation as prominent members were recruited into war work. For example Lady Denman of the WI was appointed Chairman of the Women's Land Army and Dr Genevieve Rewcastle, President of the CWL, resigned to serve as a surgeon in the Navy. At local level, as James Hinton has documented, it was common for leaders and members of established women's organisations to join the WVS in order to co-ordinate war work within their local communities.[10]

In spite of these problems and the general upheaval that wartime brought, voluntary women's organisations continued with many of their

regular national and local activities throughout the war years. Empha-
sising the importance of these 'normal' activities, Lady Denman stressed
that it was 'essential that the Women's Institutes, in their anxiety to help
at a time of war, do not lose sight of their functions in peace time.'[11] She
also encouraged members 'to keep up morale and to prevent life in an
emergency from becoming wholly disorganised.'[12]

Closer co-operation between national women's organisations was
an important feature of the wartime experience for voluntary women's
societies. In September 1939 and at the instigation of the WI and TG,
the National Council of Social Service[13] called a conference of women's
groups to discuss problems resulting from the evacuation of women and
children.[14] The outcome of this meeting was the establishment of the
Women's Group on Problems Arising from Evacuation, later renamed
the Women's Group on Public Welfare (WGPW). From 1943 the WGPW
oversaw the establishment of Standing Conferences of Women's Organisations (SCWO), set up to co-ordinate the work of the WGPW at the local
level.[15] These bodies were effective in drawing together women active at a
local level from a range of different women's organisations but, as James
Hinton has suggested, the work of the SCWOs also revealed 'tensions
between professional women and organised housewives, and ... the
continuing hostility of Labour women to the middle-class organisations
in general.'[16]

Membership of the WGPW included the WI, TG and the NCW and
the Churches Group affiliated to the new organisation that represented the
MU and the CWL.[17] The success of the WGPW in recruiting a wide range
of women's groups led the TG to declare in *The Townswoman* in April 1944
that it was the recognised co-ordinating body for 'all the women's organisations of repute.'[18] Under the chairmanship of the Labour MP Margaret
Bondfield, the WGPW proposed to act 'as a two-way channel of information between statutory authority and the ordinary citizen (particularly
the housewife) ... to meet a very real present-day need.'[19] Its primary
objective was 'to bring the experience of its constituent organisations to
bear on questions of public welfare especially those affecting women and
children'. In addition, the new body hoped to strengthen the 'good understanding between town and country people' and develop 'social activities
in the light of wartime experience.'[20]

By January 1940, 735,000 unaccompanied children and 166,300
mothers with 260,000 young children had been evacuated from London,
Manchester, Liverpool and other areas at risk from German bombers.[21]
In 1943, the Minister of Health, Ernest Brown, praised all those women
who had agreed to take evacuated mothers, children and war workers

into their homes. The Minister underlined the fact that the evacuation scheme was

> simply an appeal to the richest and oldest and deepest feelings of women. The call to share their homes with strangers, with other women's children, was, as the Government well knew, asking a tremendous lot. The women have responded greatly. Had they not done so, the scheme would have completely broken down.[22]

In spite of these enthusiastic words, the evacuation of tens of thousands of women and children to reception areas was fraught with difficulties.[23] The fact that the scheme did not end in failure was thanks not only to the efforts of individual women and their families but also to the work of national and local women's societies. These groups did their utmost to improve conditions both for evacuees and host families in the reception areas. Members of WIs and TGs were particularly concerned about the health and welfare of some of the children who came from the cities to live in their towns and villages.[24]

Lady Cynthia Colville, President of the TG, expressed her concern when she wrote that 'large-scale evacuation has laid bare the hidden things of English life, many ugly and terrifying.'[25] Nina Woods, Central President of the MU, echoed this view when she remarked in December 1939 that the experience of evacuation had 'brought to some people a seamy side of national life which they did not know existed.'[26] These comments reflect the reaction of upper- and middle-class women involved in social and moral reform to reports about the conditions of inner-city life and the supposed inability of a minority of working-class mothers to care for their children.[27]

What some members of the WI and TG did discover when they took evacuated children into their homes was the reality of the deprivation and poverty experienced by mothers and their children living in disadvantaged areas.[28] Many of these children suffered from malnutrition and diseases including head lice and scabies.[29] Bed-wetting was another common, though perhaps not surprising problem, amongst children separated from their home and family for the first time. Tensions between evacuated mothers and host families were inevitable when families were expected to share a home together. It was reported that some evacuated mothers were 'dirty, verminous, idle and extravagant' and were either 'unable or unwilling to care for their children.'[30] On the other hand many evacuated mothers resented the experience of having to live by someone else's rules. As one young mother wrote 'I couldn't stick it any longer. We were treated like bits of dirt by the locals.'[31]

In an effort to overcome these difficulties, local women's groups established day centres for evacuated mothers and children in the reception areas. In November 1939, the Worthing TG opened a club for the 1,200 mothers and 2,000 children billeted in their locality. A fee of one penny per week was required to cover the cost of tea and the rent of the hall for the Saturday afternoon meeting. While their children were cared for by local Girl Guides, evacuated mothers were given time to relax and socialise away from their overcrowded and stressful living conditions.

Club members were encouraged to take up sewing and knitting as well as to participate in other typical guild activities such as amateur dramatics and singing competitions. Reporting on the success of this project, the January 1940 edition of *The Townswoman* concluded 'the mothers are most appreciative of the club, where they may spend a happy and sociable afternoon with freedom from their children.'[32] The fact that these meetings also gave host families some time to themselves in their own homes was undoubtedly another beneficial aspect of the guild's clubs.

The Executive Committee of the MU urged its members to invite 'lonely or homesick' mothers to the Union's weekly meetings. Once again, sewing, knitting and light entertainment were common pursuits undertaken by the women who attended.[33] The MU was anxious to attract evacuated women to their meetings because of the realisation that many of the mothers and their children were 'entirely ignorant of our Holy Faith'. It was hoped that attendance at Union meetings would draw more women into the Church of England, and the Central Council called on diocesan branches in reception areas to 'let those from outside join in meetings to help them learn the power of prayer.'[34]

These efforts to reach out to evacuated mothers and their children could be construed as middle-class women seeking to impose their beliefs and standards on the working-class. As James Hinton has argued there is no doubt that these organisations and their leaders were class conscious and often viewed working-class women as benefiting from the advice and guidance given by their middle-class superiors.[35] It would be wrong however to dismiss out of hand the attempts of these groups to provide practical support and friendship to evacuated women as patronising or controlling. To do so would ignore the fact that their efforts did make some contribution to helping women cope with the difficulties experienced living with strangers far away from home.

As individual women's societies did what they could to provide clubs and leisure activities for evacuated women, the WGPW drew attention to the problems of children evacuated from the larger towns and cities. On the recommendation of the WI, the Hygiene Committee of the WGPW decided to investigate the 'low standard of customs and living of a small section of women and children evacuated from towns'.[36] In 1943, the findings of this investigation were published in *Our Towns: A Close Up*. This report focused on the health and behavioural problems prevalent amongst a small section of evacuated children. Out of this investigation came the proposal that all children over the age of two should attend nursery schools so that they could develop 'initiative, self-respect and a sense of citizenship'.[37]

The report also focused on the alleged poor standards of 'mother-craft' skills shown by a small but significant number of evacuated mothers. It was suggested that the apparent inability of these women to knit and sew or cook 'without a tin opener' was due primarily to a lack of domestic training. The committee recommended that future wives and mothers should be educated in home-craft so that they would have the necessary skill to 'build-up a housewife's routine' as well as keeping up their 'personal appearance'.[38] This emphasis on the importance of domestic-science training for young working-class women and girls was not a new idea. As Anna Davin has documented, 'lady visitors' and 'schools for mothers' dated back to the late nineteenth century and were seen as a way of 'teaching the ideology as well as the skills of domesticity, and more generally instilling habits of regularity, obedience, punctuality and discipline'.[39]

John Macnicol suggests that *Our Towns: A Close Up* presented a very negative and often selective view of working-class mothers and their children.[40] Nonetheless it would be wrong to assume that the groups involved in the WGPW were only interested in altering the moral behaviour of these women and imposing middle-class values. The persistent efforts of societies such as the MU, WI and the NCW to improve maternity services and social welfare provision for women and, as will be discussed in the next chapter, housing conditions, should not be ignored. It demonstrated their belief that the state had a responsibility to provide for the poor and disadvantaged in society and to ensure that the environment in which they raised their families was 'fit for purpose'.[41]

To this end the TG organised a conference for members to discuss the *Our Towns* report in London in March 1944, which was attended by sixty representatives from over twenty-one federations. The three main subjects for debate were listed as 'the book; and the problems of housing in relation to the book; and housing and planning for the future'.[42] It can be argued therefore that the experience of evacuation and the publication of *Our Towns* only strengthened the resolve of voluntary women's societies to campaign for social welfare reforms in the immediate post-war period.

As work with evacuated women and children continued, middle-class housewives' associations became involved in a number of other schemes designed to help the national war effort. These activities included the preservation of surplus fruit supplies, knitting for the troops and encouraging members to participate in 'make do and mend' classes. The work of the WI in organising local fruit-canning schemes and jam making was so successful that it remains the activity most often associated with the WI movement today.[43]

With the support of the Ministry of Agriculture, who provided local institutes with recipes for jam and a guaranteed supply of sugar, the WI supplied hospitals and canteens with jam and canned fruit throughout the war.[44] *Home and Country* reported that during 1944, 1,174 preservation centres had been set up.[45] In response to the success of the WI fruit preservation initiative, the WGPW encouraged other women's organisations in towns to set up their own centres for canning and processing fruit grown in gardens and allotments. By 1942, the TG was operating over a hundred local fruit-preservation centres. The Minister of Food, Lord Woolton, thanked the women involved in the scheme for 'the industry and the resource which they displayed in dealing at short notice with large quantities of perishable fruit ... some thousands of pounds of fresh fruit, which might otherwise have been wasted, have been made into jam and put into consumption by their efforts.'[46]

In 1941, the WGPW, assisted by the Boards of Education and Trade, had launched a national 'make do and mend' campaign in order to reduce demand for cotton and linen during wartime. The aim was to encourage women to repair and renovate their old clothes instead of buying new ones for themselves and their families. Societies affiliated to the WGPW supported the 'make-do and mend' campaign and local societies set up classes and groups for members. Mothers were taught ways of repairing and renovating the family's clothes as well as given tips on how to turn their own dresses into fashionable new garments. An indication of the success of this campaign was reflected in the fact that, by September 1943, 20,000 'make-do and mend' classes had been set up throughout the country.

The sewing and knitting skills of women were also put to wartime use by organisations including the CWL, WI and TG. Members were encouraged to knit 'comforts' for the armed forces, as they had done during the First World War, as well as for evacuees and bombed-out families. By the end of the war, the WI reported that its members had knitted over 160,000 garments.[47] In February 1940, the CWL set up a Comforts Depot to supply local branches of the League with wool to knit gloves, vests, jumpers and other 'comforts' for the troops.

Finished garments were sent to the League's Comforts Depot for collection and were then shipped out to troops serving in Eastern Europe and to sailors in the merchant navy. By 1941, knitting parties had been established in most local branches of the League as well as TG and WI throughout the country. Such was the success of this project that by August 1941 the CWL reported that over 6,000 knitted garments had been received by the Comforts Depot.[48]

Just as it had done in the First World War, the CWL provided huts, canteens and hostels for members of the armed forces and for women working in munitions factories for the duration of the war.[49] By the end of the war, the League had set up seventy-four huts, canteens and hostels in Britain and six hostels in the Middle East. In England, these facilities were run by local branches of the League and members volunteered to cook and serve meals to the troops in their area.

In January 1941, the Nottingham City Section of the CWL reported that canteen work was now the principal activity of the branch. Similar reports came from the League's Darlington and St Leonard's branches whilst members of the Westminster branch had the use of a mobile canteen catering for civilians in the bombed out areas of London.[50] Canteen work was also undertaken by the TG with members setting up canteens in towns where servicemen and women were stationed, providing them with a place to eat and relax away from the army camp.[51]

The domestic nature of the voluntary work undertaken by women's societies described here did not challenge traditional assumptions about the role of women within the home. Working in clubs and canteens, knitting for the troops and the production of jam and preserves was, as Caroline Merz has argued, 'an extension of, rather than an alternative to, women's normal domestic duties'.[52] Nonetheless these domestic and voluntary activities gave housewives and mothers, many of whom were ineligible for compulsory national service, the opportunity to contribute in a very active and public way to the war effort.[53] Their achievements were acknowledged in September 1943, when Ernest Brown admitted, 'I should not be doing my duty as Minister of Health if I did not recall the work of those many thousands of women without any uniform at all.'[54] Lady Denman added her own personal endorsement of the work done by members of WI and other women's societies, arguing that their efforts showed that 'we [women] are taking our small share in winning the victory which we believe will come.'[55]

In sharp contrast to the voluntary war work of middle-class women, the conscription of women into the industrial labour force did call into question, at least in the short term, the traditional role of women in society. This was in spite of the fact that significant numbers of working-class women were employed in the textile industry and in the new light industries, like engineering during the inter-war years.[56] In 1941, the National Service (No. 2) Act ordered all women between the ages of eighteen and forty to register for full-time war work. Many of these women were required to work in the chemical, engineering and shipbuilding industries traditionally dominated by men. In addition, over 500,000 women were recruited into the civil service.[57] Married women with domestic responsibilities or children under the age of fourteen were exempt from National Service. The government, however, urged married and single women of all ages to volunteer for war work.[58] It was this significant influx of women into the wartime labour force that led voluntary women's societies to reassess their position on the employment of women outside the home.[59]

As a result of continuing labour shortages, the government widened the eligibility for National Service in 1943 to include housewives and mothers with children over the age of fourteen and women between the ages of forty and fifty. Housewives were directed into local part-time work. By the end of that year an estimated 7,750,000 women were in paid employment, forty-three per cent of whom were married.[60] The employment of married women in such significant numbers outside the home was a matter of concern for voluntary women's societies. In particular, the MU and the CWL were anxious about the deleterious effect of working mothers on the stability of family life. As Sonya Rose has suggested, 'by fulfilling their wartime obligations and engaging in war work, British women jeopardised their "civic virtue" if they appeared in any way to be neglecting their maternal duties.'[61]

Although women with children under the age of fourteen were excluded from compulsory war-work, they were not prevented from entering the workforce and indeed were encouraged to do so. Married women were welcomed back into the public service with the suspension of the marriage bar for women teachers and civil servants.[62] In December 1943, the CWL and the MU met to discuss the 'bad effect on home life of mothers doing full time war work'. It was agreed to send a letter to the Ministry of Labour urging that 'married women with young children living at home should only be accepted for full-time work under very exceptional circumstances.'[63]

As the MU and the CWL suggested, not all married women were happy with the idea of entering the workforce. Many were concerned about the double burden they would face with a full-time job and housework. In 1941, a survey of 1,000 women questioned for a Wartime Social

Survey revealed that thirty-two per cent of respondents were reluctant to volunteer for war work because of their domestic responsibilities and their unwillingness to leave home.[64] Women were also disinclined to volunteer until they were sure about their conditions of employment.[65] Uncertainty about wage rates, working hours and childcare were identified as the principal reasons why married women were slow to enter the wartime labour force.

In an attempt to accelerate the recruitment of women workers a conference was held in September 1941 at the Ministry of Labour and National Service. At this meeting, representatives from various women's groups, including the CWL and NCW, informed Ministry officials that married women were most concerned about wage rates, working conditions in factories and job security once the war was over. Until the government made clear the terms under which women were to be employed, it would be difficult to persuade them to volunteer for war work.[66] If working conditions were improved, women's societies, including the CWL, declared their willingness to organise meetings encouraging women to join the workforce.[67]

This admission is telling as it illustrates the confidence that voluntary women's organisations had in voicing their concerns to government officials with regard to women's paid work. Moreover it demonstrates an awareness of the power and agency that women's groups now had in mobilising women for war work. Undoubtedly voluntary women's organisations supported the war effort and were keen for women to play their part, but not at any price. In wartime, more than ever, these groups felt it was their duty to speak out on behalf of housewives and mothers to ensure that their members were not exploited and that their domestic role was protected.

Denise Riley has argued that during the war 'women were not able to use their power as workers to push through changes to the sexual division of labour by making demands of the state, employers and their husbands.' This she suggests underlined 'the limited nature of the gains for women in the war.'[68] It is true that voluntary women's groups were not challenging traditional gender roles. This was never their intention. But contrary to Riley's argument they were able to use their power to improve working conditions for women, at least in the short term, and this sense of empowerment remained evident in their campaign work both during the war and throughout the post-war years.

Further evidence to suggest that voluntary women's groups were in a position to call for enhanced working conditions for women emerges in the March 1943 edition of *The Mothers' Union Journal*. Here Violet

Markham wrote that 'a fair deal stripped of all favour and privilege is what any decent woman who is proud of her citizenship wants when working side by side with men at a time like the present.'[69] The government did act on the advice of women's societies by reducing the working hours of women in industry to ten hours a day and instructing employers to take on local married women as part-time workers.[70] It was clear, therefore, that although organisations such as the MU and CWL did not approve of mothers with young children working outside the home, they showed little hesitation in making representations to the government on behalf of women workers during wartime. Even more significantly, their concerns were listened to and addressed.

The Second World War gave voluntary women's groups the opportunity to prove beyond doubt that their members were willing to do their bit, just like their soldier husbands and sons, to secure victory for the nation. Following the outbreak of war, the MU, CWL, NCW, WI and TG were successful in maintaining their 'normal' activities as well as contributing to the war effort in many innovative and important ways. In addition they co-operated with wartime bodies such as the WGPW and the WVS to maximise the effectiveness of women's wartime contribution.

Participation in the war effort gave voluntary women's groups the opportunity to voice their concerns about the welfare and status of women at the very highest levels of government and they were effective in persuading the government to act upon their advice on a number of occasions. As a result, they became ever more aware of the power of their own agency to influence social policy and to bring about legislative reforms which would enhance the lives of their members. This newfound confidence was evident not only in their wartime campaigns but also in their demand that the views of housewives and mothers must be at the heart of plans for post-war reconstruction.

Wartime campaigns: the demand for equal pay

Throughout the 1920s and 1930s, feminist societies including the NUSEC, the London and National Society for Women's Service and the WFL had continuously campaigned for the introduction of equal pay for women workers.[71] This demand was also backed by organisations representing the interests of working-class women, most notably the Women's Sections of the Labour Party and the WCG, and by mainstream women's groups including the YWCA and the NCW.[72] By 1935, however, women's average earnings in the industrial sector were between 37.3 and 55.9 per cent of the wage paid to male workers.

Women working in the public sector received up to 80 per cent of average male earnings.[73] Public service unions including the National Union of Women Teachers, the National Association of Women Civil Servants and the Council of Women Civil Servants supported the campaign for equal pay in the public sector and worked alongside women's organisations in an effort to bring about this reform.[74] The NCW also supported this call for equal pay for civil servants and in 1930 had passed a resolution for 'the adoption of the principle of equal pay for men and women civil servants of the same grades and seniority'.[75]

In April 1936, the House of Commons voted by a majority of eight to introduce equal pay in the civil service.[76] This result reflected the cross-party support for pay reform but the decision was quickly overturned when the Prime Minister, Stanley Baldwin, immediately called for a vote of confidence in the National Government. In response, Eva Hartree, President of the NCW, condemned this decision, claiming that it 'caused much resentment not only among women's organisations but among other supporters of the principle [of equal pay]'.[77] Both the Labour and Conservative administrations argued against the implementation of equal pay on the grounds that during a period of economic depression such a large increase in public spending would not be feasible.[78] Refusing to accept this explanation the NCW reaffirmed its position when it stated that 'on economic grounds and as a matter of common justice, a piece of work whether carried out by a man or a woman, should receive reward according to its value and not for any other reason'.[79]

The NCW, along with the YWCA and working-class women's organisations, also objected to unequal pay rates in the private sector during the 1930s. In 1935, the NCW condemned the fact that women working in the clothing and textile industries received lower rates of pay than men.[80] One member of the Council's Executive described this situation as a scandal, suggesting that 'the whole status of women is kept down by inequality of pay and opportunity'.[81] Yet in spite of the continued efforts of campaigners, equal pay in both the public and private sectors remained an elusive goal throughout the 1930s.

The outbreak of war in September 1939 presented women's organisations with a new opportunity to highlight the inequalities in pay and conditions experienced by women workers. As thousands of women joined the armed forces and were recruited into wartime employment, it became increasingly obvious that the vast majority of women workers would continue to earn lower rates of pay than men.[82] This fact was confirmed in 1941 when the conscription of women into the industrial workforce was not accompanied by equal pay legislation. The Woman

Power Committee had tried to persuade the national government to include an equal pay clause in the National Service (No. 2) Act but this proposal was rejected on the grounds that such a move could lead to nationwide industrial action.[83] Unsurprisingly, the government's decision was condemned by women's societies involved in the equal pay campaign.

The feminist SPG urged women to demand equal pay when registering for war work.[84] At the same time, the NCW voiced its objection to the fact that women in the ARP Service were paid lower rates than men. In May 1941 the YWCA highlighted the injustice of unskilled women in the transport and engineering industries earning less money than unskilled men.[85] Yet in spite of all these protests it was the establishment of the Equal Compensation Campaign Committee (ECCC) in October 1941 that succeeded in drawing wider support for the implementation of equal pay during wartime. This committee was set up by a number of women's groups, including the NCW, to protest against the Personal Injuries (Civilians) Act.[86] Under the terms of the act, women who were prevented from working because of a war injury were to receive less compensation from the government than men.

Such blatant discrimination outraged many women, including those not actively involved in the equal pay campaign. In January 1943, the WI reported that the majority of its local institutes were in favour of equal compensation payments.[87] Following a well-organised and highly publicised parliamentary campaign, the ECCC won the support of over 200 MPs and in April 1943 the government was forced to back down and award equal compensation payments to men and women.[88]

The success of the equal compensation campaign had important implications for the equal pay debate. It had now been established that women and men were entitled to the same rate of compensation when not at work so logically it could be argued that they also had the right to the same pay when in work. As a result, supporters of equal pay were optimistic that the government would review its policy on equal pay. Hopes were raised in September 1943 when the government invited 6,000 representatives of the country's leading women's societies, including the MU, CWL, NCW, WI and TG, to a National Conference of Women in London. In his opening address to the conference, Ernest Bevin, the Minister of Labour and National Service, told the women that the government wished to pay 'tribute and express our gratitude to the women of the country for the magnificent contribution they have made to the war effort'.[89]

Yet in spite of all the lavish praise of women's work, the Chancellor of the Exchequer confirmed during the meeting that the government had no intention of changing its position on equal pay. The decision was a major blow to all of the women's organisations involved in the equal pay campaign for so many years. The NCW, sceptical about any political party having a willingness to change the law on pay, had already dismissed the government's 'innumerable bouquets' pointing out that it would be 'far better and more just to give women the proper rate for the job'.[90]

Undeterred and inspired by the triumph of the equal compensation campaign, an Equal Pay Campaign Committee (EPCC) was set up in January 1944 to co-ordinate the work of women's societies campaigning for equal pay.[91] The campaign committee focused on the common grades of the civil service, where men and women performed the same work but received differential pay rates. Founding members of the EPCC included the NCW, the National Association of Women Civil Servants and the British Federation of Business and Professional Women (BFBPW). Soon afterwards the YWCA and the WI joined the campaign and by 1946 seventy-two women's societies had affiliated, representing some four million women.[92] On affiliating to the EPCC the WI informed its membership that 'institutes are now taking part in the battle for equal pay waged by other women's organisations for the past thirty years.'[93]

For some time the WI had objected to the fact that women working in agriculture received lower pay than men and in 1928 had written to the Ministry of Agriculture complaining about the lower wage rates set for women agricultural workers.[94] As the equal pay campaign gathered pace during the early 1940s, the WI demonstrated its willingness to become more involved and to extend its demand for equal pay to all occupational sectors. At its annual conference in June 1943, the Bures WI (West Suffolk) branch tabled a resolution 'that men and women should receive equal pay for equal work', which was carried by a large majority. Copies of this resolution were then sent to the Ministries of Labour and Education, the Treasury, the Federation of British Industries and the Trades Union Congress.[95]

The CWL and MU did not join the EPCC on the grounds that equal pay was a political and potentially divisive issue. However it is impor- tant to note that the CWL and MU had not felt compelled to dissociate themselves from resolutions in support of equal pay passed by the NCW throughout the 1920s and 1930s. This decision would imply that neither group objected in principle to equal pay for women workers. Interestingly it was reported in the July 1936 edition of *The Catholic Women's League Magazine* that a debate on equal pay for equal work had taken place at a meeting of the Westminster Diocesan Branch and the motion in favour had been carried by a large majority.[96] There is no evidence to suggest, however, that either group ever contemplated a national campaign in order to bring about this legislative change.

The TG also refused to support officially the EPCC's campaign on the grounds that it was a political question. The Guild did however acknowledge the importance of this issue for women and announced that its members were split fifty-fifty on whether or not equal pay for equal work should be implemented. Some considered it 'indefensible that women's employment should play second fiddle to men's' while others believed that 'women should not be paid at the same rate as men for the same work.'[97] It is important to note that although the TG did not speak out publicly in favour of equal pay, it would appear that the Union's Executive did have some sympathy with the campaign. During the height of the equal pay campaign in 1943, individual guilds were encouraged 'to learn about the feminist propagandist societies so that their members can hear about them, join them and work for them if they so wish.'[98] There is also evidence that individual guilds were debating this issue during the 1940s, and in 1945 the Woodthorpe guild voted to support the measure.[99]

By March 1944 the EPCC, under the chairmanship of the Conservative MP Mavis Tate, had collected 160 signatures from MPs calling for a Parliamentary debate on equal pay in the civil service. Support was also forthcoming from the National Union of Women Teachers and the Woman Power Committee.[100] Later that month when the 1944 Education Bill was discussed in the Commons, the Conservative MP Thelma Cazalet-Keir, speaking on behalf of the Tory Reform Group, proposed an amendment to abolish differential pay rates between male and female teachers. The teaching profession was viewed as an ideal test case for equal pay as the duties performed were exactly the same for men and women.

The government immediately rejected the equal pay clause but when put to the vote it was passed in the Commons by 117 votes to 116. This victory once again illustrated that a significant number of MPs from all political parties now accepted that equal pay for women was a legitimate demand. For Churchill and the Cabinet, fears about cost and possible industrial unrest outweighed any thoughts of reform and the Prime Minister called for a vote of confidence in the government. In the ensuing Commons debate the equal pay amendment was removed from the bill.

Now clearly aware of the strong support for equal pay, both within parliament and beyond, the government announced that a Royal Commission on Equal Pay would be set up to investigate and report on its 'social, economic and financial implications.'[101] Like many of those involved in the campaign, the WI was pessimistic about the value of a Royal Commission and viewed it as a stalling tactic. The WI Executive remarked that the commission signified 'a turn away from progressive action back to consideration, which has already lasted too many years and is by many regarded as a sop'.[102] Nevertheless, the EPCC agreed to suspend its activities until the commission published its report.

Both the NCW and the WI, along with other members of the campaign committee, gave evidence to the Royal Commission on Equal Pay. All of these groups defended the right of women and men doing similar work to earn the same wage.[103] When the Royal Commission on Equal Pay published its report in October 1946 it gave a clear picture of the inequalities in pay, both in the public and private sectors, based on the gender of the worker. The report stated that there was no logical reason why equal pay for equal work should not be introduced in the civil service.[104]

The commission however was unable to make any specific recommendations for legislative change and did acknowledge that immediate implementation of equal pay would be unwise in view of the post-war economic crisis.[105] Following the publication of the report the WI defended the position of women in industry arguing that 'if a woman, despite her lesser physical strength and shorter industrial life, does in fact weave as much cloth, or sell as many bus fares as her male counterpart, it is surely only fair that she be paid the same wage?'[106]

The EPCC resumed its activities in November 1946 and in December wrote to all members of the House of Commons urging them to bring pressure to bear on the government to 'make an early announcement of their intention to carry it [equal pay] into effect for all employment over which they have direct responsibility'.[107] On 30 January 1947 the committee organised a mass meeting at the Central Hall, Westminster, attended by 2,000 women representing seventy-seven women's societies and nine trade unions.[108] Speakers included members of the three main political parties and a resolution was adopted expressing indignation at the long delay in establishing the principle of equal pay. The Labour government was urged to 'give a lead by implementing the policy of Equal Pay for Equal Work in all Government and public employment NOW'.[109] Although the Labour party had agreed to the principle of equal pay for equal work, the post-war Labour government confirmed in June 1947 that it would not introduce equal pay in the public service on the grounds that 'it would be wholly inflationary in its results'.[110]

In spite of this setback the EPCC continued to press for pay reform and held a second mass meeting in Westminster on 10 June 1948. Once again some 2,000 people attended and a resolution was passed demanding the immediate implementation of equal pay for equal work in all government and public employment.[111] At the end of the meeting it was reported that hundreds of women, led by the Chairman of the EPCC, Thelma Cazalet Keir MP, marched to the House of Commons where extra police were called in as the women stood outside the lobbies chanting 'We want equal pay now.'[112]

At the national level the NCW and the WI remained active members of the EPCC in the immediate post-war years and supported the committee's campaign to keep the issue of equal pay at the top of the political agenda. It would appear, however, that the majority of local branches and institutes did not join the campaign for equal pay. In 1948 and again in 1949 the NCW reported that support for equal pay amongst the branches was meagre with few providing any information on their work for the equal pay campaign.[113] Similarly, the WI Executive urged its members to get involved in the campaign. However, there appears to have been little response to a request from Thelma Cazalet Keir for institutes to raise the question of equal pay at local political meetings and report back to the EPCC.[114]

Lack of local support for equal pay could be put down to the fact that many individual NCW members and WI members were not themselves engaged in paid work in the late 1940s.[115] In addition the government had made it clear that no reform would be introduced during a period of austerity. The majority of local groups may have preferred to direct their public campaigning to more urgent and relevant issues such as housing. Nevertheless, both the NCW and the WI remained active members of the EPCC throughout the late 1940s and early 1950s.

Updates on the progress of the campaign were regularly reported in their respective journals and members of the NCW were reminded that it was 'up to us to get equal pay by Parliamentary pressure, through MPs and prospective candidates, bye elections and demonstrations.'[116] In 1947 the WI reassured members that its involvement in the campaign was appropriate 'since the principle of equal pay as a basic justice has been accepted by all political parties [and so] cannot possibly be considered as a matter of party politics.'[117] In 1955 victory was finally achieved when the Conservative government announced it would introduce equal pay to the civil service on a gradual basis, and as a result the EPCC disbanded.[118]

The involvement of the NCW and the WI in the equal pay campaign and in particular their campaigning activities during wartime were significant and yet have often been overlooked in historical accounts.[119] These two groups firmly believed that a women's primary duty was to care for her husband and children and that paid work for mothers should only be embarked upon if women could accommodate both roles. In spite of this they were not in any way disinterested in women's working conditions.

In fact they believed that any discrimination based on gender was to be abhorred. In supporting the principle of equal pay, voluntary women's groups demonstrated that the issue could no longer be marginalised or dismissed as a political or feminist demand. With more and more women entering the paid workforce, equal pay was becoming an increasingly important issue for all women, including housewives and mothers. Moreover, equal pay for equal work was a social right of citizenship and as such the NCW and WI believed that they had a duty to win this right for women workers.

Wartime campaigns: the employment of women police

The outbreak of the Second World War brought renewed attention to a second long-running campaign instigated by feminist, political and voluntary women's organisations.[120] This was the demand for the appointment of women police to every police force in the country. Arguing from moral rather than feminist principles, women's societies emphasised the important role of policewomen in safeguarding the welfare of vulnerable women and children. It was on these distinctly moral and welfare grounds that the NCW had led the campaign for the employment of women police throughout the 1920s and 1930s.

During the First World War the NUWW (later the NCW) became one of three groups to set up voluntary women police patrols.[121] Patrolling parks, cinemas and other public places likely to be frequented by servicemen, the patrols were there to ensure that good moral behaviour prevailed at all times. Unlike the police matrons whose work was limited to the supervision of female detainees,[122] the voluntary patrols marked a new development in police work as women took to the streets. By the end of 1915 there were 2,301 women patrols in 108 towns and cities in Britain and Ireland.[123]

The work of voluntary patrols was so successful that in September 1918, Sir Nevile Macready, the Police Commissioner, proposed the establishment of a women's police force in the Metropolitan area. It is significant that the NUWW patrols were selected to provide this service on the grounds that they would limit their duties to domestic and moral welfare work and so not pose a threat to the established male police force.[124] The policewomen employed by the Metropolitan Police Force acted as auxiliaries and did not have the power of arrest. Nevertheless, the official recognition given to the work undertaken by women police was a significant step forward in the campaign for women police. In 1920 and again in 1924 two select committees (the Baird and the Bridgeman Committees) recommended the employment of women police. However, public spending cuts in 1922 meant that the numbers of women police employed by the police force remained nominal.[125] In 1924 there were only sixty-eight attested (with powers of arrest) and thirty-seven non-attested policewomen in England and Wales in comparison with 54,945 policemen.[126]

Apart from the cost factor in employing policewomen for special duties, a significant number of local police commissioners appeared reluctant to accept the idea of women in the police force. The principal objection was the assumption that police work, like soldiering, was an unsuitable job for a woman. For others the work performed by women police was seen as an extension of welfare work. This, it was argued, could be undertaken by untrained police matrons and so did not require trained women police officers.[127] Lack of support among chief constables for the appointment of women police was reflected in the fact that by 1928, 142 out of a total of 181 local police forces were without the services of a single policewoman.[128]

Louise Jackson writes that the inter-war campaign for the appointment of women police was made up of a 'broad coalition of viewpoints.'[129] Feminist arguments in favour of women police focused on the legal rights of women and children whilst voluntary women's groups such as the NCW and the YWCA emphasised the important role of policewomen in safeguarding the welfare of vulnerable women and children. During the 1920s and 1930s, the NCW spearheaded the campaign for the appointment of women police on the grounds that cases involving women and children were best dealt with by women. Setting out its demands in 1929 the Council argued that patrolling in public places, inspecting common lodging houses and the supervision of female prisoners in court were duties women were more competent to carry out than men. The Council also advised that policewomen should only ever take statements from women and children. In order to oversee the incorporation of women into the police force, the Council requested that a woman of senior rank be appointed to the Metropolitan Police in London and that a woman assistant inspector be appointed at the Home Office to co-ordinate the work of policewomen and to advise chief constables in the selection and training of policewomen.[130]

It is important to note that even though the NCW focused on the suitability of women police for special protective duties, it did not accept that policewomen once appointed should be treated any differently from their male colleagues. In June 1929 the Council, working with the NUSEC, requested that women appointed to the police force should have the same status, powers and conditions of service as male officers. It was also hoped that regulations defining the duties of policewomen should be drawn up without further delay.[131]

In October 1931 and as result of continuing pressure from women's societies and MPs, including Lady Astor, Eleanor Rathbone and Sir Arthur Steel Maitland, statutory regulations for policewomen were issued by the Home Office. For the first time attested policewomen were given uniform conditions of pay and service, although they were paid lower wages than men. Women eligible for police work had to be unmarried or widowed and between the ages of twenty-two and thirty-five and their duties were usually restricted to patrolling, dealing with women and children, clerical work, plain clothes duty and detective work.[132]

Much to the chagrin of women's societies, the employment of women police was left to the discretion of chief constables and local watch committees who were under no obligation to appoint female officers.[133] In July 1934, the NCW presented a petition to the Home Office calling for the employment of more women police. Members of women's organisations, including the WI and the YWCA, had collected over 6,000 signatures for the petition. In addition the NCW urged the Home Office to ensure that protection duties relating to women and children be made compulsory for policewomen.[134]

The Home Office immediately rejected these demands, as it was unwilling to interfere with the 'local discretion' of individual chief constables.[135] The following year the NCW, supported by the WI, MU and CWL, once again urged both the Home Office and regional watch committees to increase the number of women police they employed. A resolution was sent to local police authorities calling on them to 'appoint an adequate number of trained and attested policewomen who shall include among their duties the taking of statements from women and children when allegations of sexual offences are under investigation, and such detective duties as can most appropriately be performed by women'.[136] The Executive Committee of the TG also showed its support for the campaign, calling on members to 'examine the position regarding women police' and to 'urge the local chief constable to make provision for policewomen where necessary'.[137]

Reports of local campaigns for women police during this period included a joint effort by the Brighton and Hove branch of the CWL and the Lewes WI in 1938 to press for the appointment of more women police in the East Sussex area.[138] The Oldham and Bolton branches of the NCW also reported their involvement in the woman police campaign and the Nottingham branch was actively involved in local campaigning for a number of years.[139] Yet in spite of the persistent demands of women's societies, progress was slow and by 1939 only 45 out of 183 police forces in England and Wales had appointed policewomen.[140]

In much the same way as the outbreak of the war gave added urgency to the question of equal pay, it also energised activists campaigning for the employment of women police. In 1939 the government announced its intention to set up a Women's Auxiliary Police Corps (WAPC) to supplement the regular police force during wartime. Women recruited to the WAPC had no police powers and their duties were restricted to clerical and canteen work as well as driving and maintaining police vehicles. Jackson writes that as the war continued, the work of the WAPC expanded to include the patrolling of railway terminals 'to prevent prostitutes "molesting servicemen", as well as the supervision of air-raid shelters to prevent undesirable sexual activity'.[141]

Organisations involved in the women police campaign supported the use of women for such patrols, as they too wanted to protect the moral welfare of women during wartime. Groups such as the MU and CWL were concerned that young women and girls might be tempted to loiter around army camps and fall into prostitution, and women's societies appealed to the Home Office and local police chiefs to set up more women patrols to prevent this happening, just as they had done during the First World War.

In response the Home Office issued a circular to police authorities encouraging but not compelling them to employ full-time policewomen to undertake regular police duties, including patrol work.[142] Once again a significant number of chief constables proved unwilling to employ women police in their forces. By 1940 there were ninety-nine attested and twenty unattested policewomen serving in England and Wales. This meant that 138 out of a total of 181 police forces still did not employ women police.[143] Realising that more affirmative action was needed, the NCW, in collaboration with twenty other women's societies, set up the Women's Police Campaign Committee (WPCC) in June 1940.

Membership of this new committee included the MU, WI and the YWCA. Feminist societies such as the WFL and the working-class WCG also supported the work of the committee. It was hoped that these organisations could work together 'in order to secure justice and humanity in the treatment of women, girls and children' by ensuring that the 'appointment of a percentage of fully trained women police in every force should be made compulsory'.[144] In April 1944, the campaign committee organised a conference in London to protest against the Home Secretary's continued refusal to make the appointment of women police obligatory. Some 500 representatives of seventy national women's societies, including the WGPW, attended this meeting, which was chaired by Margaret Bondfield MP.

William Temple, the Archbishop of Canterbury and husband of the MU Vice-President, addressed the conference and stated that

> There is always a need for the work of women police – war only adds to this urgency. The demand for more women police is quite an old question – I regard its history with dismay because it is extremely discreditable to my sex. It seems that the main obstacle has been sheer, downright, stark prejudice.[145]

These stern words and strong public condemnation by the Archbishop of the government's failure to act and the publicity surrounding the conference proved extremely effective.

This time the Home Secretary's response was immediate and he requested that every police authority in England and Wales should see 'as a matter of urgency to the appointment of adequate numbers of women police'.[146] This instruction meant that the government had finally acknowledged the need for the compulsory appointment of women police and was willing to insist that policewomen must be employed by every police force in the country. This admission was a major triumph for those who had campaigned for women police for over twenty years, most notably the NCW. Having now achieved its central objective, the WPCC was disbanded and the campaign for women police brought to an end. It is worth noting however that the numbers of women serving in the police force remained marginal in the post-war years, with just over 3,000 policewomen serving in England and Wales in 1963.[147]

The involvement of voluntary women's organisations in the campaign for women police supports the argument that this campaign was more about the protection of women and children and the moral welfare of women than egalitarian demands for equal opportunity.[148] There is no doubt that those involved in the campaign equated the needs of women within the justice system with those of vulnerable children. Moreover the emphasis placed on women's sexual behaviour and the risk of transgression supports Carol Smart's suggestion that women were viewed 'as powerful and powerless, as sexual agents but also as victims, as dangerous but in need of protection'.[149] During wartime these contradictions were more pronounced than ever. As Rose argues, women had to remain sexually respectable to be good citizens despite the fact that male sexual promiscuity within the armed forces was condoned and soldiers were issued with condoms when posted overseas.[150]

Nonetheless, conservative motives in calling for the appointment of women police should not diminish the significance of the campaign. Once again evidence is provided of the ability of women's organisations to take a stand on a particular issue, bring that issue to public attention and in the case of women police, persuade the authorities to implement reform. Voluntary women's organisations played a crucial role in this campaign and through their agency and activism succeeded in winning for women the right to be processed by other women when embroiled within the criminal justice system.

Sonya Rose has argued that the war years 'saw a renaissance of active interest on the part of women's groups in improving the status of the housewife and mother'.[151] This exploration of the activities of voluntary women's organisations during wartime would appear to support such a view. However, the involvement of housewives' associations in war work, their active engagement in campaigns for equal pay and the appointment of women police cannot be viewed in isolation. The MU, CWL, NCW, WI and TG, through their action on issues ranging from divorce law reform, maternity services, family allowances and healthcare provision, had championed the interests of housewives and mothers throughout the 1920s and 1930s. Their wartime work represented continuity rather than the revival Rose suggests. As the following chapters will demonstrate, this commitment to improving women's lives and the status of housewives and mothers continued well into the post-war years.

Notes

1 WL, 5/FWI/A/2/2/06, Box 40, NFWI Archive, *National Federation of Women's Institutes 22nd Annual Report, 1938* (1938), p. 3.

2 *The Mothers' Union Workers' Paper*, 310 (October 1939), p. 247.

3 Clements, 'Feminism, citizenship and social activity', pp. 17–30. On women in wartime see for example H. Smith, 'The Effect of the War on the Status of Women', in H. Smith (ed.), *War and Social Change: British Society in the Second World War* (Manchester: Manchester University Press, 1986), L. Noakes, *War and the British: Gender, Memory and National Identity 1939–1991* (London: I. B. Tauris, 1998) and P. Summerfield, 'Women, War and Social Change: Women in Britain in World War II', in A. Marwick (ed.), *Total War and Social Change* (Basingstoke: Macmillan, 1988).

4 Clements, 'Feminism, citizenship and social activity' and Hinton, *Women, Social Leadership and the Second World War*.

5 S. O. Rose, *Which People's War? National Identity and Citizenship in Britain 1939–45* (Oxford: Oxford University Press, 2003), p. 107.

6 *Ibid.*

7 *The Catholic Women's League Magazine*, 335 (November 1939), p. 14. MSH, Central Council Minutes, Vol. 11 (1937–42), 'Minutes of the Mothers' Union Central Council', December 1939, p. 215.

8 During the war, 470,000 women served in the armed services, joining the Auxiliary Territorial Service, the Women's Auxiliary Air Force, or the Women's Royal Naval Service. The Women's Land Army recruited 30,000 women while 375,000 women

were involved in civil defence work. See Pugh, *Women and the Women's Movement*, p. 274.

9   Women's Group on Public Welfare, *Our Towns: A Close Up* (Oxford: WGPW, 1943), p. 2.

10 Hinton, *Women, Social Leadership and the Second World War*, pp. 35–65.

11 *Home and Country*, 21:7 (July 1939), p. 260.

12 *Home and Country*, 21:2 (February 1939), p. 56.

13 The National Council of Social Service was established in 1919 to assist the work of voluntary organisations and provide a link between them and the relevant statutory authorities.

14 Hinton, *Women, Social Leadership and the Second World War*, p. 177.

15 For an account of the work of local SCWOs in Nottingham, see Clements, 'Feminism, citizenship and social activity', pp. 162–227. See also Hinton, *Women, Social Leadership and the Second World War*, pp. 35–65.

16 Hinton, *Women, Social Leadership and the Second World War*, p. 179.

17 Other members of the WGPW included the Labour Party's Women Sections, the SJCWWO and the WCG. For a full list see Hinton, *Women, Social Leadership and the Second World War*, p. 178.

18 *Ibid.*

19 WL, Pamphlet Collection, *Women's Group on Public Welfare Report 1939–1945* (1945), p. 4.

20 *Ibid.*

21 Although many women and children evacuated in September 1939 subsequently returned home, there remained over 150,000 evacuated children living in reception areas in the autumn of 1943. Women's Group on Public Welfare, *Our Towns: A Close Up*, p. 2.

22 WL, Pamphlet Collection, *The National Conference of Women, called by H.M. Government, Report of Proceedings, Tuesday 28 September, 1943, Royal Albert Hall, London* (1943), p. 11.

23 See J. Macnicol, 'The Effect of the Evacuation of Schoolchildren on Official Attitudes to State Intervention', in Smith (ed.), *War and Social Change*.

24 Lancashire, Sussex, Yorkshire and Kent were among the 'safe' areas designated by the Government.

25 Merz, *After the Vote*, p. 22.

26 MSH, Central Council Minutes, Vol. 11 (1937–42), 'Minutes of the Mothers' Union Central Council', December 1939, p. 196,

27 Macnicol, 'The Evacuation of Schoolchildren', pp. 24–28.

28 In 1940 the WI published the results of a survey of local WI responses to the evacuation scheme. The report *Town Children through Country Eyes* highlighted the poverty and neglect experienced by children in their care. See Andrews, *The Acceptable Face of Feminism*, p. 116.

29 As Macnicol points out, the problem of head lice was more to do with living in cramped living conditions than with poor parenting. Macnicol, 'The Evacuation of School Children', p. 18.

30 Women's Group on Public Welfare, *Our Towns: A Close Up*, p. 3.

31 D. Sheridan (ed.), *Wartime Women: A Mass Observation Anthology* (London: Phoenix, 1990), p. 64.

32 Cited in Merz, *After the Vote*, p. 23.

33 *The Mothers' Union Workers' Paper*, 310 (October 1939), p. 247.
34 MSH, Central Council Minutes, Vol. 11 (1937–42), 'Minutes of the Mothers' Union Central Council', December 1939, p. 196.
35 Hinton, *Women, Social Leadership and the Second World War*, pp. 48–49.
36 Women's Group on Public Welfare, *Our Towns: A Close Up*, p. 106.
37 *Ibid.*, p. 106.
38 *Ibid.*, pp. 105–106.
39 Davin, 'Imperialism and Motherhood', p. 38. See also J. Bourke, *Working Class Cultures in Britain 1890–1960* (London: Routledge, 1993), p. 68.
40 Macnicol, 'The Evacuation of Schoolchildren', p. 27.
41 For a discussion of more radical interpretations of *Our Towns*, see J. Welshman, 'Evacuation, Hygiene and Social Policy: The *Our Towns* Report of 1943', *Historical Journal*, 42 (1999).
42 *The Townswoman*, 11:9 (May 1944), p. 131.
43 As one WI worker remarked in an interview to the *Guardian* newspaper, 'Oh dear, not the jam thing again'. *Guardian* (24 April 1994).
44 Andrews, *The Acceptable Face of Feminism*, pp. 100–120.
45 *Home and Country*, 27:1 (January 1945), p. 2.
46 Merz, *After the Vote*, p. 29.
47 *Home and Country*, 27:7 (July 1945), p. 132.
48 *The Catholic Women's League Magazine*, 356 (August 1941), p. 6.
49 The YWCA also provided huts and canteens for women in the services throughout the war.
50 *The Catholic Women's League Magazine*, 347 (November 1940), p. 8.
51 Merz, *After the Vote*, p. 25
52 *Ibid.*
53 During the war years, an estimated 8,770,000 women remained full-time housewives working within the home.
54 *The National Conference of Women*, p. 11.
55 *Home and Country*, 21:10 (October 1939), p. 369.
56 For an account of women's work in industry during the 1920s and 1930s, see M. Glucksmann, *Women Assemble: Women Workers in the New Industries of Inter-war Britain* (London: Routledge, 1989).
57 Summerfield, 'Women, War and Social Change', p. 97.
58 *Ibid.*, p. 103.
59 For a detailed discussion about the employment of women during the Second World War see P. Summerfield, *Women Workers in the Second World War: Production and Patriarchy in Conflict* (London: Routledge, 1984).
60 In 1931, married women made up sixteen per cent of the female workforce. Braybon and Summerfield (eds), *Out of the Cage*, p. 167.
61 Rose, *Which People's War?*, p. 120.
62 The NCW had protested against the marriage bar during the 1930s as 'unjust, uneconomic and contrary to the public interest'. *NCW Handbook 1933–34* (1934), p. 78.
63 MSH, Central Council Minutes, Vol. 12 (1943–47), 'Minutes of the Mothers' Union Central Council', December 1943, p. 80. The British Council of Churches also expressed concern about the negative impacts on family life when mothers engaged in paid work. Rose, *Which People's War?*, p. 120.

64 See Summerfield, 'Women, War and Social Change', p. 104.

65 A 1941 Mass Observation survey showed that the women were unhappy with the lack of information from government sources about wage rates, working hours and childcare facilities. *Ibid.*

66 During the early years of the war, women conscripted into the wartime industries faced a twelve-hour day which left little time for shopping, housework and other domestic duties which they still had to perform.

67 *The Catholic Women's Magazine*, 358 (October 1941), p. 3.

68 D. Riley, 'Some Peculiarities of Social Policy Concerning Women in Wartime and Postwar Britain', in M. R. Higonnet, J. Jenson, S. Michel and M. Collins Weitz (eds), *Behind the Lines: Gender and the Two World Wars* (New Haven: Yale University Press, 1987), p. 261.

69 *The Mothers' Union Journal*, 192 (March 1943), p. 25.

70 The number of female part-time workers had increased from 380,000 in June 1942 to 900,000 in June 1944. Smith, 'The Effect of the War on the Status of Women', p. 216.

71 Smith, 'British Feminism in the 1920s', in Smith (ed.), *British Feminism in the Twentieth Century*, p. 49 and H. Smith, 'British Feminism and the Equal Pay Issue in the 1930s', *Women's History Review*, 5:1 (1996).

72 Thane, 'The Women of the British Labour Party and Feminism', pp. 133–34.

73 Pugh, *Women and the Women's Movement in Britain*, p. 96 and Smith, 'The Problem of "Equal Pay for Equal Work" in Great Britain during World War II', *Journal of Modern History*, 53 (1981), p. 654.

74 Smith, "British Feminism and the Equal Pay Issue in the 1930s", pp. 97–110.

75 *NCW Handbook 1930–31* (1931), p. 84.

76 Smith, 'The Problem of "Equal Pay for Equal Work"', p. 654.

77 WL, Pamphlet Collection, *NCW Report of the Council Meeting and Conference, Southport, June 29–July 2, 1936* (1936), p. 14.

78 Trade union support for the 'family wage' and the cheap labour already supplied by unskilled women workers were other reasons why both the government and private industry were unwilling to introduce equal pay. Pugh, *Women and the Women's Movement*, pp. 96–97.

79 *NCW Handbook 1937–1938* (1938), p. 109.

80 Women working in the dressmaking and women's light clothing trade were paid seven pence per hour while men received one shilling per hour. WL, Pamphlet Collection, *NCW Report of the Council Meeting and Conference, Leicester, October 14–18 1935* (1935), p. 40.

81 *Ibid.*

82 In 1940 the 'Extended Employment of Women' agreement guaranteed the 'men's rate for the job' for women working in the engineering industry but this only applied to women doing exactly the same work as men. Smith, 'The Problem of "Equal Pay for Equal Work"', p. 657. See also P. Thane, 'Towards Equal Opportunities? Women in Britain since 1945', in T. Gourvish and A. O'Day (eds), *Britain Since 1945* (Basingstoke: Macmillan, 1991), pp. 184–185.

83 Smith, 'The Problem with "Equal Pay for Equal Work"', pp. 656–667.

84 *Ibid.*, p. 660.

85 *News For Citizens* (May 1941), p. 1. The majority of women workers continued to be paid less than men during the war years with women earning on average fifty

to seventy per cent of men's wages. Smith, 'The Problem with "Equal Pay for Equal Work"', p. 658.

86 The committee, chaired by the Conservative MP Mavis Tate, included representatives of the British Federation of Professional and Business Women, the Woman Power Committee and the WFL.

87 *Home and Country*, 25:1 (January 1943), p. 1.

88 Smith, 'The Problem of "Equal Pay for Equal Work"', pp. 661–664.

89 *National Conference of Women*, p. 2.

90 *Women in Council*, 30 (November 1942), p. 3.

91 See A. Potter, 'The Equal Pay Campaign Committee: A Case-Study of a Pressure Group', *Political Studies*, 5 (1957).

92 WL, Box 263, Equal Pay Campaign Committee Archive. See also Rose, *Which People's War?*, p. 116.

93 WL, 5/FWI/G/2/3/039, Box 259, NFWI Archive, *Home and Country*, 27:1 (January 1945).

94 WL, Pamphlet Collection, *National Federation of Women's Institute Annual Conference Report, 1928* (1928).

95 National Federation of Women's Institutes, *Keeping Ourselves Informed*, p. 45.

96 *The Catholic Women's League Magazine*, 297 (July 1936), p. 11.

97 *The Townswoman*, 11:2 (October 1943), p. 17.

98 *Ibid.*, p. 18.

99 Clements, 'Feminism, citizenship and social activity', p. 213.

100 Smith, 'The Problem of "Equal Pay for Equal Work"', p. 666.

101 *Ibid.*, pp. 669–671.

102 *Home and Country*, 26:6 (June 1944), p. 85.

103 Thane, 'Towards Equal Opportunities?', p. 190.

104 *Ibid.*, pp. 190–191. There was no agreement on the payment of equal rates in industry and as a result three members of the commission, Dame Anne Loughlin, Miss L. Nettlefold and Dr Janet Vaughan, submitted a minority report supporting equal pay for female industrial workers.

105 Thane, 'Towards Equal Opportunities?', p. 191.

106 *Home and Country*, 29:1 (January 1947), p. 78.

107 WL, Box No. 263, EPC Archive, letter from H. C. Hart, Honorary Secretary of the EPCC to all members of the House of Commons, 11 December 1946.

108 *Women in Council*, 19:7 (March 1947), pp. 1–4.

109 *Ibid.*, p. 1. Two speakers at the meeting, Liberal MP Megan Lloyd George and the Labour MP Barbara Castle, were both honorary members of the NCW.

110 *Equal Pay for Equal Work: A Black Record 1914–1949* (London: EPCC, 1949), p. 4.

111 WL, Box 260, B15/2, EPC Archive, typed report of EPCC Meeting, 10 June 1948.

112 WL, Box 260, B15/2, EPC Archive, *The National Association of Women Civil Servants Newsletter*, July 1948, p. 2.

113 *NCW Handbook 1947–1948* (1948), p. 42 and *NCW Handbook 1948–1949* (1949), p. 39.

114 The results of this survey were to be presented at the June meeting but there is no evidence that the information was either received or given out. *Home and Country*, 2:30 (February 1948), p. 65.

115 Pat Thane writes that during the late 1940s two out of every three women did not work outside the home. Thane, 'Towards Equal Opportunity?', p. 197.

116 London Metropolitan Archive, London (hereafter LMA), ACC/3613/1/72, NCW Archive, 'Parliamentary and Legislative Committee minutes, Thursday 15 May 1947'.

117 WL, 5/FWI/G/2/3/043, Box 260, NFWI Archive, *Home and Country*, 29:8 (August 1947).

118 Following this decision the EPCC dissolved itself in December 1955. For a detailed account of the equal pay campaign during the early 1950s see H. Smith, 'The Politics of Conservative Reform: The Equal Pay For Equal Work Issue, 1945–1955', *The Historical Journal*, 35:2 (1992).

119 Joyce Freeguard does explore the role of the NCW and WI in this campaign. See Freeguard, 'It's time for women of the 1950s', pp. 96–125.

120 For example, Pat Thane writes that the Women's National Liberal Federation actively supported the campaign for women police throughout the inter-war years. P. Thane, 'Women, Liberalism and Citizenship', in E. Biagini (ed.), *Citizenship and Community: Liberals, Radicals and Collective Identities in the British Isles, 1865–1931* (Cambridge: Cambridge University Press, 1996), pp. 85–86.

121 The two other groups were the Women Police Volunteers and the Women Police Service. See A. Woodeson, 'The First Women Police: a force for equality or infringement?', *Women's History Review*, 2:2 (1993). See also L. Jackson, *Women Police: Gender, Welfare and Surveillance in the Twentieth Century* (Manchester: Manchester University Press, 2006), pp. 18–20 and A. Woollacott, '"Khaki Fever" and Its Control: Gender, Class, Age and Sexual Morality on the British Home-Front in the First World War', *Journal of Contemporary History*, 29 (1994).

122 Since 1883, the police force had employed matrons to sit with women detained in police cells or awaiting trial. See B. Weinberger, *The Best Police in the World: An Oral History of English Policing* (Aldershot: Scolar Press, 1995), p. 110.

123 Woollacott, '"Khaki Fever" and Its Control', p. 335. See also P. Levine, '"Walking the Streets in a Way No Decent Woman Should": Women Police in World War I', *Journal of Modern History*, 66:1 (1994).

124 Woollacott, '"Khaki Fever" and Its Control', p. 335.

125 Proposals to disband the Metropolitan women police force in 1922 were only averted by the intervention of the NCW and influential supporters including the Archbishop of Canterbury and Lord Aberdeen. E. Tancred, *Women Police 1914–1950* (London: NCW, 1950), p. 10.

126 In the Metropolitan area one hundred policewomen were employed in comparison with 20,381 policemen. J. Carrier, *The Campaign for the Employment of Women as Police Officers* (Aldershot: Avebury, 1988), p. xviii.

127 Weinberger, *The Best Police Force in the World*, p. 92.

128 Carrier, *The Campaign for the Employment of Women as Police Officers*, p. 169.

129 Jackson, *Women Police*, p. 19.

130 Tancred, *Women Police 1914–1950*, p. 11.

131 *Ibid.*

132 See Carrier, *The Campaign for the Employment of Women as Police Officers*, pp. 244–249 and Weinburger, *The Best Police in the World*, p. 93.

133 Carrier, *The Campaign for the Employment of Women as Police Officers*, p. 14.

134 It was also requested again that a woman police inspector be appointed to the Home Office. Tancred, *Women Police 1914–1950*, pp. 18–20.

135 *Ibid.*, p. 21.

136 *NCW Handbook 1936–37* (1937), p. 101.

137 *National Union of Townswomen's Guilds Annual Report 1934* (1934), p. 38.

138 *The Catholic Women's League Magazine*, 327 (January 1939). p. 4.

139 *NCW Handbook 1935–36* (1936), p. 94. See also Clements, 'Feminism, citizenship and social activity', p. 210.

140 One-sixth of those women were not attested constables. Cited in Weinberger, *The Best Police in the World*, p. 92.

141 Jackson, *Women Police*, p. 25.

142 WL, Pamphlet Collection, M. H. Cowlin, *Women Police in War Time: What is the WAPC?* (leaflet published by the NCW in November 1939), p. 3.

143 *NCW Handbook 1940–41* (1941), p. 73.

144 *Ibid.*

145 Tancred, *Women Police 1914–1950*, p. 28.

146 In October 1944, the Home Secretary announced that a Woman Staff Officer was to be appointed to H.M. Inspectors of Constabulary. *Ibid.*, p. 29.

147 Weinberger, *The Best Police in the World*, p. 98.

148 See Carrier, *The Campaign for the Employment of Women as Police Officers*, p. 252.

149 C. Smart, 'Disruptive Bodies and Unruly Sex', in C. Smart (ed.), *Regulating Womanhood* (London: Routledge, 1992), cited in Jackson, *Women Police*, p. 171.

150 Rose, *Which People's War?*, p. 119.

151 *Ibid.*, p. 144.

6

Housewives and citizens:
post-war planning and the post-war years

I n September 1943, Winston Churchill told delegates attending the National Conference of Women that the support women had given to the war effort 'will be found to have definitely altered those social and sex balances which years of convention had established'.[1] Echoing this view one year later, the Minister for Reconstruction, Lord Woolton, informed members of the NCW that the government 'must see to it that the progress of reconstruction gives [women] a fair deal in return'.[2] In spite of these assurances, voluntary women's societies were determined that the opinions of women would be represented at all levels of post-war planning. Megan Lloyd George MP, member of the NCW and WI, expressed this view when she insisted that women 'shall be brought in to assist the Government in planning ... not so much because we think we have a right, although we have earned that right ... but because we really have a definite contribution to make'.[3]

Voluntary women's groups were just as emphatic as Lloyd George in defending the right of women to be involved in post-war planning and were optimistic that once the war was over the status of women in post-war society would be enhanced. In October 1941, the NCW passed a resolution calling on the government to guarantee that 'when the present emergency is over women citizens shall have a status identical with that of men'.[4] Reiterating this hope in 1943, Mrs Home Peel, then President of the NCW, told her members that

> the time has surely come for the government to give some indication of the attitude they propose to adopt towards women after the fighting has ceased. It is unthinkable that the reserves of women power, which the war has brought to light, should be lost to the nation after the war.[5]

This chapter will consider the involvement of the MU, CWL, NCW, WI and TG in plans for post-war reconstruction. The submissions of these groups to the Beveridge Committee and their views on the nascent welfare state have been discussed in Chapter 4. Here their involvement in plans for post-war housing and their engagement with debates about the role of women in post-war society will be considered. Their motive, as always, was to safeguard the stability of family life and promote the traditional role of women as wives and mothers. They did not, however, expect women to retreat into the family home after years of war work. Instead, women were encouraged to be active citizens who as housewives and workers would assist in the national recovery. In return, voluntary women's societies expected and campaigned to ensure that women would benefit from, in the words of the WI, all the 'new social services and improved amenities that are the right of every citizen'.[6]

Post-war reconstruction and the family: homes fit for housewives

In 1941, the National Government began to plan for social and economic recovery once the war had ended in an effort to avoid a return to the economic difficulties of the inter-war years. Simultaneously, post-war planning provided an opportunity to boost the morale of citizens so that they could have hope for a future free from the worst excesses of poverty and privilege.[7] Housewives' associations in particular looked forward to a time when families would be reunited and the wartime disruption of everyday life would be brought to an end.

The preservation of family life in the aftermath of the war was one of the central objectives of post-war reconstruction.[8] Conscription, the employment of over seven million women in the labour force and the evacuation of children from their family homes raised fears about the long-term stability of family life. Women's societies were amongst those most concerned. In December 1941, the MU warned members that 'the family life of the nation' must be safeguarded and 'based on Christian foundations'.[9] Two years later *The Mothers' Union Workers' Paper* suggested that family life had been

> badly disrupted and broken owing to the separation for long periods of husbands and wives, to the new types of work for women and to the attraction of wage earning. Many young wives will find it immensely difficult to settle down into the quiet routine of household jobs after the hustle and noise and cheery companionship of factory or office life.[10]

In order to facilitate the smooth transition from the workplace to the home, women's societies argued that the standard of living for housewives and mothers would have to be improved if young women were to be persuaded to take up their traditional domestic role.

As the previous chapters have suggested, fears about the falling birth rate coupled with concerns about the employment of large numbers of married women during wartime gave women's societies the perfect opportunity to highlight the importance of housework and motherhood. With the government considering plans for post-war reconstruction, women's groups were in a strong position to argue that the working conditions of housewives and mothers needed to be improved.

This they did by effectively drawing attention to the need for adequate maternity services, family allowances paid to mothers, home-helps and a range of other social welfare benefits for wives and mothers. Yet in spite of these achievements, women's societies remained convinced that further reforms were necessary. All such reforms would encourage more women to marry and start a family once the war had ended thereby sustaining family life and protecting the role of the mothers within the home.

Furthermore, the publication of *Our Towns: A Close Up* in 1943 had highlighted in stark terms the effects that extreme poverty, unemployment and bad housing could have on the physical and moral welfare of women and children. Members of WI, TG and other women's societies had themselves witnessed at first hand the malnutrition, ill health and unruly behaviour of some evacuees in their care. Rather than just condemning working-class mothers for supposed failures in rearing their children, voluntary women's groups instead looked to the state to ameliorate these social problems and lobbied for reform.

If the opinions of women were to have any influence upon the government's reconstruction programme it was imperative that local and national planning committees included female representatives and considered evidence from women's societies. In October 1941, the NCW called on the government to guarantee that women 'shall have full opportunity for putting their demands for reforms affecting their status before any body appointed to deal with post-war reconstruction.'[11] Although few women were appointed to committees, women's societies were able to ensure that a feminine voice was heard by giving evidence to various committees, for example the NCW memorandum on social insurance submitted to the Beveridge Committee.[12]

Unsurprisingly, housing policy was one aspect of post-war planning that was of particular interest to voluntary women's societies. The inter-war years had witnessed on-going housing shortages and the persistence of slum conditions. For example, in 1931 70,000 houses in Manchester were condemned as unfit for human habitation and in London over 30,000 of the city's poor were living in basement dwellings.[13] Housing in rural areas could be just as bad with homes lacking hot or cold running water, electricity and adequate sewage systems. In 1935 an estimated 42,000 rural homes were deemed overcrowded and by the end of 1937 it was reported that approximately 57,000 houses in the countryside were unfit for habitation.[14]

This housing crisis continued despite the fact that four million houses had been built during the 1920s and 1930s, the majority of which were in new estates situated on the outskirts of towns and cities. Families moving to these areas benefited from the superior housing conditions, but found that they were living far from friends, family and jobs, in areas with few shops, playgrounds or other basic amenities. For both middle-class and working-class women this meant the break-up of traditional kinship and support networks leaving many women isolated in their new homes.[15] For all of these reasons and the obvious link between good housing standards and a happy home life, voluntary women's groups campaigned for better housing throughout the 1920s and 1930s. In doing so they worked alongside feminist and political women's societies as well as organisations representing the voluntary housing sector.[16]

The connection between housing and a stable family life can also be extended to the concept of good and active citizenship. Elizabeth Darling, in her work on the voluntary housing sector during the 1930s, has established a link between the provision of well-designed affordable housing and the practice of good citizenship, particularly for working-class housewives. Darling argues that British designers of labour-saving homes, most notably the well-known housing consultant Elizabeth Denby, hoped that less time spent on housework would allow wives and mothers more time to participate in public life and so ensure that every woman could become 'a citizen as well as a housewife.'[17]

Similarly Gillian Scott, writing on the involvement of the WCG in the inter-war housing debate, has argued that the Guild believed labour-saving on housework and engagement with life outside the home were inextricably linked. This was a view endorsed by a senior guildswoman in 1925 when she stated that 'women's emancipation will never be complete until the chains of black-leading, war on smoke and the eternal dusting are forever shaken off.'[18] Time spent on housework was also becoming a matter of concern for middle-class housewives. Although many middle-class households still had at least one domestic servant it was clear that a dwindling number of working-class women were willing to work in service when other more lucrative occupations were available. As a result, middle-class women faced the reality of having to take on all of their own housework for the first time.[19]

It was in the context of debates on housing provision, design, house-work and concerns about the impact that bad housing had on family life, that representatives of thirty women's organisations came together in the mid-1930s to form the Women's Housing Conference. Included in the list of societies represented were the NCW, the MU and the CWL, along with a wide range of other women's groups, housing associations and professional bodies.[20] A memorandum drawn up by the Special Committee of the Women's Housing Conference in February 1936 outlined the key concerns of this new body. Overall the aim was to ensure 'that the needs of the working woman on whom the wellbeing of the home and family depends' were catered for in the housing schemes of all public authorities.[21]

In addition the memorandum stated that the views of housewives and mothers on housing design should be made known to the Ministry of Health's Central Housing Advisory Committee. Local authorities should consult with groups of women before housing plans were passed. The co-option of women onto the Housing and Estates Committees of Local Authorities was recommended so that the views of women were made known at local level. The need for improved housing for large families was highlighted, echoing concerns frequently voiced by the CWL and the MU. These views reflected wider anxieties during the 1930s about decreasing family size and falling population levels.

A second area of concern raised by the CWL, MU and the NCW during these years was the housing needs of old and single people, indicating that housewives' associations did not confine themselves only to the interests of married women with families. The Women's Housing Conference advised that more suitable accommodation was required for old and single people and that all new housing estates should include this variety of housing. The memorandum also requested that new develop-ments should have better amenities including schools, churches and halls as well as health clinics, shopping centres and children's playgrounds. To do so would help overcome problems of loneliness experienced by house-wives living in these new estates.[22]

In order to implement these recommendations, a Women's Advisory Housing Council (WAHC) was set up by over thirty women's socie-ties on 15 December 1936. Included amongst the groups represented on the council were the CWL and the NCW, and the aim of this new body was to draw attention to the '[housing] needs of the working housewife and mother'.[23] The council made representations both to the Ministry of Health and to local housing committees calling for improvements in public and private housing schemes. Well-equipped kitchens, indoor bathrooms, hot running water, gardens and playgrounds were listed as the basic design features which should be included in every new home and housing estate.[24] These features would not only make the lives of housewives and mothers easier but would ensure that women had time to engage in 'good and active citizenship'.

The WI and TG were also involved in the campaign for better housing throughout the inter-war years, and Margaret Andrews has explored the involvement of the WI in campaigning for improvements to rural housing and water supplies throughout the 1920s and 1930s.[25] Local authorities were lobbied to provide a far greater number of rural homes with piped water and modern sewage systems and there is evidence that institutes became very involved carrying out surveys of local housing provision and presenting their evidence to local housing committees. It was hoped such representation would overcome existing problems for housewives with regard to interior design as 'it is astonishing how many new cottages are still built with the larder facing south or the sink in the wrong place.'[26]

The TG, whose membership consisted of women living in urban areas, was primarily concerned with the housing needs of women in towns and cities. In addition, the Guild was concerned about the welfare of women moving to live in new suburban housing estates far from family and friends. Guild members were encouraged to stand for local housing committees, to set up guilds in suburban areas and to recruit new members from amongst the recently arrived families in new housing estates. As well as voicing their opinion on housing standards, the TG were also concerned about the isolation and loneliness that some women might feel in their new homes, a problem which could be overcome by joining the local guild and meeting other women in a similar situation.

The outbreak of the Second World War brought an end to new building and development programmes as manpower and resources were diverted into the war effort. By the early 1940s it was already obvious that there would be a major housing shortage after the war. The 1941 blitz and subsequent flying bomb attacks demonstrated the destructive power of German bombing raids, which left over 475,000 homes destroyed by the end of the war.[27] Women's groups emphasised the need for every family to be accommodated in high quality housing if traditional family life was to be restored once hostilities ended. There is no doubt that the participation of voluntary women's organisations in the inter-war housing debate had given them both confidence and experience. This in turn facilitated an intensification of their campaign for housing reform during the war years.

In May 1942 a Women's Housing and Planning Conference was held at the Royal Institute of British Architects in London at the behest of a number of women's organisations, including the NCW, the WI, the TG, the WCG, the WAHC and the WGPW. The discussion points from the conference highlighted continuities with the inter-war housing campaign but also reflected the new energy and determination amongst women's groups that any plans for housing provision after the war must take into account the views of women. An increase in labour-saving devices in modern homes, adequate water supplies in rural areas, the need to survey the views of women on housing and the need for more female representation on national and local housing committees were pinpointed as key issues.

The conference concluded that there 'cannot be too much discussion on this issue [housing] while it is still fluid' and that 'housework should not be regarded as an end in itself, but as a means to a happy family life.'[28] Furthermore, the WAHC insisted that the voices of women must be heard in the housing debate on the grounds that it was the housewife who

> has the personal experience of housing needs and knows better than any architect or designer what is wanted to provide labour saving fitments, heating and washing conveniences and what arrangements of rooms will bring most comfort to the family and help the mother in the economical management of the home.[29]

The ideal opportunity for voluntary women's organisations to voice their opinions on post-war housing came in May 1942, when as part of the government's plans for reconstruction, the Ministry of Health set up a new housing subcommittee to investigate the future possibilities for housing policy. The Design of Dwellings Committee was chaired by the Earl of Dudley and was tasked with considering ways in which the design of homes and the layout of suburban housing estates could be improved. The results of the committee would inform guidelines for future planning schemes. The Ministry of Health, responding to the demands of women's groups, appointed seven women to the committee, three of whom were WI members and two members of the WCG.[30] In addition seventeen women's organisations, including the WAHC, the WGPW, the WCG, the TG, the WI, the NCW and the MU, were invited to submit evidence outlining the housing needs of their members.[31]

In order to ascertain the views of women on housing, a detailed housing questionnaire was drawn up by the WAHC on behalf of the WGPW with a total of forty-seven questions to be answered.[32] The questionnaire was then sent out to women's organisations including the MU, the TG and the WI. The survey requested members of these organisations to describe the kind of houses they would like to live in and asked a wide range of questions relating to the design and layout of kitchens, bedrooms and bathrooms. Recipients were also asked to suggest ways in which the everyday burden of housework could be reduced and to comment in detail on labour-saving designs that would make the running of the home more economical.

A full analysis of the TG responses to the housing questionnaire appeared in its journal *The Townswoman* in June 1943. It was reported that 11,753 members in 281 guilds had answered the questionnaire, thereby reflecting the views of a cross section of urban women. Guild members were congratulated for expressing their opinions demonstrating that 'the average woman's point of view ... in relation to her work as a housewife must be taken into consideration in town planning, and now is the time for this point to be considered.'[33]

In June 1942 the WI sent the WAHC housing questionnaire to each of its County Federations and received replies from forty-five counties with reports from approximately 1,500 institute branches. A pamphlet was then published detailing the results of the questionnaire and it was reported that 'many Institutes said they had never enjoyed anything so much' and that the exercise had given rural women the chance to 'give vent to pent-up feelings.'[34] Once again the importance of obtaining the views of women on housing was emphasised with the words that 'the house matters to a rural working woman infinitely more than to a working man; she has to look after it, she has to arrange it for her man and her children: her knowledge is the real, practical knowledge that counts.'[35]

Although the CWL did not submit evidence directly to the Design of Dwellings Committee, the views of Catholic women were reflected in the evidence given by the National Board of Catholic Women (NBCW). This organisation, which represented a number of Catholic women's groups, focused on the housing needs of families. With regard to the design of local authority housing it was argued houses with a large kitchen-living room, scullery and small parlour were best. Mindful of the needs of families, three-bedroom houses were required to allow parents, boys and girls to sleep separately with separate beds for each child. It was also argued that housing schemes should make provision for larger families by designing houses with small single rooms for older children.

In response to the WAHC survey, the MU collected 5,000 answers to the questionnaire from seven dioceses: London, Birmingham, Chelmsford, Exeter, Llandaff, Mammoth and Ely. Comfortable, spacious and affordable modern houses for families were the top priority for MU members and it was reported in *The Workers' Paper* that the housing survey had highlighted the need for family homes with 'not less than three or four bedrooms for families, for children do grow up and want more space. One would think the planners were convinced that children didn't ever grow up.[36]

The MU's enthusiasm for family housing was linked closely to its belief in the importance of traditional family life and during the war the organisation was increasingly concerned that poor housing would deter couples from marrying and having large families once the war had ended. This concern was reflected in its evidence to the Royal Commission on Population when the Union made clear its view that the greater availability of large houses would encourage parents to have more children.[37]

As a representative organisation of over one hundred women's groups, the NCW drew up its own separate memorandum for the Dudley Committee addressing the needs of the lower-paid professional classes. Recommendations included gas and electric heating, windows for easy cleaning and well-planned estates with ample amenities such as shops, laundries, libraries and playgrounds.[38] The Council blamed inter-war housing policy for the proliferation of isolated urban housing estates with few facilities and warned that such 'mistakes in rehousing must not be repeated'.[39]

Before submitting the findings of the women's housing questionnaire to the Dudley Committee, the WGPW analysed the 40,000 replies and compiled a comprehensive report. A survey of this size inevitably reflected a wide variety of opinions but there was a good deal of uniformity when it came to describing the essential features of an ideal home. Privacy, space and simplicity emerged as the three most important considerations. The survey revealed that the majority of women questioned wanted a three-bedroom house with a garden and an upstairs bathroom. Downstairs there should be a parlour, a kitchen/scullery and a living room for everyday use by the family. Large bright rooms with soundproof walls were recommended and it was suggested that the corners in all rooms should be rounded to make the sweeping of floors less cumbersome. Tiled bathrooms, kitchens with built-in cupboards and draining boards were simple but important features which would reduce the daily workload of the housewife. The demand for hot running water upstairs and downstairs, made repeatedly during the inter-war period, appeared frequently in all replies.[40]

The housing questionnaire is significant for a number of reasons. It gave thousands of women the opportunity to describe the kind of labour-saving homes they hoped to live in after the war. At the same time, it allowed voluntary women's societies another opportunity to impress upon their members how important it was for women to speak out on public questions affecting their own lives and the lives of their families.

There is evidence that the survey succeeded in arousing the interest of local branch members in the housing debate. In June 1943, *The Towns-woman* reported that guild members taking part in the housing inquiry had 'visited existing housing schemes; they had lectures from architects, from town councillors, and from experts on special aspects of housing'.[41] Likewise, members of the MU in London and Coventry, where some of the most destructive bombing had taken place, were said to be taking an active part in discussing post-war housing policy.

In July 1942 the Central Council of the MU advised members to consider standing for election to local housing committees, or failing that to ensure that they voted for suitable candidates to represent the views of women in local government.[42] Having urged women in 1934 to vote for suitable men for public office it is significant that eight years later the Union was now happy to endorse and encourage the candidacy and election of women to local government. This change of heart reflects shifting perceptions of women's role in public life and indicates that it was becoming increasingly commonplace for women to take up official roles instead of relying on men to represent their interests for them.[43]

The publication of the Design of Dwellings Report in 1944 was a triumph for women's organisations and was a vindication of the years spent campaigning on housing.[44] Many of the recommendations included in the report mirrored the responses of women to the housing question-naire. The report proposed, for example, that kitchens should be well equipped with gas and electric cooking appliances, cupboards, draining boards and ventilated larders.[45] Increased floor space, tiled bathrooms and a living room with a dining recess or a dining kitchen were amongst the report's other recommendations. Referring to the design of housing estates, it advised that all new developments should contain a mixture of houses, flats and maisonettes.[46] The report also recognised the needs of larger families, thereby reflecting the specific concerns of CWL and the MU. Although it based its standard house plan on a family of five, it was acknowledged that families with more than three children would require additional space, and that this fact should be accommodated in future housing plans.[47]

The Design of Dwellings Report was instrumental in shaping post-war housing policy and its recommendations set national minimum housing standards in official *Housing Manuals* published after the war.[48] By 1951, 900,000 houses had been built with the help of government subsidies, the vast majority of which provided low-cost local authority housing for working-class families.[49] Although housing shortages and housing standards continued to be a significant problem during the late

1940s and 1950s, the impact that the MU, CWL, NCW, WI and TG had on housing policy during wartime should not be underestimated.

The fact that the recommendations of these groups were included in the Design of Dwellings Report and then later incorporated into public housing schemes is significant. It illustrates that the agency and activism generated by mainstream women's organisations on the question of housing in post-war planning was both effective and successful. As a result, these groups were able to exert their influence on national housing policy. Moreover, the housing campaign also allowed voluntary women's organisations to establish the right of housewives and mothers to contribute to public debates and show that their participation was of value to all members of the community.

Post-war reconstruction and domesticity: housewives, workers and citizens

The war years brought many new challenges to voluntary women's organisations. As the last chapter suggested, all five of the organisations included in this study successfully negotiated the demands made on them during the war and emerged more confident and self-assured about their public role in representing the interests of housewives and mothers. However, one of the key changes that occurred during wartime, which would have a longer-term impact on housewives' associations, was the growing number of mothers taking up paid work. These new opportunities for housewives and mothers created something of a dilemma for voluntary women's groups as they wished to support the war effort and the contribution of women workers, but at the same time firmly believed that young children should be looked after at home, by their mothers.

In evidence to the Royal Commission on Population, mainstream women's organisations repeatedly emphasised this point. Speaking on behalf of its affiliated societies, the NCW argued that young children 'are best brought up in the home, we all realise that'.[50] This view was shared by working-class women's societies. In its evidence to the commission the SJCWWO made it clear that when a family's finances allowed it, women with young children should remain at home because 'far from desiring to go out to work they want to have a proper standard in the home to enable them to do their job as a housewife and mother'.[51] Similarly, the Fabian Women's Group informed the commission that 'women must be whole-hearted full-time mothers'.[52] Feminist organisations also shared this belief. As Jane Lewis writes 'on the whole, post-war feminists accepted that women's most vital task was that of motherhood'.[53]

There is evidence to suggest that the consensus amongst women's organisations giving evidence to the Royal Commission on Population was shared by many women at this time. A survey of working-class teenage girls in 1945 revealed that most aspired to marriage and motherhood and believed that 'a women's first duty is to look after her own home'.[54] In 1943 a study of women's attitudes towards paid work had reported that forty-three per cent of young women aged between 18–24 and 25–34 intended to give up work after the war. The most common reason given for their decision to stop working was the prospect of marriage and starting a family. This finding backed the assertion made by women's groups that mothers with young children should and would want to look after their own children at home.[55] The popularity of marriage and motherhood revealed in these wartime surveys was played out in the dramatic increase in the number of marriages taking place during the period 1945–48. The subsequent post-war baby boom meant that the birth rate, in decline throughout the 1930s, peaked in 1947 at 20.6 births per 1,000 of population.[56]

What is interesting and significant about this rousing endorsement of marriage and motherhood is that these views were most prevalent amongst younger women, many of whom were as yet unmarried. Older married women did not necessarily share the same views. The 1943 wartime survey revealed that a significant number of older married women hoped to continue working once the war had ended. Thirty-nine per cent of married women and forty-nine per cent of married women with children questioned in 1943 expressed their intention to remain in employment after the war.[57] For some married women the experience of war work had given them confidence in their abilities as paid employees and provided them with an independent income for the first time.

This new development did not go unnoticed by voluntary women's organisations, whose memberships included significant numbers of older married women. In March 1944, the MU acknowledged in evidence to the Royal Commission on Population that there may be 'a growing reluctance on the part of women to lose the economic independence they enjoyed before marriage or through war work'.[58] When questioned by a member of the commission about the advisability of mothers going out to work, the NCW and the MU defended a mother's right to work in certain circumstances.

Rosamond Fisher, Central President of the MU, told the commission that 'speaking as a feminist I say yes [to mothers working] but speaking as a mother I would say let her have a career provided it does not stand in the way of having babies … but it almost always does.' Mrs Fisher went on to argue on behalf of working mothers, pointing out that it was hard for people not to have a career when people of my generation could do voluntary work ... and nobody ever criticised them for that or for leaving their babies ... [but today] if a young woman takes up a career and leaves her baby she is severely criticised. I think it a little hard to argue that a woman should not continue her career if she has a baby, but the baby must come first.[59]

In her statement, Fisher not only described herself as a feminist, a rather surprising admission for the President of the MU, but also supported the idea that some mothers had the right to decide whether or not they would continue working after they had children. Acknowledging the opportunities that charitable work had given upper and middle-class women in the past, she believed that middle-class professional women should be encouraged to return to work as soon as their children had grown up. On the other hand, however, the Union advised working-class mothers to avoid unskilled labour and concentrate on caring for their families. The implication appeared to be that middle-class women would always have more to contribute to society through paid work than their working-class equivalents.[60]

The NCW, in its evidence to the Royal Commission on Population, also defended the right of women to have a career as well as a family. However, like the MU, the Council stressed that the welfare of the children must come first. In order to ensure that women with young children could stay at home, the Council proposed a 'dual role' for married women. This would allow mothers to pursue a career before they started a family, and then return to it when their children had grown up.[61] Once again the decision to continue with a career once children were older was seen only as an option for middle-class women who could afford to interrupt their careers and rely for a time on their husband's income. For the vast majority of working-class women there was little choice but to go out to work if the family's income could not support a new baby.

In spite of the very obvious class bias expressed here, the suggestion made during the 1940s by both the MU and the NCW, that women had the right to marriage, motherhood and a career, was nothing short of radical. Traditionally, family life and a career were regarded as mutually exclusive for women. The fact that the MU and NCW acknowledged that some married women would want to continue working after they had children reflects their long-held belief that housewives and mothers, as citizens, had a significant contribution to make to society and that contribution included participation in paid work.

The occupations that the MU and NCW considered of value were very much rooted in respectable middle-class careers for women, for example teaching, medicine and social work. Nonetheless, the fact that mothers were being encouraged to take up these roles by conservative middle-class women's organisations in the late 1940s is of great significance and has not often been acknowledged by historians. Indeed Denise Riley writes that in 1945 'the dominant rhetoric described the figures of woman as mother and woman as worker as diametrically opposed and refused to consider the possibility of their combination.'[62] Yet it was at this very time that highly respected and influential housewives' organisations were foreseeing a future where mothers would take up employment and successfully combine paid work and motherhood.

This recognition on the part of voluntary women's groups that some mothers would wish to continue working after the war reflected the reality of changing work patterns for women in the late 1940s and throughout the 1950s. Although the percentage of all women workers fell from fifty-one per cent in 1943 to forty per cent in 1947, the number of married women working outside the home gradually increased during the post-war period.[63] By 1951 forty-three per cent of women workers were married.[64] One reason for this increase was the urgent demand for additional workers in the export industries to offset the post-war balance-of-payments deficit. In 1947, the Labour government launched a major recruitment campaign of radio appeals and newspaper advertisements, appealing to married women to help solve the country's financial crisis by making themselves available for work in industry.[65]

Just as they had done during the war, voluntary women's groups accepted that their members had a duty as citizens to assist the government in its plans for a national recovery. In response to the appeal for women workers, the NCW recognised that 'the participation of women [in industry] is necessary to secure the increased production on which the future of this country depends in the present national crisis.'[66] The Council supported the efforts of local branches to assist in the government's recruitment drive. Mrs Cockcroft, a prominent Halifax member, was praised for holding a public meeting urging women to work part-time in the regional textile industry.[67]

The CWL, however, expressed concern about the government's policy. Stella Given Wilson, President of the League, warned that Catholics must be watchful to safeguard the home and family and ensure that paid work for mothers did not conflict with a happy family life.[68] Given Wilson was not alone in having reservations about married women working in industry. In an effort to protect the stability of family life and allow mothers with young children to stay at home, both the MU and the NCW made representations to ministers requesting that mothers with children of school age should be excluded from the recruitment drive.

In 1947 the MU wrote to the Ministry of Labour advising that undue pressure should not be put on young mothers to return to work. In his reply, the Minister assured the Union that 'instructions have been given that there should be no effort to recruit mothers of very young children and there should be no pressure ... brought to bear on women whose home responsibilities prevented them from going to work.'[69] The minister went on to confirm that he believed 'a woman's first duty is to her home', a sentiment warmly welcomed by the majority of women's organisations at this time.[70]

Although reassured by the Ministry of Labour, the NCW felt compelled to request that the government see to it that women who did return to work were offered fair terms of employment. In October 1947 the Council passed a resolution calling on the authorities to 'exert themselves to help the women workers with regard to their remuneration and conditions of work, and in such matters as the provision of transport and shopping facilities.'[71] It will be recalled, however, that the Labour government refused to accede to any request for equal pay throughout its period in office on the grounds of cost. Nor is there any evidence to suggest that women workers were singled out for special treatment with regard to transport and shopping during these years.

The demand for married women workers in occupational sectors other than heavy industry also increased during the late 1940s. Job opportunities for women expanded in light industries such as electrical engineering, where women were engaged in low paid, unskilled and repetitive jobs. In addition the removal of the civil service marriage bar in 1946, the recruitment of married women teachers in 1948 and the creation of new jobs for women within the welfare state all increased the employment opportunities for married middle-class women.

In the immediate post-war years it is clear therefore that voluntary women's groups were beginning to adjust to the notion of mothers working outside the home. Whilst accepting some mothers would and should work, these groups remained committed to actively promoting the domestic role of women. They continued to believe, as they always had done, that women were at the centre of family life and that the needs of the family must be the primary concern of wives and mothers. This was particularly significant at a time when the number of marriages ending in divorce was on the increase.[72]

Yet in spite of their firm belief in marriage and motherhood, the MU, CWL, NCW, WI and TG also believed that they still had a duty to encourage their members to engage in public life. If women were to devote themselves exclusively to home and family, or engage in paid work, then they would have less time to join voluntary women's organisations and be good citizens. In order to prevent falling memberships and their ability to represent the 'woman's point of view', these groups needed to ensure that women continued to be involved in public life so that their collective agency could be utilised to campaign on issues of local and national importance.

One way in which housewives' associations encouraged their members to be good and active citizens in the immediate post-war years was to urge them to do what they could to assist in the national recovery. The imposition of economic austerity in the late 1940s made exceptional demands on the patience and goodwill of all women, and housewives in particular. During the war many women had felt it their duty to put up with the hardships of wartime rationing, regarded as the fairest method of distributing limited supplies. It was acknowledged in *Home and Country* in January 1944 that a good system of rationing ensured that 'a considerable section of the population were better fed than ever before'.[73] As a result, women's groups co-operated with the Ministry of Food throughout the war and members of the WI and the TG had advised women on the best use of rations to provide healthy meals for their families.[74]

The end of the war did not bring any relief to the housewife whose responsibility it was to feed and clothe her family, regardless of scarce resources. Rationing remained in force for another eight years and in 1946 bread, the staple diet of many families, was rationed for the first time.[75] Such action was deemed necessary by the Labour government to overcome the serious deficit in the balance of payments. As a result, a policy of austerity was introduced which restricted foreign imports and increased taxation on domestic consumption.[76] Having already experienced six years of rationing, the government was anxious to emphasise the necessity of austerity if the country was to overcome the post-war economic crisis. Housewives had a key role to play in the success of this policy. As Ina Zweiniger-Bargielowska observes 'housewifery was no longer regarded as a private concern but rather as a central component of the war effort and post-war reconstruction.'[77] It was hoped that housewives in particular would support the government's economy drive and accept, as they had done during the war, that it was their duty as citizens to participate in the national recovery.

Nonetheless, discontent grew amongst women about the long hours they spent standing in queues after the end of the war. In July 1945, two housewives from London, Irene Lovelock and Alfreda Landau, set up the

British Housewives' League (BHL) and collected 17,000 signatures from 'ordinary housewives' protesting about the prevalence of queues, which were then presented to parliament.[78] The BHL was at its most active during 1946 and 1947 when it became an outspoken critic of bread rationing and the Labour government's austerity programme.

The League organised public meetings and marches to protest against the continuing shortages. These events attracted considerable press attention, resulting in dramatic headlines such as 'British Housewives National Revolt Campaign'.[79] With an active membership of some 15,000 mainly middle-class women, public protests were organised in cities including Liverpool, Glasgow, Leeds and London.[80] However the BHL failed to attract a widespread membership or win political respect and was often viewed by contemporaries as a Tory front whose principal aim was to agitate against the Labour government.[81] James Hinton has, however, challenged this view and argued that the organisation remained non-partisan and

> represented a possibility that women would revolt against austerity in ways which would fundamentally challenge the constructive 'mend and make do' ethos which informed the role of the 'housewife' in 1940s Britain: but the possibility was never realized.[82]

One reason why the BHL failed to become an influential women's organisation was its inability to win the support of large mainstream women's groups. The MU, CWL, NCW, WI and TG did not endorse the League's campaign, objecting to its outspoken criticism of the government and more particularly to its militant tendencies. In August 1945, the NCW organised its own Anti-Queue Conference to discuss the problem of food and clothing queues. Just as concerned about the hardships endured by women due to the continuing shortages, the Council advocated co-operation with the authorities in making the best use of scarce resources rather than confrontation to overcome the difficulties housewives experienced.[83]

In February 1946 it was announced that supplies of bacon, poultry and eggs were to be cut. Five months later, bread was rationed for the first time, a clear sign that things would get worse before they got better. The BHL organised protests against the introduction of bread rationing and collected some 600,000 signatures objecting to the new restrictions.[84] Voluntary women's groups once again took a more conciliatory line and tried to explain to their members why such harsh measures were required to ensure that everyone got their fair share.

In the April 1946 edition of *The Mothers' Union Workers' Paper*, Rosamond Fisher gave guidance on the problem of food shortages. She highlighted the plight of the starving and homeless in Europe and reminded members that 'queues and shortages are trying and tiring, but what are they compared to the broken hearts of mothers and wives [in Europe].'[85] The TG and WI were also willing to support the Labour government's rationing policy and agreed that members of both organisations could volunteer to work as Food Leaders for the Ministry of Food, giving advice to housewives on how to make the best of their rations.[86]

In spite of this support for the government's policy of austerity, both the WI and TG were careful to avoid any accusation of political bias. The WI made it clear that although it was willing to assist with the implementation of bread rationing, it remained a non-political organisation.[87] Likewise, the TG issued a memorandum to all local guilds informing them that they could not pass resolutions on any controversial issue, including bread rationing. The National Executive Committee warned that in most cases political parties sponsored protests against bread rationing, most likely a reference to the activities of the BHL.[88]

It was hardly surprising, however, that some local guild members would wish to express their dissatisfaction at the continued cuts in the ration. One local member of the TG, Constance Hill, took it upon herself to go against the instructions of the National Executive and organised a housewives' protest in Liverpool. She told a meeting of 700 women that 'the smiling mother of yesterday is the bad-tempered mother of today … we are under-fed, under washed, and over-controlled.'[89]

Whilst individual members of mainstream organisations may have identified with the highly publicised protests of the BHL, most women accepted that rationing was the only equitable way to deal with food shortages. In August 1946, one month after bread rationing had been introduced, opinion polls showed that seventy per cent of housewives felt they could manage in spite of the ration cuts.[90] This meant that voluntary women's groups could continue to co-operate with the Labour government's programme of austerity in the knowledge that the majority of members supported this policy.

Calls upon housewives to once again exercise their duty as citizens came in 1947 when a coal shortage resulted in a national fuel economy drive. Voluntary women's organisations were approached by the authorities to assist in the campaign and following a request by Sir Stafford Cripps, President of the Board of Trade, the NCW and WI agreed to do their utmost to heighten public awareness about the need for food and fuel economies. Both groups worked with local authority recovery committees, set up to encourage all members of the community to produce more food and participate in salvage and fuel economy schemes set up by the government.[91]

Speaking in October 1947, Lady Albemarle, President of the WI, discussed ways in which institute members could respond to the government's 'call for good citizenship'.[92] It was decided to launch Operation Produce, a scheme similar to the wartime fruit-preservation project, which urged every WI member to produce an extra 10 lb of home grown food. Locally produced food would cut down on the demand for transport and fuel and ensure a good supply of fresh fruit and vegetables for the family. Any surplus produce was sold to the public at WI markets.[93]

The need to ration essential goods during a period of economic austerity was accepted by leading housewives organisations and they demonstrated their willingness to assist the government in the administration of food and fuel economy schemes on numerous occasions. In return for this co-operation, the leadership of the MU, CWL, NCW, WI and TG hoped that housewives would be treated fairly by the authorities. One outstanding grievance raised by women's organisations during this period was the fact that household linen, sheets and towels, could only be purchased with personal clothing coupons. This meant that housewives, whose primary responsibility was to look after the home, were invariably left with fewer clothing coupons than other members of the family.[94]

In an effort to resolve this apparent injustice, the MU appealed directly to Sir Stafford Cripps to end restrictions on the supply of sheets to housewives.[95] In spite of this formal request, no change in the existing rationing arrangements was immediately forthcoming. In April 1947 the WI National Executive sent a deputation to the Board of Trade to highlight the hardships endured by rural women 'owing to the shortages of bed linen and curtains, country shoes and wellingtons'.[96] Little progress was made in relation to the supply of shoes and boots but the June edition of *Home and Country* reported that women could now purchase blankets and sheets with separate coupons.[97] This was a small but nonetheless important victory for housewives during the difficult years of the late 1940s.

Women, including housewives and mothers, did benefit from the introduction of major social welfare reforms during the post-war years, many of which had been recommended in the Beveridge Report. These measures included the payment of family allowances to mothers, improved maternity benefits for working mothers and new and higher rates of benefit payments. The NHS, inaugurated in 1948, did much to enhance the quality of life for women during the post-war years. Moreover, new employment opportunities for women were created with the coming of state welfare. The expansion of education and health services created exciting and rewarding new career options for many women.

Yet in spite of all of these significant developments, the immediate post-war years continued to be a struggle for many housewives who had to manage with meagre rations, cope with poor housing conditions and learn to juggle paid work with domestic responsibilities. The failure of both the Labour government and private employers to introduce equal pay for women workers contributed to the fact that the majority of women workers continued to earn lower rates of pay than men. By the end of the 1940s, the promise made by the Minister for Reconstruction, Lord Woolton, of a 'fair deal' for women, remained unfulfilled.

The post-war years did, however, provide voluntary women's organisations with the opportunity to highlight once again the importance of active citizenship for women. Encouraging members to play their part in the rebuilding of the nation, the MU, CWL, NCW, WI and TG claimed a role for women as responsible members of the community whose input was essential if Britain was to recover. This role involved co-operating with the government in its national austerity programme and supporting measures such as rationing and fuel economy schemes. In return, mainstream women's groups insisted that the state had to consider the opinions of women when it came to plans for reconstruction.

To this end, voluntary women's groups were successful. They did succeed in influencing post-war housing policy and the government did acquiesce to their demands not to put undue pressure on mothers with young children to go out to work. Throughout the 1940s, government committees and royal commissions into a range of important topics including housing provision, social welfare reform and equal pay, had sought out the views of these organisations. In responding to their requests, middle-class women's groups ensured that housewives had a voice right at the heart of government and that their opinions influenced public policy. Having achieved this level of success during the 1940s, voluntary women's groups saw no reason not to continue with their work on behalf of women citizens in the decades that followed.

Notes

1   *National Conference of Women*, p. 6.
2   *Women in Council*, 41 (November 1944), p. 10.
3   WL, Pamphlet Collection, 'Extract from Megan Lloyd George's address to the National Conference of Women, September 1943', *National Conference of Women*, p. 38.
4   *NCW Handbook 1941–42* (1942), p. 64.
5   *Women in Council*, 41 (November 1943), p. 1.
6   *Home and Country*, 31:7 (July 1949), p. 143.
7   See Vincent, *Poor Citizens*, pp. 112–132.

8 See J. Finch and P. Summerfield, 'Social Reconstruction and the Emergence of Companionate Marriage, 1945–59', in D. Clark (ed.), *Marriage, Domestic Life and Social Change: Writings for Jacqueline Burgoyne (1944–88)* (London: Routledge, 1991), pp. 7–11.

9 MSH, Central Council Minutes, Vol. 11 (1937–42), 'Minutes of the Mothers' Union Central Council, December 1941', p. 345.

10 *The Mothers' Union Workers' Paper*, 354 (June 1943), p. 129.

11 *NCW Handbook 1941–42* (1942), p. 64.

12 By the end of 1943, the Ministry of Agriculture had set up nine committees to discuss war and post-war subjects. Membership of these committees was made up of seventy-eight men and four women. Of the forty-one committees set up by the Ministry of Food, only one committee included a woman representative while the Board of Education's five committees consisted of seventy-one men and seventeen women members. See M. Goldsmith, *Women and the Future* (London: Lindsay Drummond Ltd, 1946), p. 81.

13 Lewis, *Women in England 1870–1950*, p. 28 and J. Burnett, *A Social History of Housing 1815–1985* (London: Methuen, 1986), p. 243.

14 WL, 5/FWI/D/12/2, Box 138, NFWI Archive, 'Notes for VCOs on Rural Housing, 1938'.

15 See Roberts, *A Women's Place* and Vincent, *Poor Citizens*, pp. 87–89.

16 For a detailed discussion of the inter-war housing campaign see C. Beaumont, 'Where to Park the Pram? Voluntary Women's Organisations, Citizenship and the Campaign for Better Housing in England, 1928–1945', *Women's History Review* 22:1 (2013).

17 Elizabeth Denby was a key figure in the voluntary housing sector and one of a number of influential women involved in housing design and housing reform during the inter-war period. She also advised the WGPW on housing issues. See E. Darling, '"A Citizen As Well As a housewife": New Spaces of Domesticity in 1930s London', in H. Heynen and G. Baydar (eds), *Negotiating Domesticity: Spatial Productions of Gender in Modern Architecture* (London: Routledge, 2005), pp. 49–64.

18 *Co-operative News* (31 January 1925), p. 12, cited in G. Scott, '"Workshops Fit for Homeworkers": The Women's Co-operative Guild and Housing Reform in Mid-Twentieth Century Britain', in E. Darling and L. Whitworth (eds), *Women and the Making of Built Space in England 1870–1950* (Aldershot: Ashgate, 2007), p. 168.

19 In 1931 over two million women had been employed in domestic service but by the early 1950s this number had been reduced to 750,000. P. Summerfield, 'Women in Britain since 1945: Companionate Marriage and the Double Burden', in J. Obelkevich and P. Catterall (eds), *Understanding Post-war British Society* (London: Routledge, 1994), pp. 60–62.

20 These included: London Labour Party (Women's Committee), St Joan's Social and Political Alliance, Fabian Group, National Women Citizens Association, Women's National Liberal Federation, Royal Institute of British Architects (Women's Committee) and a number of London housing associations. For the full list see Public Record Office, London (hereafter PRO), HLG 36/3, 'Memorandum of the Women's Housing Conference' (n.d., c.1936).

21 *Ibid.*

22 *Ibid.*

23 *The Catholic Women's League Magazine*, 304 (February 1937), p. 16.

24 *The Catholic Women's League Magazine*, 309 (July 1937), p. 45.

25 Andrews, *The Acceptable Face of Feminism*, pp. 79–99.
26 WL, NFWI 5/FWI/D/1/2, Box 138, NFWI Archive, General Public Affairs, 'Quarterly Notes on Public Questions', June 1938.
27 Burnett, *A Social History of Housing*, p. 285.
28 BL, *Women's Housing and Planning Conference* (28 May 1942).
29 *The Mothers' Union Workers' Paper*, 354 (June 1943).
30 *Home and Country*, 26:9 (September 1944), p. 140.
31 Fifty-seven organisations in total gave evidence to the Committee. A. Ravetz, 'A View from the Interior', in J. Attfield and P. Kirkham (eds), *A View From the Interior: Feminism, Women and Design* (London: The Women's Press, 1989), p. 199. For an account of the evidence of working-class women's groups to the Design of Dwellings Committee see Scott, '"Workshops Fit for Homeworkers"'.
32 WL, WFM/D19/WM2/12/3/2, WGPW Archive, 'Planning and Equipment of the Post-War Home: Questionnaire' (1942).
33 *The Townswoman*, 11 (November 1943), p. 130
34 WL, 5/FWI/D/1/2/67, Box 144, NFWI Archive, 'Evidence for the Central Housing Advisory Committee's Sub-Committee on the Design of Dwellings' (reprinted January 1946).
35 *Ibid.*
36 *The Mothers' Union Workers' Paper*, 345 (June 1943), p. 136.
37 BL, Evidence No. 11, The Royal Commission on Population, 1944–49, 'The Mothers' Union written evidence to the Royal Commission on Population', March 1944.
38 'Design of Dwellings', Household Service League Supplement, *Women in Council*, 27 (July 1942).
39 *Ibid.*, p. 3.
40 'The Report of the Women's Advisory Housing Council Questionnaire', *The Mothers' Union Workers' Paper*, 354 (June 1943), p. 136.
41 *The Townswoman*, 10 (June 1943), p. 130.
42 *Ibid.*
43 *The Mothers' Union Journal*, 157 (August 1934), p. 20.
44 *Design of Dwellings: Report of Central Housing Advisory Committee* (London: HMSO, 1944).
45 Burnett, *A Social History of Housing*, p. 298.
46 A. Ravetz, 'Housing the People', in J. Fyrth (ed.), *Labour's Promised Land? Culture and Society in Labour Britain 1945–51* (London: Lawrence and Wishart, 1995), p. 155.
47 *Design of Dwellings*, p. 14.
48 John Burnett writes that in the immediate post-war years official *Housing Manuals* 'accepted and even exceeded the Dudley recommendations'. However by the end of the 1940s growing economic pressures resulted in a relaxation of standards with room sizes, the number of bedrooms and additional WCs falling victim to the cuts. See Burnett, *A Social History of Housing*, pp. 297–300.
49 *Ibid.* p. 300.
50 BL, The Royal Commission on Population, 1944–49, 'NCW oral evidence to the Royal Commission on Population', 29 September 1944.
51 BL, The Royal Commission on Population, 1944–49, 'The Standing Joint Committee of Working Women's Organisations oral evidence to the Royal Commission on Population', 16 March 1945.
52 Riley, 'Some Peculiarities of Social Policy', p. 268.

53 Lewis, *Women in Britain since 1945*, p. 24.
54 P. Jephcott, *Rising Twenty: Notes on Some Ordinary Girls* (London: Faber and Faber, 1948), cited in C. Langhamer, 'The Meanings of Home in Postwar Britain', *Journal of Contemporary History*, 40:2 (2005), p. 360.
55 G. Thomas, *Women and Industry: An Inquiry into the Problem of Recruiting Women to Industry Carried Out for the Ministry of Labour and National Service* (1943) cited in P. Summerfield, 'Women, War and Social Change', p. 108.
56 See Smith, 'The Effect of the War on the Status of Women', pp. 220–221.
57 *Ibid.*, p. 107.
58 BL, The Royal Commission on Population, 1944–49, 'The Mothers' Union oral evidence to the Royal Commission on Population', March 1944. Penny Summerfield has also suggested that the wartime experience of work 'was regarded by many participants as a key phase in terms of personal change and development'. Summerfield, 'Women, War and Social Change', p. 96.
59 BL, The Royal Commission on Population, 1944–49, 'The Mothers' Union oral evidence to the Royal Commission on Population', 13 October 1944.
60 'Mothers in Jobs', *Mothers in Council* (March 1947), p. 46.
61 BL, The Royal Commission on Population, 1944–49, 'NCW oral evidence to the Royal Commission on Population', 29 September 1944.
62 Riley, 'Some Peculiarities of Social Policy', p. 260.
63 For a detailed breakdown of women's participation in the post-war workforce see Summerfield, 'Women, War and Social Change', pp. 98–99.
64 In 1931 sixteen per cent of female employees were married. This figure rose to forty-three per cent in 1943 at the height of wartime recruitment but fell again to forty per cent in 1947. By 1951 forty-three per cent of women workers were married. *Ibid.*, p. 100.
65 Pugh, *Women and the Women's Movement*, p. 287.
66 *Women in Council*, 20:11 (November 1947), p. 9.
67 *NCW Handbook 1948–49* (1949), p. 67.
68 *The Catholic Women's League Magazine*, 437 (August 1948), p. 4.
69 *The Mothers' Union Workers' Paper*, 408 (January 1948), p. 3.
70 *Ibid.*
71 *Women in Council*, 20:11 (November 1947), p. 9.
72 Between 1936 and 1939 the average number of divorce petitions filed each year was 7,500. This yearly average increased to 39,000 between 1945 and 1948. Pugh, *Women and the Women's Movement*, p. 270.
73 *Home and Country*, 26:1 (January 1944), p. 3.
74 The WI participated in the government's Food Advice Campaign providing nutritional information to women at travelling exhibitions and domestic science demonstrations.
75 I. Zweiniger-Bargielowska, 'Bread Rationing in Britain, July 1946–July 1948', *Twentieth Century British History*, 4:1 (1993).
76 I. Zweiniger-Bargielowska, 'Rationing, Austerity and the Conservative Party Recovery after 1945', *Historical Journal*, 37:1 (1994).
77 I. Zweiniger-Bargielowska, *Austerity in Britain: Rationing, Controls and Consumption, 1939–1955* (Oxford: Oxford University Press, 2000), p. 99.
78 J. Hinton, 'Militant Housewives: The British Housewives' League and the Attlee Government', *History Workshop Journal*, 38 (1994), p. 132 and Campbell, *The Iron Ladies*, p. 74.

79 *Daily Mail* (15 February 1946).

80 Hinton, 'Militant Housewives', p. 145.

81 E. Wilson, *Only Halfway to Paradise: Women in Post-war Britain: 1945–1968* (London: Tavistock, 1980) and Campbell, *Iron Ladies*.

82 Hinton, 'Militant Housewives', p. 150.

83 *NCW Annual Report 1946* (1946), p. 6. On queuing see also Zweiniger-Bargielowska, *Austerity in Britain*, pp. 117–119.

84 Hinton, 'Militant Housewives', p. 135.

85 *The Mothers' Union Workers' Paper*, 388 (April 1946), p. 97.

86 *National Union of Townswomen's Guilds Annual Report 1946* (1946), p. 36.

87 *Home and Country*, 28:8 (August 1947), p. 121.

88 *National Union of Townswomen's Guilds Annual Report 1946* (1946), p. 36.

89 Cited in Hinton, 'Militant Housewives', p. 133.

90 Polls of July and August 1946 cited in J. Hinton, 'Women and the Labour vote, 1945–50', *Labour History Review*, 57:3 (1992), p. 61.

91 *Home and Country*, 20:9 (September 1948), p. 154.

92 *Home and Country*, 29:11 (November 1947), p. 191.

93 *Home and Country*, 31:3 (March 1949), p. 103.

94 During the war, the WCG and the Labour Party Women Sections had protested to the government about this anomaly but were unable to bring about any change in procedure.

95 *The Mothers' Union Workers' Paper*, 397 (January 1947), p. 6.

96 *Home and Country*, 29:5 (May 1947), p. 89.

97 *Home and Country*, 29:6 (June 1947), p. 101.

Domesticity, modernity and women's rights: voluntary women's organisations and the women's movement 1950–64

What is a wife? A woman who sets jam to jell, children to rights and her hair for a Saturday night out ... why does she do it? Because somebody thinks she's wonderful-and she wants to go on keeping it that way. (*Woman*, 27 April 1963)

The image of the 'ideal woman' flashed on all sides of Magazines ... is of a pretty creature whose highest function is to pamper her skin and create the 'house beautiful' ... the assumption [is] that the frilly little woman, pottering at home, is serving mankind to the [best of her ability]. (*The Townswoman*, February 1963)

The 1950s and early 1960s have often been portrayed as a time when women succumbed to the prevailing ideology of domesticity, spurred on by post-war affluence, the rise of mass consumption and fears that mothers going out to work would give rise to a generation of juvenile delinquents.[1] Lynne Segal writes that the 1950s were represented by a 'tense domesticity and anxious conformity ... when a seemingly endless and all embracing consensus held sway throughout almost every Western nation'.[2] However, as historians engage in a closer examination of women's lives during these years a disconnect begins to emerge between the idealised domesticity so often presented in women's magazines and popular culture and the reality of women's lives in mid-twentieth century Britain.[3]

The magazine image of the 'modern wife', devoted to her home and family, working happily in her labour-saving kitchen, is undermined by the increasing numbers of married women going out to work, the rise in the divorce rate and the emergence of the housewife as a consumer and the guardian of consumer interests.[4] Rather than representing a period of consensus, the 1950s and early 1960s instead signified a time of confusion, uncertainty and change with regard to the role of women in post-war society. As Conekin, Mort and Waters have written of the 1950s, 'the modern in this period was a hybrid affair, assembled out of tales about the past as well as narratives of the future'.[5]

The MU, CWL, NCW, WI and TG were at the heart of this debate about the future role of women. It is crucial, however, to recognise that their desire to replace the image of the 'frilly little women' with an altogether more positive representation of the modern housewife as a good and active citizen represents continuity, not change. This chapter will demonstrate that all five women's organisations, having success-fully campaigned on behalf of wives and mothers throughout the 1930s and 1940s, continued to represent the interests of their members in the decades that followed. Their agency and activism succeeded in drawing public and political attention to a wide range of old and new issues impacting on women's lives in the 1950s and early 1960s. Moreover, these organisations played a key role in articulating the concerns and anxieties of housewives as they adapted to their changing role in British society.

Housewives and citizens: voluntary women's organisations and the role of women in the post-war years

Despite assumptions that the 1950s and early 1960s were a time when the women's movement went into decline, housewives' associations continued to attract new members and remained popular, vibrant and influential organisations throughout these years. In 1954 WI membership peaked at 467,000 women in 8,178 institutes. The same year, membership of the MU for England, Wales, Scotland and Ireland was given as 481,623 women in 11,409 branches. The TG continued to expand and by 1954 had set up 1,634 guilds resulting in an approximate national membership of 131,000 women. Membership of the CWL remained fairly constant throughout the 1950s with a yearly average of 22,000 women. In 1955 an exact figure of 22,186 members was recorded. Similarly the NCW maintained its affiliated membership during these years and in 1952 confirmed that it had 89 branches and 97 affiliated societies.[6]

One of the reasons why these organisations remained popular was their continued commitment to offer housewives a wide variety of educa-tional, social and leisure activities. So important was this aspect of their work that in 1950 the MU decided to broaden its local branch activity to include 'drama, book clubs and talks on national and international affairs as well religious education in an effort to appeal to the wives of professional men', and to ensure that it could compete with the growing popularity of the WI and TG.[7]

In addition to providing women with activities outside the home and supporting their work within it, the MU, CWL, NCW, WI and TG also continued to speak out on behalf of housewives and mothers on local and national issues and remained dedicated to encouraging women to be active citizens who participated fully in post-war society. These goals were expressed by Lady Brunner, Chairman of the WI, at its AGM in May 1952. She told the thousands of rural housewives gathered that

> Our Institute membership is a two-way traffic. It brings us out from our homes but it should send us back with enhanced skill in the crafts and duties that are needed to make a home, with a kindlier and more understanding approach to our neighbour, with minds open to new ideas and a wider knowledge of our heritage, and a deeper sense of responsibility as citizens.[8]

Similarly, the MU reminded its members in 1964, especially those with young children, that they must keep in touch with the world outside their homes, take up voluntary work and attend evening classes, all to ensure that they are not regarded primarily as housewives but also as valued members of society.[9]

The representation of the modern housewife as an intelligent, responsible and valued member of society was a key objective shared by all five voluntary women's organisations throughout the 1950s and early 1960s. As a result the MU, CWL, NCW, WI and TG firmly rejected the image of the 'perfect housewife' so prevalent in women's magazines such as *Woman* and *Woman's Own*. Interestingly it was the MU, arguably the group with the most traditional views on domesticity, that launched an outspoken attack on this idealised image of the housewife. In its journal, *MU News*, it condemned magazines which suggested that the ultimate status symbol for women was 'still a man', and that women aspired only to marriage so that they could be the happy wife with 'radiant skin and a larder filled with home-baked bread'. This image of the 'perfect wife' did a great disservice to women in the post-war period and readers were warned not to make an 'idol out of domesticity'.[10]

It is evident that during these years a new discourse emerged amongst voluntary women's organisations with regard to the 'true' nature of domesticity and the role of housewives in the post-war years. This debate reveals the tension which existed between the popular image of the modern housewife, blissfully immersed in her family life, smiling happily from the pages of women's weekly magazines, and the efforts of voluntary women's groups to show that domesticity for women meant more than total devotion to home and family.

For voluntary women's organisations being a housewife also meant being a good citizen. Through their domestic role women had the opportunity to make a valuable contribution to public life. Modern women, as experts in domesticity, had the experience and knowledge to engage in politics, become involved in community issues, have an opinion on consumer standards and have the right to comment on the delivery of public services.

As a result, understandings of housewifery in the 1950s and 1960s may not be as straightforward as previously assumed. The time has come to challenge the portrayal of housewives 'as bored, isolated, exploited victims forced into a narrow role under patriarchy'.[11] Instead, as Ina Zweiniger-Bargielowska writes of domesticity in the 1950s, 'the picture was certainly more complex, employment did not necessarily result in female liberation or greater equality, and full-time housewifery was a locus of female power both within the family and in wider society'.[12]

The popularity of women's magazines at this time, *Woman* for example had a weekly circulation of almost 3.5 million in the late 1950s, meant that voluntary women's groups had to work hard to convince wives and mothers that domesticity provided a power base for female activism.[13] In order to ensure that members were aware of their duty as citizens, all five organisations continued to offer educational opportunities to women, which included training in democratic processes, public speaking as well as short courses and lectures on a wide variety of themes. The WI opened Denman College, a residential college for members, in 1948 and throughout the 1950s and 1960s it offered practical and educational courses to members.[14]

Reflecting on the role and status of women in post-war society was another key preoccupation. In 1953 the TG organised a social studies conference on the theme of 'The Woman Citizen in a Changing World'. The conference, which was heavily oversubscribed, focused on the achievements of women citizens and the legal position of women. Following the conference, guilds were encouraged to study these subjects at local meetings.[15] In September 1960 the North Surrey Federation of the TG held a residential course at Ruskin College Oxford, on the 'Status of Women', run by the Workers' Educational Association. Themes explored during the three-day course included women in industry, women and the family, and women and public life, and it was reported that 'within an hour of arrival at the college the transformation from housewife to student was complete'.[16]

A survey of annual reports throughout these years reveals that all five organisations were discussing and researching a wide diversity of topical issues ranging from road safety, anti-litter campaigns, nuclear power and weapons testing, the peace movement, air pollution, prostitution and mental health services, to name but a few. Each year AGMs were held (often in prestigious locations such as the Royal Albert Hall or the Royal Festival Hall) where resolutions were passed reflecting the concerns of the organisation and follow-up action taken through letter-writing campaigns, deputations to parliament and surveys carried out by individual organisations on public services in their local areas. As WI members were reminded in 1954, 'the WI gives us training in democratic citizenship and this great Annual Meeting is our yearly inspiration'.[17]

In 1953 the TG announced its intention to become more outspoken on public questions when it passed by overwhelming majority two resolutions: the first allowing the movement to express its views on national affairs and the second giving mandatory powers to the Executive Committee to lobby government departments and other public bodies on matters subject to resolutions.[18] This change in policy indicated that the TG, along with the MU, CWL, NCW and WI, clearly envisaged a dynamic role in public life during the 1950s and 1960s. Such a role was deemed essential to ensure that the voices and opinions of women were made known at a time when they continued to be under-represented in public life.[19] In 1961 members of the TG were reminded of 'the good that can accrue to the population as a whole when a large body of women, after informed debate, act in unison and make their composite voice heard in the land'.[20]

It would appear that the views of voluntary women's groups were valued throughout the 1950s and early 1960s. On numerous occasions they were invited to submit evidence to governmental enquires and royal commissions. For example, the NCW and MU provided evidence to the 1951 Royal Commission on Marriage and Divorce. The NCW submitted evidence to the Committee of Enquiry on Homosexual Offences and Prostitution, which reported in 1957. In 1956 the WI and MU contributed to the Ministry of Health's inquiry into the welfare of children in hospital. In 1959 the MU was again invited to submit evidence to the government's Departmental Committee on Artificial Insemination.

Voluntary women's organisations also organised their own confer-ences and investigations into issues of national concern and invited government representatives to attend. For example, in November 1950 the WI held a conference on 'Crime and Responsibility' at which the Home Secretary gave the keynote address.[21] This desire on the part of the government to listen to the views of housewives may be explained by Conservative Party policy during the 1950s, which set out to appeal directly to women voters. As Ina Zweiniger-Bargielowska suggests, 'the

Conservative Party made a considerable effort to win over female support both in terms of organisation and policy.[22] Many issues of concern to voluntary women's groups, for example equal pay, consumer standards and women's position within the welfare state, were amongst those tackled by Conservative governments throughout the decade.

The activities of the MU, CWL, NCW, WI and TG in providing educational opportunities and lobbying on public questions opened up to women a wide range of activities and pastimes which extended well beyond 'the kitchen sink'. Persuading housewives that they had choices on how to spend their time, they also encouraged members to take up voluntary work within their local communities. Volunteering had been a strong tradition within each organisation for many years and one that had been strengthened by their involvement with the WVS in the war years.

During the 1950s and early 1960s these groups reported that members were active in a wide variety of voluntary work, whether it be taking up positions as local councillors or working with charitable organisations. For example, members of the MU and CWL were involved in providing support and advice for foreign girls arriving in London looking for work. In 1958 a kiosk was set up at Victoria Station so that the girls could register for assistance on arrival.[23] Other forms of voluntary action included visiting old people, befriending mental health patients and raising money for local services such as 'meals on wheels'. In 1953 the MU announced that members in Liverpool were being recruited by hospitals as 'baby cuddlers' to provide comfort to sick and premature babies.[24]

It is clear therefore that through all of their activities voluntary women's organisations sought tirelessly to demonstrate that domesticity should not result in women being isolated in their own homes, concerned only with the welfare of their husbands and children. Instead voluntary women's groups rejected this 'old-fashioned' version of domesticity and envisaged their role as facilitators in encouraging women to participate fully in local and national affairs. This was a much more modern interpretation of domesticity for women in the post-war years and one which it was hoped would empower women rather than limiting their lives to home and family. This view was reiterated at the 1962 AGM of the WI when members were told that 'the woman of today wants to be of use in the world but she does not know how to set about it alone. We can offer her the machinery.'[25]

Housewives and workers: voluntary women's organisations
and attitudes to working mothers in the post-war years

There is no doubt that the MU, CWL, NCW and WI were keen to
encourage members to get involved in activities outside their homes. But
when it came to paid work for mothers they continued to express reservations, just as they had done throughout the 1940s. After the war an
increasing number of wives and mothers chose to engage in paid work
and in doing so they too challenged traditional constructions of domesticity.[26] Dolly Smith Wilson has argued that working mothers tried to
establish a 'new image of motherhood by citing the benefits employment
provided their families'. She goes on to argue that 'in this new definition,
a good mother was not solely one who stayed at the beck and call of her
family, but one who nurtured their self-reliance and independence by
not being constantly available, as well as providing goods and pleasures
otherwise out of reach of the family.'[27]

Whilst voluntary women's organisations wholeheartedly supported
the view that housewives should not be at the 'beck and call' of their
families, they did not believe that mothers with young children should
go out to work. As the previous chapter has indicated, the increasing
numbers of married women and mothers engaging in paid work in the
1940s had led the MU, CWL and NCW to call on the government to
exclude mothers with young children from all recruitment drives. These
groups recognised the valuable contribution that middle-class women in
the professions could make to the workforce but urged married women
to interrupt their careers when their children were young and to only
consider returning to work when their children were of school age.

This acceptance of a 'dual role' for women in the 1940s illustrates that
voluntary women's organisations were grappling with the issue of how to
combine paid work with family life a decade before the publication of the
seminal text *Women's Two Roles: Home and Work*, published in 1956 by
Alva Myrdal and Viola Klein.[28] Like voluntary women's groups, Myrdal
and Klein supported the concept of married women working, as long as
the welfare of the family was not compromised. The easiest way to achieve
this balance was for wives and mothers to return to the workforce once
their children were of school age and for them to seek part-time work.
This influential report was published at a time when the increase in the
number of part-time positions available reflected the demand for this
type of work and the reality that married women and mothers did want
to work outside the home.[29]

As the numbers of wives and mothers going out to work expanded, the difficulties of managing this 'dual role' and the impact it would have on family life became an issue of concern. In 1956 the NCW, through its Public Health and Child Welfare Sectional Committee, sent out a questionnaire to its branches in sixty-five towns and districts to gather information on 'the effects on the family of the employment of married women with children'.[30] Reporting on the findings of the survey in April 1957 it was confirmed that replies were received from all over the country and that branches had consulted experts in their local areas including probation officers, women teachers, health visitors and GPs.

The survey revealed that the main motive for married women working was economic, due to the 'rising cost of living, the higher standards expected in the home today and the higher rents of modern local authority housing'. The ability to purchase items such as 'good clothes for the family, toys for the children and television were mentioned in nearly every reply'. However, the report also noted that another frequently mentioned factor was 'the desire of many married women for some form of economic independence, and this must not be underestimated'.[31] This finding echoed the views expressed by the MU and NCW to the Royal Commission on Population, where they acknowledged that some women would want to earn their own living through paid employment.

In terms of the social impact of working mothers on family life the responses to the NCW survey were varied. In cases where the mother had good organising abilities, a co-operative husband and a stable marriage, 'no apparent ill-effects were felt'. Overall it was generally agreed that where mothers worked 'the home was not less well kept, nor were meals neglected or children less clean' and when suitable child-care arrangements were made by the mother 'the children did not appear to suffer'.[32]

Nonetheless concern was expressed in most replies as to the effect of 'deprivation of a mother's care on very young children' and that mothers of children under three years of age should only take part-time work'. In addition to this stipulation it was noted that there was general agreement that 'if her working hours correspond to the children's school hours there are no ill-effects' and there was 'an overwhelming consensus of opinion that there had been no increase in juvenile delinquency due to mothers taking up employment'.[33] This view supported research carried out in the late 1940s by the WGPW, which had concluded that 'there was no conclusive evidence that this [mothers working] was a cause of neglect'.[34]

To argue that working mothers did not necessarily contribute to the problem of juvenile delinquency was a bold statement to make in the 1950s. As Smith Wilson has shown, it was common at this time for local magistrates, police officers and social workers to claim that working mothers contributed to the problem of youth crime.[35] Moreover the views of David Winnicott and John Bowlby on the link between maternal deprivation and delinquency were extremely influential during these years and resulted in the common perception that when young people engaged in crime the working mother was to blame.[36]

The results of this NCW survey are important not only for presenting a more positive perception of working mothers but also for identifying the difficulties that working mothers experienced as they adapted to their 'dual role' in ever greater numbers. The findings of the survey highlighted the lack of official support on the part of government and local authorities for mothers in employment. The lack of publicly subsidised nurseries was condemned and it was reported that no plans were in place for future support. The overall conclusion was that, in the eyes of the state, balancing domestic responsibilities and employment was the responsibility of the individual, in this case the mother.[37]

One of the specific problems faced by working mothers identified in the survey was finding someone to care for their children after school and during school holidays. What the NCW hoped was that industry would adjust to the needs of working mothers, for example allowing women to work evening shifts when their husbands had returned home from work. Accepting that this might prove difficult it was also argued that local councils should provide more after-school care and holiday clubs for the children of working mothers.[38]

The NCW was not the only voluntary women's organisation concerned about the impact of the 'dual role' for housewives. In an article entitled 'Mothers at Work', published in September 1957 in *Home and Country*, the WI acknowledged that many married women now went out to work and that the modern woman had the right to 'find fulfilment in work profitable both to herself, her family and to the community'.[39] The difficulties faced by mothers working had to be acknowledged, for example what to do when children were ill, required after-school care or care during school holidays.

The article went on to suggest that women's organisations such as the WI should bring pressure to bear on parliament, local authorities and business to create 'married women' jobs allowing mothers to fit their work around school hours.[40] In highlighting this issue the National Executive of the WI was responding to requests from its own members. In a letter sent by the Kemsing institute to the WI Central Secretary in April 1957, it was suggested that the organisation should call on employers to permit women workers the flexibility to collect their children from school. Employers should also consider allowing mothers to stay at home when children were ill so as to avoid sick children being sent to school. The institute argued that it was important for the WI to take a stand on such matters as this would demonstrate that members were 'not old fogeys living in the past' but women who were trying to deal with 'a problem of modern times'.[41]

Similarly the TG, instead of condemning mothers for going out to work, supported the introduction of new initiatives to assist working mothers. Readers of *The Townswoman* were told in September 1963 that 'some may disapprove of working mothers but it is going to happen so we need to plan for it.' Amongst the ideas put forward to support working mothers were day nurseries, summer camps, staggered school holidays and refresher courses facilitating the entry of older married women into the professions.[42] The TG, like the MU and NCW, wished to encourage middle-class, well-educated women back into the workplace, ideally when their children had reached school age. In 1962 members were asked to consider

> how little encouragement there is for the married woman who wants to go and do a job of work…the wastage of brain and talent must be considerable when they take on work far below their capacity, as they usually do.[43]

The debate surrounding the advantages and dangers of mothers working raged on throughout the 1950s and early 1960s. What was clear however was the fact that ever increasing numbers of wives and mothers were choosing to go out to work and that the impact of this 'dual role' on traditional notions of domesticity would be long-lasting.[44] In December 1957 the MU published in its journal *Home and Family* an article entitled 'A Mothers' Place'. The article, by Brenda Brooke, was part of a series of 'challenging articles' and sought to inform readers about the impact paid work could have on their family life. Women contemplating employment were advised to think how they would feel about someone else caring for their children. They were warned 'if you hand them to someone else, you are throwing away one of the most precious gifts you will ever have bestowed on you.'[45]

What is most striking about this article is the response it received from MU members. In the June 1958 edition of *Home and Family*, letters objecting to the article were published and the editor of the journal felt compelled to clarify that Brooke's argument was directed 'against the full-time employment of mothers with young children'.[46] Two of the three letters published attested to the value and satisfaction that the authors felt in undertaking part-time work and the third letter, from a full-time mother, stated that 'far from scorning many of the women who do this [engage in paid work], I frankly admire many of them.'[47]

By the early 1960s the MU appears to have accepted that mothers would work outside the home but continued to argue that such arrangements must always take into consideration the needs of young children. Responding to a 1964 campaign by the government to encourage more married women to return to the teaching profession, the Union accepted that many married women 'can return to teaching, especially part-time, without jeopardising their family ... [but] the needs of the family should always come first.'[48]

Similarly, the CWL recognised that some mothers would work outside the home, but hoped mothers with young children would wait until their children were older before doing so. In 1953 the League's Salford branch proposed to the National Council that the organisation should explore the possibility of campaigning for more financial help to be made available to young mothers. This, it was, argued may dissuade them from going out to work. A heated debate ensued with some members pointing out that economic pressures were not the only reason why mothers engaged in paid work. Others suggested that whatever the financial situation, mothers had a moral responsibility to look after their own children and 'people could not be made moral by Acts of Parliament'. It was finally agreed that the League should instead consider any 'educative possibilities' to encourage mothers of young children to stay at home, and the resolution was referred back to branches for further discussion.[49]

The fact that mainstream women's organisations acknowledged that mothers would work outside the home, and at times even encouraged well-qualified women to do this as long as their children were of school age, was a radical challenge to the popular image of the 1950s and 1960s housewife. More pragmatic than women's magazines, organisations like the MU, CWL, NCW, WI and TG accepted the reality that increasing numbers of housewives and mothers would go out to work. Rather than condemning these women as 'bad mothers', voluntary women's organisations became increasingly concerned about the difficulties women would encounter when trying to balance paid work with motherhood. As a result they advocated on behalf of those struggling to adapt to this 'dual role'. In doing so they demonstrated that domesticity for women in the 1950s and 1960s could be reconstructed to incorporate the good wife, mother, citizen and worker.

Housewives and women's rights: voluntary women's organisations, female agency and the women's movement

Debates about the vigour of the feminist movement during the 1950s and early 1960s have preoccupied historians for a number of years.[50] These decades have traditionally been viewed as a time when feminist pressure groups went into decline, unable to challenge the prevailing ideology of domesticity. In addition the introduction of the welfare state had ushered in many of the social welfare reforms demanded by women's groups during the 1930s and 1940s, leaving feminist groups with difficult decisions to make about their future role.

It has also been suggested that the emergence of the WLM in the late 1960s and early 1970s contributed to the perception that the previous two decades represented years of inactivity within the women's movement. Joyce Freeguard has written that for activists involved in second-wave feminism, 'women of the 1950s were seen to stand outside feminist history, except as examples of the oppression that the 1960s feminists sought to eradicate.'[51]

New research into female activism in the 1950s and early 1960s has now extended beyond the study of post-suffrage feminist societies to include a more diverse range of women's organisations. For example, Freeguard has explored the role of a number of women's groups, including the Married Women's Association (MWA), the WGPW, the Council of Married Women (CMW) and the British Federation of University Women (BFUW), in feminist campaigns of the 1950s.[52] Like Freeguard, Linda Perriton has argued that the British Federation of Business and Professional Women continued to campaign on issues of women's equality in the post-war years.[53] Samantha Clements, in her work on women's organisations in Nottingham, also highlights the continued agency and dynamism of women in the city at this time.[54]

This chapter has already illustrated how the MU, CWL, NCW, WI and TG continued to speak out on behalf of housewives and mothers during the 1950s and early 1960s, and yet their activities have often been ignored or underestimated by historians. Margaret Andrews, in her history of the WI movement, identifies a withdrawal from public debate by the WI during these years and asks in the final chapter of her book 'Can Flower Arranging Be Feminist?'[55] Similarly Martin Pugh, writing about the demise of feminism in the 1950s, states that the TG in the 1950s had 'become a conventional women's organisation.'[56]

What the records of mainstream voluntary women's groups reveal, however, is the vast array of campaigns and causes these groups engaged with throughout these years. This engagement in public life continued despite the fact that all five remained steadfast in their desire to be portrayed as non-feminist and non-party-political. As a result they continued to avoid any taint of affiliation with the three main political parties and were quick to deny any feminist tendencies. For example, in 1949 the WI, giving evidence to William Beveridge's enquiry into voluntary action, stated that the organisation was 'not a feminist body'.[57] Nevertheless they continued to champion causes relevant to the lives of housewives and mothers and to assert the citizenship rights of women. Their principal motive in carrying on with this work was to enhance the lives of women and to safeguard the stability of family life.

It is impossible to do justice here to all of the campaign work undertaken by voluntary women's organisations during the 1950s and early 1960s.[58] Instead an overview of a number of specific campaigns will be provided to illustrate the continued activism and agency on the part of the MU, CWL, NCW, WI and TG. These are: the on-going debate with regard to the liberalisation of divorce, the demand that the earnings' limit placed on widows' allowances be revised, the right of parents to visit their children in hospital and the removal of turnstiles from public lavatories.

Divorce and divorce law reform remained controversial topics amongst voluntary women's organisations during the 1950s and early 1960s. The number of divorce petitions peaked at the end of the war in 1946 at 41,704 and rose to 137,400 during the years 1956 to 1960.[59] This rise can be attributed to the 1949 extension of Legal Aid to include divorce cases and the growing acceptability of divorce within British society. However, as Claire Langhamer suggests, access to divorce remained restricted throughout these years, as it was founded on the notion of matrimonial offence.[60] It was not until the passing of the Divorce Law Reform Act 1969 that the principle of 'no fault' divorce was introduced into British law.

The question of divorce law reform emerged after the war in 1951 when Eirene White MP introduced a Private Members Bill to the House of Commons. Her bill proposed that a marriage could be dissolved if the couple had lived apart for seven years and there was no prospect of reconciliation. In response to the bill, the Labour government announced its intention to set up a new Royal Commission on Marriage and Divorce.[61] This move was welcomed by the NCW who, with a number of other women's groups including the MWA, NWCA and the BFUW,[62] had been lobbying the government since 1949 to investigate the 'present high rate of broken marriages and divorce'.[63]

As Joyce Freeguard has argued, women's organisations, both feminist and mainstream, worked together to ensure that the views of women on divorce were presented to the Royal Commission. The NCW and MU, in addition to eleven other women's groups including the MWA, the YWCA and the WCG, submitted memorandums.[64] In its evidence the NCW made clear that representing ninety-seven affiliated societies, including church groups (MU and CWL), and a number of the 'more extreme feminist societies', it could not present a united front on the subject of divorce. The Council instead reiterated that its policy had always been to promote 'the welfare and stability of the family and the encouragement of the highest public and private morality for both sexes'.[65]

Amongst the recommendations put forward by the NCW to the Commission was the need to establish equality within the law. To this end, female co-respondents in divorce cases should be liable to costs and damages in the same way as male co-respondents. The Council also raised the important issue of financial arrangements between husbands and wives and urged that wives should be 'entitled to a portion of the joint income of husband and wife for her own separate use'.[66]

This demand reflected the organisation's belief that the financial dependency of wives on their husbands left women vulnerable and undermined the 'mutual respect' necessary for a successful marriage. The NCW also asked the Commission to consider the plight of mothers and children when a husband left and then sold the family home or where a wife was driven to leave her husband due to his bad behaviour. In both cases the wife and children would become homeless.[67] This concern with regard to the financial position of women in marriage was echoed in the evidence given by a number of other women's groups, for example the MWA, CMW and the WCG.[68]

The Royal Commission reported in 1956 and supported the view that marriage should be seen as a joint partnership between husband and wife. It fell short of recommending that wives should have a legal right to a portion of her husband's income. In response the NCW announced that it regretted 'that so few constructive proposals were put forward to provide practical means to ensure a sound economic basis for this partnership'.[69] Overall the Commission's desire to strengthen the principle of marriage as a lifelong commitment 'led it ultimately to recommend no significant change in the existing divorce laws'.[70]

The MU was also invited to contribute to the Commission and did so in May 1952. In its submission the Union asserted that 'marriage is a relationship that can only be severed by death' and that the current rise in the divorce rate had 'minimised the importance of family as the natural unit of society'.[71] Cordelia Moyse writes that the Commission was unconvinced by the evidence put forward by the MU on the grounds that it was 'of little practical use'.[72] The Union's refusal to recognise that divorce might be appropriate in some cases and its failure to provide statistics to prove that the children of divorced parents suffered disproportionally, did much to undermine its position.[73]

By the early 1950s it would appear that the uncompromising stance taken on divorce by the MU and its refusal to allow divorced women to become members had left it 'out of step' with wider public opinion. The leadership of the Union was aware of this fact and increasingly found it necessary to publicly defend its position on divorce. In 1950 Mrs Remson Ward, the Union's Central Secretary, explained to members that divorced women, even if they were the 'innocent' party, could not join as 'no one who has been party to divorce can promise to uphold marriage as a lifelong relationship'.[74]

The Union maintained its hardline approach to divorce throughout the 1950s and early 1960s despite ever-increasing divorce rates and the 'growing assumption within the Church that modern society was inherently secular and that the Church could not expect social policy formation to be grounded in terms of traditional Christian morality'.[75] In 1961 the Union once again called on members to oppose the Matrimonial Causes (Breakdown of Marriages) Bill, as this would lead to 'no fault' divorce.[76] However, by 1964 the realisation that such intransigence could threaten its future success led the Union to advise members that 'we must change our public image from the present one of the "anti-divorce" lot ... to an image of Christian women in action'.[77] As a result of these concerns the Union embarked on a major reassessment of its 'three objects' in 1969 and three years later divorced women were finally admitted as members.[78]

In keeping with Catholic social teaching, the CWL maintained its position in opposing divorce throughout the 1950s and early 1960s. Although not called upon to give evidence to the Royal Commission, the League confirmed that it would 'work even further in its endeavours to safeguard the sanctity of marriage and family life' and that members 'can all fulfil their sacred role as upholders of the Catholic home and family'.[79] In light of the number of marriages ending in divorce, the League suggested ways to help and support couples whose marriages might be in trouble. One example given was the setting up of parochial babysitting schemes to allow couples to spend more time together. The League also supported the greater availability of conciliation services for married couples. It would appear that the CWL took a more pragmatic approach to divorce than the MU. In 1951 it stated that 'we shall not object to an improvement in the "machinery" of Divorce – if the evil institution must exist, nothing is to be gained by its working inefficiently and inhumanly, as it often does today'.[80]

The WI and TG did not speak out on divorce during these years on the grounds that it was a sectarian issue. However both groups shared the concerns expressed by the NCW and other women's groups with regard to the financial position of wives and mothers. Despite having welcomed the introduction of the welfare state, voluntary women's groups recognised that they needed to monitor all legislative matters with regard to women's pension rights, income tax allowances, the financial entitlements of divorced women and widows' pensions. Involvement in such campaigns was justified on the grounds that women as citizens, performing an important role within the home, had the right to adequate financial support from the state.

Using traditional campaign tactics, including lobbying and letter writing, mainstream women's groups challenged any attempt to discriminate against married women within the legal system that would leave them vulnerable to poverty. Their concern was the financial status of women, and in particular the very real threat of poverty for widowed, separated and divorced women and their children. This coincided with the 're-discovery of poverty' in the late 1950s and 1960s, which revealed that despite state welfare certain groups within society were still at risk of living in poverty.[81]

One issue attracting the particular attention of voluntary women's groups was the earnings limit placed on widows' allowances. In 1950 the WI passed a resolution calling on the government to raise the amount of earnings allowable for women in receipt of widowed mother's pension. The resolution, along with evidence of the hardship experienced by widowed mothers, was sent to the Minister for Insurance.[82] Responding to these requests, the government announced in 1955 that the National Insurance Advisory Committee would review the earnings rule and in May 1956 the Committee recommended an increase to 60 shillings per week to the earnings allowed by widowed mothers.[83]

Despite this increase the issue remained a matter of concern for women's organisations throughout the 1950s and early 1960s. In 1957 the Salford branch of the NCW proposed a resolution highlighting the poverty experienced by widowed mothers. Based on statistics revealing that thirty per cent of widowed mothers were living on National Assistance, the resolution called on the government to increase once again the amount of earnings allowable.[84] The executive of the NCW subsequently agreed to support action on this issue as 'members felt it was an important matter and everything possible should be done.'[85]

To draw attention to this new campaign a meeting was organised in Manchester in February 1958. The meeting, attended by representatives of a number of women's groups and professional organisations, unanimously resolved that 'deductions from widowed mothers' allowances in respect of earnings are a great injustice, involving hardship and frustration and inviting evasion, and should be abolished.'[86] Those attending the meeting were asked to contact their MP to voice their discontent on this matter. A few months later on 16 July 1958, a deputation organised by the NCW and representing its affiliated members attended the House of Commons. The deputation met with MPs from both the Labour and Conservative parties and discussed ways to generate support for the campaign to abolish the earnings rule for widowed mothers.[87]

The TG had no reservations about supporting this particular campaign and in 1957 it passed its own resolution on the question of widows' earnings. Arguing that where a widow's earnings exceeded £2 10s per week 'the law should be amended to a figure more in keeping with the present cost of living, and [the TG] urges the Minister of Pensions and National Insurance to give the matter his urgent attention.'[88] A copy of the resolution was sent to the Minister and to all women MPs in the hope that they would support the campaign. The TG passed a second resolution on this issue in 1960 requesting that the earnings allowance be increased and once again this was forwarded to the Minister.[89]

In late 1959 the NCW announced its support for the 1960 National Insurance (Widowed Mothers) Bill. The bill, sponsored by William Griffiths MP, proposed to amend the 1946 National Insurance Act so that the earnings rule in relation to widowed mothers would be abolished.[90] Branch members of the NCW were asked to write to their MP to back the bill and the Council carried out a survey of 127 widowed mothers to ascertain the scale of the problem. The results of the survey were sent as a memorandum to the Secretary of the National Insurance Advisory Committee 'as a comment upon and protest against the inadequacy of the government regulation.'[91] The survey revealed the real hardship faced by widowed mothers with more than ninety per cent of respondents stating that they could not provide a home for their children on £5 a week plus the allowances. All those questioned stated that they 'would not be able to save to cover times of sickness' whilst '98 per cent said they never had a holiday.'[92]

As the extent of this problem became known, the MU took the decision to support calls to abolish the earnings rule. In April 1960 the Union wrote to William Griffiths to confirm its approval of his bill and stated that if widows 'are fortunate enough to make satisfactory arrangements for their children and to find employment they should be entitled to keep all they earn to help them to maintain their home'.[93] The bill achieved a second reading in the House of Commons but failed to become law.

Despite this setback the campaign by women's groups to abolish the ruling on widows' earnings continued unabated. In March 1963 the NCW reported that the Council, along with representatives from the SPG and ODC, had joined a deputation organised by the Status of Women Committee to the Minister of Health to discuss the issue of widowed mothers' earnings.[94] It was also announced that plans for widowed mothers to lobby the House of Commons on Tuesday 21 May were underway. All branches were asked to let headquarters know of any widowed mothers who would be willing to attend the Commons on that day and to send details of hardship cases involving widowed mothers to the Ministry of Pensions and National Health.[95]

In 1964 the TG passed a third resolution on the issue of widows' earnings, this time calling for the abolition of the earnings rule. Copies of the resolution were sent to the three main political parties and in reply both the Liberal and Labour Party confirmed their intention, if elected, to abolish the earnings rule.[96] Some satisfaction on this issue was finally achieved when in 1964 the MU welcomed news that the earnings limit for widowed mothers would be increased to £7 per week. No doubt expressing the view of a number of women's groups, the Union added however that 'it would still like the earnings limit to be abolished.'[97]

Two other campaigns spurred voluntary women's groups into action during these years: the right of parents to visit children in hospital and the removal of turnstiles from public lavatories. It could be argued that in highlighting these issues, housewives' associations were becoming less vocal on the citizenship rights of women. Hospital visits and access to public WCs could be viewed as rather minor matters. Nevertheless, the evidence would suggest that visiting sick children and turnstiles were important issues for members of voluntary women's groups. In response the national leadership, recognising the power they had to bring about legislative change, decided to launch campaigns so that parents could regularly visit children in hospital and women could more easily access WCs. Here the personal became political and these activities should be considered alongside the other campaigning activities of the MU, CWL, NCW, WI and TG.

In the early 1950s the welfare of children in hospital became a growing concern for the WI and the MU. As a result, both groups began to lobby the government and local health authorities to instruct hospitals to allow parents to visit their sick children on a daily basis. In 1950 the WI passed a resolution requesting that hospital management committees allow parents to visit their children more regularly, a right which was often denied. Despite a 'lively' debate amongst members on this issue, with some arguing that decisions on hospital visits should be left to the experts, it was reported that the resolution passed by a 'good majority'.[98]

As Ruth Davies writes, the whole question of visiting rights for parents came under public scrutiny in the 1950s. This was in part due to greater awareness about the impact of maternal deprivation, popularised by the work of Winnicott and Bowlby, along with wider changes 'in society and systems of hospital care'.[99] Between 1949 and 1956 the Ministry of Health issued three directives calling on hospital authorities to allow the daily visiting of children but many hospitals continued to resist.[100]

In 1953 the WI welcomed the Ministry of Health's latest directive to all hospital authorities urging them to allow daily visiting of children.[101] The same year the Watch and Social Problems Committee of the MU took up the issue. In common with the WI, some members of the Committee expressed reservations about whether or not it was advisable for parents to visit daily. The risk of infection and the fact that children may become 'over-excited' were cited as reasons to limit visits. However, members of the Committee who themselves had experience of children being admitted to hospital persuaded their colleagues that daily visiting was a good thing and that it was 'far less upsetting for the children'.[102]

In 1954 the MU invited members to report on the situation in their own areas with regard to hospital visits for parents of sick children. The Central Council reminded members that local action could be very effective, giving the example of the MU in Huddersfield who, working with other interested groups, had successfully persuaded the local hospital to allow daily visiting.[103] Reporting on the progress of the campaign in July 1955, the MU informed members that out of 1,362 hospitals admitting children, sixty-two per cent now allowed daily visiting compared to twenty-five per cent of hospitals in 1952.[104]

When in 1956 the government set up a committee, under the chairmanship of Sir Harry Platt, to investigate the welfare of children in hospital, the MU and WI were invited to give evidence. Both groups enthusiastically complied and in their submissions strongly supported the argument that daily parental visits would be beneficial to sick children and aid their recovery. The Platt Committee published its report in 1959 and despite the resistance of the medical profession and hospitals recommended that 'parents should be allowed to visit their child whenever they can, and try to help as much as possible with the care of the child.' It also advised that consideration should be given to 'the admission of mothers with their children, especially if the child is under five years of age'.[105]

The MU welcomed the findings of the report and was pleased that 'many of the points made by the MU were included', in particular the recommendation that children who do not receive regular visitors should be visited by a volunteer and that playrooms should be provided in hospitals for the siblings of sick children.[106] However, despite the publication of the report, parental visiting rights remained a contentious issue throughout the late 1950s and 1960s with some hospitals ignoring government advice. In August 1962 the MU noted that 750 hospitals were still refusing to allow daily visiting. Once again the Union felt compelled to call on the government to take immediate action 'where restrictions are still in force'.[107] Such was the strength of feeling on this matter that in 1961 a new organisation, Mother Care for Children in Hospital, was set up to campaign specifically for the implementation of the Platt Committee's recommendations, and its work continued well into the late 1960s and 1970s.[108]

Alongside raising important questions about divorce law reform, the pension rights of widows and parental visiting rights, voluntary women's groups were also prepared to voice their concerns on more practical issues impacting on women's lives. At its 1956 AGM the WI passed a resolution calling for the removal of turnstiles from public lavatories. This new design feature, brought in to replace the old penny-in-the-slot method, was condemned on a number of grounds. Supporters of the resolution argued that the turnstiles were problematic for 'the stout, those with a suitcase and handbag, the expectant mother and those with young children'.[109]

During the debate on this resolution, members were informed that local institutes were taking action on this issue but that it was now time for a national campaign. Local authorities needed to be targeted, and in the words of Mrs Clarke of Littleham WI, 'it is up to us to persist … to demand and keep demanding that every women's convenience should be made convenient to every woman'.[110] Members were warned that this was a serious issue despite the fact that men seemed to treat it as 'a music hall joke'. The resolution that the WI 'take necessary action to ensure the abolition of turnstiles in all women's conveniences' and in doing so seek the co-operation of 'kindred women's organisations' was passed by a large majority.[111]

In 1959 the NCW passed its own resolution for the removal of turnstiles. Daphne Glick writes that the Council was successful in persuading Barbara Castle MP to table a bill for the abolition of turnstiles although this did not progress beyond its first reading.[112] The Council however remained undeterred and in May 1961 stated that it 'had no intention of giving up the battle'. Letters were sent to the WI and TG as well as to women editors of all the national newspapers in an attempt to gain support for the campaign. The Council also requested that affiliated societies write to the Minister calling on him to ban turnstiles from all public conveniences.[113]

On 28 July 1961, a deputation organised by the NCW and including representatives from the WI and MU, visited the Minister of Housing and Local Government. The issue of turnstiles was discussed and it was reported that the examples of hardship presented to the Minister had made an impact.[114] Following this meeting it was announced in November 1961 that loans for public conveniences with turnstiles were to be permanently withdrawn and local authorities were requested to remove turnstiles from existing facilities.[115]

There is no doubt that this decision was based on the evidence presented by women's organisations. Over 2,200 turnstiles had proven defective over a five-year period. In addition people had been trapped in turnstiles on at least 150 occasions with twelve sustaining injuries.[116] The particular difficulties that mothers with young children experienced in using the turnstiles when out and about or travelling were also highlighted. Following years of persistent campaigning on the part of voluntary women's organisations, success finally came in July 1963. The new Public Lavatories (Turnstiles) Act banned the use of turnstiles in public WCs and all turnstiles were to be removed within six months.

Joyce Freeguard, writing on the activities of feminist women's organisations during the 1950s, states that 'the image that emerges of women's organisations ... is one of interconnection, co-operation, mutuality and success in their pursuit of a wide range of gender equality issues.'[117] Samantha Clements expresses similar sentiments when she writes that women's organisations during these years, 'made an important contribution in helping to make both politicians and wider society aware of the many issues of concern to women, thus raising their profile.'[118] Both of these statements can equally be applied to the work of conventional, middle-class voluntary women's organisations.

The evidence presented in this chapter demonstrates that voluntary women's groups continued to represent a dynamic women's movement in the decades following the Second World War. Working alone or in collaboration with one another and other women's groups, the MU, CWL, NCW, WI and TG successfully challenged the construction of post-war domesticity and continued to campaign on a wide range of issues of concern to housewives and mothers. The fact that a number of these campaigns brought about legislative change contradicts perceptions of the era as a time when female activism was rendered ineffectual by affluence, consumerism and domesticity. One final but significant revelation is the fact that these housewives' organisations, often dismissed as conventional and conservative, identified the personal as political long before the emergence of the WLM in the late 1960s.

Notes

1   See D. Smith Wilson, 'A New Look at the Affluent Worker: The Good Working Mother in Post-war Britain', *Twentieth Century British History*, 17:2 (2006), pp. 206–229.

2   L. Segal, *Straight Sex: The Politics of Pleasure* (London: Virago, 1994) cited in Langhamer, 'The Meanings of Home', p. 341.

3   See for example Smith Wilson, 'A New Look at the Affluent Worker', Langhamer, 'The Meanings of Home' and Birmingham Feminist History Group, 'Feminism as Femininity in the Nineteen-Fifties?', *Feminist Review*, 3 (1979).

4   See Pugh, *Women and the Women's Movement*, pp. 284–311 and M. Hilton, *Consumerism in Twentieth Century Britain* (Cambridge: Cambridge University Press, 2003), pp. 167–183.

5   B. Conekin, F. Mort and C. Waters (eds), *Moments of Modernity: Reconstructing Britain 1945–1964* (London: Rivers Oram Press, 1999), p. 3 cited in Langhamer, 'The Meanings of Home', p. 361.

6   WL, 5/FWI/A/2/2/07, Box 40, NFWI Archive, *Annual Report 1955*, BL, Mothers' Union Handbook, 1955, BL, *National Union of Townswomen's Guilds Annual Report, 1955*, *The Catholic Women's League Magazine*, 499 (March–April 1955), p. 2, BL, 'Memorandum Submitted by the NCW to the Royal Commission on Marriage and Divorce', Paper No. 83, Thursday 6 November 1952.

7   *The Mothers' Union Workers' Paper* (July 1950), p. 68.

8   WL, 5/FWI/A/2/3/08, Box 47, NFWI Archive, *NFWI Reports of AGMs*, 27 May 1952.

9   *Mothers' Union News*, 1 (January 1964), pp. 2–3.

10   *Ibid.*

11   I. Zweiniger-Bargielowska, 'Housewifery', in Zweiniger-Bargielowska (ed.), *Women in Twentieth Century Britain*, p. 161.

12   I. Zweiniger-Bargielowska, *Austerity in Britain*, p. 106.

13   During the 1950s women's magazines enjoyed a mass circulation with five in every six women in Britain reading at least one women's magazine. See Smith Wilson, 'A New Look at the Affluent Worker', p. 214 and M. Ferguson, *Forever Feminine: Women's Magazines and the Cult of Femininity* (London: Heinemann, 1983), pp. 44–64. See also R. Ritchie, 'The housewife and the modern: the home and appearance in women's magazines, 1954–1969' (Ph.D. dissertation, University of Manchester, 2010).

14   Andrews, *The Acceptable Face of Feminism*, pp. 123–145.

15   BL, *National Union of Townswomen's Guilds Annual Report, 1953*, p. 15.

16   *The Townswoman*, 27:11 (December 1960), p. 300.

17   WL, 5/FWI/A/2/3/08, Box 47, NFWI Archive, *AGM Reports, 1954*.

18   BL, *National Union of Townswomen's Guilds Annual Report, 1953*, p. 8.

19   In 1964 the number of female MPs peaked at twenty-nine, representing less than five per cent of the total of MPs. See Cowman, *Women in British Politics*, p. 127.

20 BL, *National Union of Townswomen's Guilds Annual Report, 1961*, p. 4.
21 WL, 5/FWI/G/2/3/047, Box 261, NFWI Archive, *Home and Country*, 33:1 (January 1951).
22 Zweiniger-Barielowska, 'Explaining the Gender Gap', p. 196. For a discussion of the Labour Party and the women's vote see A. Black and S. Brooke, 'The Labour Party, Women, and the Problem of Gender, 1951–1966', *Journal of British Studies*, 36 (1997), pp. 419–452.
23 In 1959 it was reported that 3,100 girls had been helped at Victoria Station and that another kiosk had been set up at Liverpool Street Station. LPL, MU/WAT/9/2, MU Archive, *MU Watch and Social Problems Bulletin*, 39 (1959), p. 5.
24 LPL, MU/WAT/1/4, MU Archive, 'MU Watch and Social Problems Committee Minutes', 18 November 1953, p. 125.
25 WL, 5/FWI/A/2/3/010, Box 40, NFWI Archive, *AGM Reports, 1962*.
26 In 1931 10.0 per cent of married women worked outside the home. This increased to 21.7 per cent in 1951 and to 45.4 per cent in 1961. By 1971 the figure had risen again to 51.3 per cent. Smith Wilson, 'A New Look at the Affluent Worker', p. 209.
27 *Ibid.*, p. 207.
28 See J. Lewis, 'Mydral, Klein, *Women's Two Roles* and Post-War British Feminism, 1945–60', in Smith (ed.), *British Feminism*, pp. 167–186.
29 Smith Wilson writes that in the 1950s and 1960s the number of part-time workers more than quadrupled and that almost all of them were married women. Smith Wilson, 'A New Look at the Affluent Worker', p. 208.
30 *Women in Council*, 28:8 (April 1957), p. 68.
31 *Ibid.*
32 *Ibid.*
33 *Ibid.*
34 Cited in Freeguard, 'It's time for the women of the 1950s', p. 129.
35 Smith Wilson, 'A New Look at the Affluent Worker', p. 210.
36 See for example D. W. Winnicott, *Getting to Know Your Baby* (London: Heinemann, 1945) and J. Bowlby, *Childcare and the Growth of Love* (London: Penguin 1953). See also Pugh, *Women and the Women's Movement*, pp. 296–298.
37 *Women in Council*, 28:8 (April 1957), p. 69.
38 *Ibid.*
39 *Home and Country*, 39:9 (September 1957), p. 269.
40 *Ibid.*
41 WL, 5/FWI/D/1/2/05, Box 138, NFWI Archive, 'Women in Industry', 'Letter to WI Central Secretary, Dame Frances Farrer from Mrs. Norman', 8 April 1957.
42 *The Townswoman*, 30:8 (September 1963), p. 243.
43 Merz, *After the Vote*, p. 46.
44 In 1964 it was estimated that seventy-four per cent of all women workers between the ages of thirty-five and forty-four were married. Central Office of Information, *Women in Britain*, p. 8.
45 BL, *Home and Family* (December 1957), p. 7.
46 BL, *Home and Family* (June 1958), p. 17.
47 *Ibid.*, p. 18.
48 LPL, MU/WAT/9/2, MU Archive, *Mothers' Union News* (July 1964).
49 *The Catholic Women's Magazine*, 491 (November/December 1953), pp. 12–13.

50 See for example: Pugh, *Women and the Women's Movement*, pp. 284–311, Bruley, *Women in Britain*, pp. 118–119, Birmingham Feminist History Group, 'Feminism as Femininity', pp. 48–65, Lewis, 'Mydral, Klein, *Women's Two Roles*', Thane, 'Women and Political Participation', pp. 23–28 and Caine, *English Feminism*, pp. 222–254.

51 Freeguard, 'It's time for women of the 1950s', p. 4.

52 *Ibid.*

53 Perriton, 'Forgotten Feminists', pp. 79–97.

54 Clements, 'Feminism, citizenship and social activity', pp. 233–260.

55 Andrews, *The Acceptable Face of Feminism*, p. 146.

56 Pugh, *Women and the Women's Movement*, p. 297.

57 W. Beveridge and A. F. Wells, *The Evidence For Voluntary Action* (London: Allen and Unwin, 1949), p. 137.

58 See also Beaumont, 'Housewives, Workers and Citizens', pp. 59–76.

59 C. Langhamer, 'Adultery in Post-war England', p. 94 and Pugh, *Women and the Women's Movement*, p. 326.

60 Langhamer, 'Adultery in Post-war England', p. 94 and L. A. Hall, *Sex, Gender and Social Change in Britain since 1880* (Basingstoke: Macmillan, 2000), pp. 150–166.

61 Hall, *Sex, Gender and Social Change*, p. 150.

62 The SPG set up the MWA in 1938. Its main aim was to regulate financial arrangements between husbands and wives. The BFUW was established in 1907 to develop links between female university graduates. See Freeguard, 'It's time for women of the 1950s', pp. 16–43.

63 LMA, ACC/3613/1/72, NCW Archive, 'Parliamentary and Legislative Committee minutes', 15 December 1949.

64 Freeguard, 'It's time for women of the 1950s', pp. 135–142.

65 BL, 'Memorandum submitted by the National Council of Women of Great Britain', Paper No. 83, 6 November 1952.

66 *Ibid.*

67 *Ibid.*

68 The Council of Married Women was formed in 1952 when the MWA split over disagreements between members over its evidence to the Royal Commission on Marriage and Divorce. See Freeguard, 'It's time for the women of the 1950s', p. 34. See also C. Blackford, 'Ideas, structures and practices of feminism, 1939–1964' (Ph.D. dissertation, University of East London, 1996).

69 Cited in Freeguard, 'It is time for women of the 1950s', p. 142.

70 Langhamer, 'Adultery in Post-war England', p. 95.

71 BL, 'Memorandum submitted by the Mothers' Union', Paper No. 10, 26 May 1952.

72 Cited in Moyse, *A History of the Mothers' Union*, p. 190.

73 *Ibid.*

74 *The Mothers' Union Journal*, 222 (September 1950), p. 12.

75 Moyse, *A History of the Mothers' Union*, p. 191.

76 LPL, MU/WAT/9/2, MU Archive, *Watch and Social Problems Bulletins*, 43 (April 1961).

77 *Mothers' Union News*, January 1944.

78 See Beaumont, 'Housewives, Workers and Citizens', p. 73 and Moyse, *A History of the Mothers' Union*, pp. 190–194.

79 *The Catholic Women's League Magazine*, 473 (October 1951), p. 2.

80 *Ibid.*

81 See T. Evans, 'Stopping the Poor Getting Poorer: The Establishment and Professionalisation of Poverty NGOs, 1945–95', in Crowson, Hilton and McKay (eds), *NGOs in Contemporary Britain*, pp. 147–163.

82 National Federation of Women's Institutes, *Public Questions Annual Record* (London: NFWI, 1956), p. 28.

83 *Ibid.*

84 *Guardian* (9 October 1957).

85 LMA, ACC/3613/01/075, NCW Archive, 'Minutes of the Parliamentary and Legislative Committee', 20 November 1958.

86 *Guardian* (27 February 1958).

87 *Guardian* (15 July 1958).

88 *The Townswoman* (January 1958), p. 9.

89 *The Townswoman* (November 1960).

90 LMA, ACC/3613/01/075, NCW Archive, 'Minutes of the Parliamentary and Legislative Committee', 19 November 1959.

91 *Ibid.*

92 *Guardian* (2 February 1960).

93 LPL, MU/WAT/9/2, MU Archive, 'Watch and Social Problems Bulletins', 40 (April 1960).

94 The Status of Women Committee was a national body responsible for coordinating the work of organisations campaigning for women's rights. It reported to the United Nations. Gordon and Doughan, *Dictionary of British Women's Organisations*, p. 138.

95 LMA, ACC/3613/01/075, NCW Archive, 'Minutes of the Parliamentary and Legislative Committee', 13 March 1963.

96 *The Townswoman* (November 1964).

97 LPL, MU/WAT/9/2, MU Archive, *Mothers' Union News*, 'Watch News' (January 1964), p. 12.

98 WL, 5/FWI/A/2/3/08, Box 47, NFWI Archive, *AGM Reports*, 14 June 1950. See also Goodenough, *Jam and Jerusalem*, p. 75.

99 R. Davies, 'Marking the 50th anniversary of the Platt Report: From Exclusion, to Toleration and Parental Participation in the Care of the Hospitalised Child', *Journal of Child Health Care*, 14:1 (2010), p. 7.

100 *Ibid.*

101 WL, 5/FWI/D/1/2/01, Box 138, NFWI Archive, 'Public Affairs News Sheets', 15 (May 1953).

102 LPL, MU/WAT/1/4, MU Archive, 'Watch Committee minutes', 17 June 1953.

103 LPL, MU/CC/1/14, MU Archive, 'Central Council minutes', 14, 'Watch Committee report', 1954, p. 410.

104 LPL, MU/WAT/9/2, MU Archive, 'Watch and Social Problems Bulletins', 26 (July 1955), p. 3.

105 Davies, 'Marking the 50th Anniversary', p. 14.

106 LPL, MU/WAT/1/4, MU Archive, 'Watch Committee minutes', 18 February 1959, p. 268.

107 LPL, MU/WAT/9/2, MU Archive, *Mothers' Union News*, 'Watch News' (August 1962), p. 21.

108 Davies, 'Marking the 50th Anniversary', pp. 15–16.

109 WL, 5/FWI/A/2/3/09, Box 47, NFWI Archive, *AGM Reports*, 6 June 1956.

110 *Ibid.*
111 *Ibid.*
112 Glick, *The National Council of Women*, p. 65.
113 LMA, ACC/3613/01/075, NCW Archive, 'Parliamentary and Legislative Committee minutes', 18 May 1961.
114 WL, 5/FWI/A/2/2/07, Box 40, NFWI Archive, *Annual Report*, 1961.
115 WL, 5/FWI/A/2/2/07, Box 40, NFWI Archive, *Annual Report*, 1961.
116 LMA, ACC/3613/075, NCW Archive, 'Parliamentary and Legislative Committee minutes', 16 November 1961.
117 Freeguard, 'It's time for women of the 1950s', p. 1.
118 Clements, 'Feminism, citizenship and social activity', p. 248.

Conclusion

The emergence of 'second wave' feminism in the late 1960s signified a new phase in the history of the women's movement. As Pat Thane writes, the WLM was 'overwhelmingly a movement of younger women and tended to be hostile or indifferent to constitutional action through parliament'.[1] This new movement rejected formal organisational structures, debated class difference and attracted significant media attention with its new, radical style of direct action and political campaigning. Moreover, the WLM for the first time challenged traditional gender roles and, in doing so, challenged the presumption that women would always find fulfilment in marriage and motherhood. As a result the WLM appeared more relevant to the lives of young women in the 1970s than the women's groups their mothers would have joined in previous decades.

Thane observes that 'there seems to have been little contact between the older and newer women's organisations' and a lack of recognition amongst WLM activists of earlier campaigns undertaken by feminist, political and voluntary women's organisations.[2] Writing in the European context, Karen Offen expresses a similar view when she suggests that in the early 1970s 'a new generation of feminists in Europe thought, in good conscience, that they were beginning from "Year Zero"'.[3] Offen has done much to fill in the gaps within the European context, but there is still much more work to be done when it comes to discovering the links between the WLM and more conservative voluntary women's groups who, as this study has established, spoke out on behalf of women, housewives and mothers in the decades before the emergence of 'second wave' feminism.

This book has focused on the history of voluntary women's groups in England, but there is plenty of evidence to suggest that in other European countries housewives organisations were also campaigning to improve the lives of women throughout the twentieth century. For example, in Ireland, the Irish Countrywomen's Association and the Joint Committee of Women's Societies and Social Workers, campaigned to secure social and economic rights for women.[4]

In France, the Catholic and conservative La Ligue Patriotique des Femmes Francaises (Patriotic League of French Women), highlighted health and welfare issues impacting on women's lives and was the most influential women's organisation in France during the 1920s and 1930s.[5] Koven and Michel have written that French women 'were far more likely to participate in maternalist activities than join feminist organisations, even though maternalism did not necessarily further their emancipation as a sex.[6] A similar situation emerged in Denmark during the 1940s and 1950s, a period in which the number of organisations for women, including housewives' associations, peaked and where 'most did not define themselves as feminist.'[7]

At first glance the apparent disjuncture between the WLM and older voluntary women's organisations appears obvious. By the mid-1960s the MU, CWL, NCW, WI and TG were all expressing anxiety about ageing memberships and were discussing ways in which they could recruit younger women into their organisations. Various initiatives were proposed such as holding meetings in the evenings so that working women could attend and updating the format and content of their journals and magazines to make them more attractive to younger readers.

By the end of the 1960s, however, only the TG could record a growth in membership with approximately 275,700 guild members in 1969.[8] In the late 1960s, membership of the MU in the British Isles had fallen to 380,000.[9] In the early 1970s, the WI recorded a membership of 442,086 rural women and individual membership of the NCW had dropped to 7,000, although the Council continued to represent nearly one hundred affiliated societies.[10] Yet despite such falls in membership the fact that these groups were still representing hundreds of thousands of women at a time when 'associations committed to the promotion of active citizenship as a core objective' were thought to have disappeared is impressive.[11]

More work needs to be done not only on the history of voluntary women's groups and their members throughout the mid to late twentieth century but also on the ability of other women's groups, both voluntary, religious and political to represent effectively the interests of women in a changing society. This study has demonstrated that conservative women's groups shared concerns and demands for social change with a wide range of other campaigning groups, for example the Labour Party Women's Sections and the WCG. It would be fascinating to learn more about the similarities and differences between these organisations and to trace their relationships with the newly emerging WLM.

For the MU, CWL, NCW, WI and TG, an ageing membership along with their continued association with conservative, middle-class, predominantly white and increasingly middle-aged values may also have deterred younger women from joining in the 1960s and 1970s. Assumptions that these groups were more interested in baking, sewing and 'making jam' than challenging gender inequalities became increasingly common during these years. Indeed it can be argued that these somewhat negative perceptions continue to this day. One of the aims of this book has been to debunk these popular myths.

There is no doubt however that voluntary women's groups do appear to have been overtaken and in some ways 'left behind' by the WLM. In addition, the success of other new and more dynamic pressure groups, for example the Campaign for Nuclear Disarmament and the Child Poverty Action Group, clearly made an impact.[12] With their ability to attract significant media attention and their use of modern campaign techniques, these groups eclipsed the MU, CWL, NCW, WI and TG as effective campaigning organisations. As a result, concerns expressed by house-wives' associations in the 1960s that they were viewed as 'old-fashioned' and reactionary appear to have been well founded.

Despite these difficulties, voluntary women's groups continued to speak out on behalf of housewives and mothers throughout the late twentieth century and all five organisations are still active today. For example, in 1965 the TG passed a resolution in favour of legalised abortion, two years before the passing of the Abortion Act 1967. In 1972 the WI called on the government to send a directive to all local authorities to insure that a full, free family-planning service was available to all women. Throughout the 1960s, the TG, WI and MU campaigned successfully for the introduction of a nationwide cervical cancer-screening programme.[13] These campaigns would suggest that voluntary women's groups had more in common with the WLM than has previously been recognised.[14]

Until more is known about the history and activities of the MU, CWL, NCW, WI and TG, along with other women's organisations during the 1960s and 1970s and their relationship, if any, with the WLM, it is difficult to make any final judgement on the links between the different strands of the women's movement. Without this knowledge it is too early to suggest that the wave metaphor, often used to describe the trajectory of the feminist movement, needs to be revised. What is clear however is that the years between so-called 'first wave' and 'second wave' feminism should no longer be called a 'silent period'.[15] This study of voluntary women's groups has shown that the history of the twentieth-century women's movement is one of continuity. Activists in a variety of women's organisations tirelessly campaigned to secure the rights of citizenship for women. In doing so they not only provided a public voice for women but also did much to improve women's lives.

Notes

1 Thane, 'Women and Political Participation in England', p. 24.
2 *Ibid.*
3 Offen, *European Feminisms, 1700–1950*, p. 3.
4 See C. Beaumont, 'Women and the Politics of Equality: The Irish Women's Movement, 1930–1943', in M. O'Dowd and M. Valiulis (eds), *Women and Irish History* (Dublin: Wolfhound Press, 1997), pp. 173–88.
5 Koven and Michel, 'Womanly Duties', p. 1100.
6 *Ibid.*
7 D. Dahlerup, 'Three Waves of Feminism in Denmark', in G. Griffin and R. Braidotti (eds), *Thinking Differently: A Reader in European Women's Studies* (London: Zed Books, 2002), p. 346.
8 BL, *National Union of Townswomen's Guilds Annual Report, 1970*. There are no figures available for the CWL.
9 Moyse, *A History of the Mothers' Union*, p. 176.
10 WL, WL, 5/FWI/A/2/2/07, Box 40, NFWI Archive, *Annual Report*, 1971 and Glick, *The National Council of Women*, p. 63.
11 H. McCarthy and P. Thane, 'The Politics of Association in Industrial Society', *Twentieth Century British History*, 22 (2011), p. 227.
12 Crowson, Hilton and McKay (eds), *NGOs in Contemporary Britain*.
13 Beaumont, 'Housewives and Citizens', pp. 70–72.
14 Amongst the demands made by the WLM were equal pay, equal education and job opportunities, free access to twenty-four-hour nurseries, free contraception and abortion on demand. Cowman, *Women in British Politics*, p. 165.
15 Dahlerup, 'Three Waves of Feminism in Denmark', p. 345.

Bibliography

Archive collections

Birmingham City Library

National Council of Women, 1928–1931, Birmingham Branch Archive. MSS 841 B

Lambeth Palace Library, London

Letters and Papers of G. F. Fisher, Archbishop of Canterbury 1945–61. Vols. 17, 105, 190, 249, 250, 265

Letters and Papers of C. G. Lang, Archbishop of Canterbury, 1928–42. Vols. 107, 113, 136, 152, 178

Letters and Papers of William Temple, Archbishop of Canterbury, 1942–44. Vol. 35

Mothers' Union Archive MU/

London Metropolitan Archive

National Council of Women Archive ACC/3613/

Mary Sumner House, London

Mothers' Union Archive (accessed 1992–95, now catalogued and located in Lambeth Palace Library)

Annual Reports of the Mothers' Union London Diocese, 1928–50

Executive Committee Minutes Vol. 12, 1937

Minute Book of the Mothers' Union, Holy Cross St. Pancras Branch, 1931–40

Minutes of the Mothers' Union Central Council, Vols. 8–12 (1927–50)

Mothers' Union London Diocese Press Cutting Collection, 1889–1934

Mothers' Union Pamphlet Collection

Modern Records Centre, University of Warwick

Trades Union Congress National Archive (Correspondence with women's organisations) MSS 292/821

YWCA National Archive MSS 243/

Public Record Office, London

Memorandum of the Women's Housing Conference (n.d., *circa* 1936), HLG 36/3

Women's Library, London

Equal Pay Campaign Committee Archive MSS 6CCS/

National Federation of Women's Institute Archive MSS 5/FWI/

National Union of Societies for Equal Citizenship Archive MSS 7AMP/D/2/3

National Women Citizens' Association Archive MSS 5NWC/

Six Point Group Archive MSS 5CMW/

WL Pamphlet Collection
Women's Forum/Women's Group on Public Welfare Archive MSS 5WFM/

Newspapers and periodicals

The Blue Triangle Gazette
The Catholic Citizen
The Catholic Women's League Magazine
The Catholic Women's Outlook
Co-operative News
Daily Mail
Guardian
Home and Country
Home and Family
Manchester Guardian
Mothers in Council
Mothers' Union News
The Mothers' Union Journal
The Mothers' Union Journal (London Cover).
The Mothers' Union Workers' Paper
National Council of Women News
News For Citizens
The Sunday Pictorial
The Tablet
Time and Tide
The Times
The Townswoman
Woman
Women in Council
The Women's Leader

Contemporary sources and pamphlets

Abbott, E. and Bompass, K., *The Woman Citizen and Social Security; A Criticism of the Proposals Made in the Beveridge Report as They Affect Women* (1943).
Barclay, E. Noel, *Marriage and Divorce* (1936).
Beveridge, W., *Social Insurance and Allied Services* (London: HMSO, Cmd 6404, 1942).
Campbell, H. M., *Maternal Mortality, Reports on Public Health and Medical Subjects # 25* (London: HMSO, 1924).
Campbell, J., *The Protection of Motherhood, Reports on Public Health and Medical Subjects # 48* (London: HMSO, 1927).
Central Office of Information, *Women in Britain Reference Pamphlet 67* (London: HMSO, 1964).

Constitution of the National Women Citizens' Association (1918).

Cowlin, M. H., *Women Police in War Time: What is the WAPC?* (1939).

Design of Dwellings: Report of Central Housing Committee (London: HMSO, 1944).

Encyclical Letter from the Bishops, *Resolutions and Reports of the Lambeth Conference 1930* (1930).

Encyclical Letter from the Bishops, *Resolutions and Reports of the Lambeth Conference 1948* (1948).

Equal Pay Campaign Committee, *Equal Pay for Equal Work* (1944).

Equal Pay Campaign Committee, *Equal Pay for Equal Work: A Black Record* (London: EPCC, 1949).

Evans, D., *The Case For Equal Pay* (1948).

Evidence for the Central Housing Advisory Committee's Sub-Committee on the Design of Dwellings (London: HMSO, 1946)

Evidence to the Royal Commission on Marriage and Divorce 1952 (London: HMSO, 1952).

Ferguson, S. and Fitzgerald, H., *Studies in Social Services* (London: HMSO, 1954).

Hubback, E., *Training For Citizenship* (London: AEC, 1935).

——, *The Making of Citizens* (London: AEC, 1942).

Hubback, E. and Simon, E., *Education For Citizenship* (London: AEC, 1934).

Memorandum Submitted by the Mothers' Union to the Royal Commission on Marriage and Divorce, 1951–1955 (London: HMSO, 1955).

Ministry of Health, *Final Report of the Departmental Committee on Maternal Mortality and Morbidity* (London: HMSO, 1932).

Ministry of Health, *Interim Report of the Departmental Committee on Maternal Mortality and Morbidity* (London: HMSO, 1930).

Ministry of Health, *Report on an Investigation into Maternal Mortality* (London: HMSO, 1937).

The National Association of Women Civil Servants Newsletter (July 1948).

National Conference of Women, called by HM Government: Report of Proceedings, Tuesday 28 September 1943, Royal Albert Hall, London (1943).

The National Council of Women, *The First Sixty Years 1895–1955* (London: NCW, 1955).

The National Council of Women: What Is It? (1929).

National Federation of Women's Institutes Annual Reports (1928–64).

National Federation of Women's Institutes Annual Conference Reports (1928–64).

National Federation of Women's Institutes Procedure at Meetings (1949).

National Federation of Women's Institutes, *Public Questions Annual Record* (London: NFWI, 1956).

National Federation of Women's Institutes, *Town Children through Country Eyes: A Survey on Evacuation* (1940).

The National Insurance Act 1946 (London: HMSO, 1946).

National Union of Townswomen's Guilds Annual Reports (1928–64).

National Union of Townswomen's Guilds Handbooks (1928–64).

NCW Handbooks (1928–64).

NCW Reports of Council Meetings and Conferences (1928–64).

Oral Evidence submitted to the Royal Commission on Population, 1944–1945 (London: HMSO, 1949).

Papers of the Royal Commission on Population (London: HMSO, 1949).

Pope Leo XIII, *Rerum Novarum: The Condition of the Working Classes* (Encyclical, 1891).

Pope Pius XI, *Quadragesimo Anno: The Social Order – Its Reconstruction and Perfection* (Encyclical, 1931).

Pope Pius XI, *Casti Connubii: Encyclical Letter of His Holiness Pope Pius XI on Christian Marriage, December 1930* (London: Sheed & Ward, 1933)

Report of the Royal Commission on Equal Pay (London: HMSO, 1946).

Report of the Royal Commission on Population (London: HMSO, 1949).

Report of the Royal Commission on Marriage and Divorce (London: HMSO, 1956)

Tate, M., *Equal Work Deserves Equal Pay* (n.d.).

Thomas, G., *Women and Industry: An Inquiry into the Problem of Recruiting Women to Industry Carried Out for the Ministry of Labour and National Service* (1943)

Ward, D., *The Christian Attitude towards Birth Control and Abortion* (1937).

——, *Marriage and Divorce* (n.d.).

Women's Group on Public Welfare, *Our Towns: A Close Up* (Oxford: WGPW, 1943).

Women's Group on Public Welfare Report 1939–45 (1945).

Women's Housing and Planning Conference (1942).

Written Evidence Submitted to the Royal Commission on Population 1944–47 (London: HMSO, 1949).

Articles and chapters

Beaumont, C., 'Women and the Politics of Equality: The Irish Women's Movement, 1930–1943', in M. O'Dowd and M. Valiulis (eds), *Women and Irish History* (Dublin: Wolfhound Press, 1997).

——, 'Citizens not Feminists: The Boundary Negotiated between Citizenship and Feminism by Mainstream Women's Organisations in England, 1928–1939', *Women's History Review*, 9:2 (2000).

——, 'The Women's Movement, Politics and Citizenship, 1918–1950', in I. Zweiniger-Bargielowska (ed.), *Women in Twentieth Century Britain* (Harlow: Pearson Education, 2001).

——, 'Moral Dilemmas and Women's Rights: The attitude of the Mothers' Union and Catholic Women's League to divorce, birth control and abortion in England 1928–1939', *Women's History Review*, 16:4 (2007).

——, 'Housewives, Workers and Citizens: Voluntary Women's Organisations and the Campaign for Women's Rights in England and Wales during the Post-war Period', in N. Crowson, M. Hilton and J. Mckay (eds), *NGOs in Contemporary Britain: Non-State Actors in Society and Politics since 1945* (Basingstoke: Palgrave Macmillan, 2009).

——, 'Where to Park the Pram? Voluntary Women's Organisations, Citizenship and the Campaign for Better Housing in England, 1928–1945', *Women's History Review*, 22:1 (2013).

Beinart, J., 'Obstetric Analgesia and the Control of Childbirth in Twentieth-Century Britain', in J. Garcia, R. Kilpatrick and M. Richards (eds*), The Politics of Maternity Care: Services for Childbearing Women in Twentieth-Century Britain* (London: Clarendon Paperbacks, 1990).

Birmingham Feminist History Group, 'Feminism as Femininity in the Nineteen-fifties?', *Feminist Review*, 3 (1979).

Black, A. and Brooke, S., 'The Labour Party, Women and the Problem of Gender, 1951–1966', *Journal of British Studies*, 36 (1997).

Blackford, C., 'Wives and Citizens and Watchdogs of Equality: Post-war British Feminism', in J. Fyrth (ed.), *Labour's Promised Land? Culture and Society in Labour Britain 1945–51* (London: Lawrence and Wishhart, 1995).

Brooke, S., '"A New World for Women?" Abortion Law Reform in Britain during the 1930s", *American Historical Review*, 106 (2001).

——, 'The Sphere of Sexual Politics: The Abortion Law Reform Association, 1930s to 1960s', in N. Crowson, M. Hilton and J. McKay (eds), *NGOs in Contemporary Society: Non-State Actors in Society and Politics since 1954* (Basingstoke: Palgrave Macmillan, 2009).

Canning, K. and Rose, S. O., 'Gender, Citizenship and Subjectivity: Some Historical and Theoretical Considerations', in K. Canning and S. O. Rose (eds), *Gender, Citizenship and Subjectivities* (Oxford: Blackwell, 2002).

Clapson, M., 'Working-Class Women's Experiences of Moving to New Housing Estates in England since 1919', *Twentieth Century British History*, 10:3 (1999).

Cohen, D., 'Private Lives in Public Spaces: Marie Stopes, the Mothers Clinics and the Practice of Contraception', *History Workshop Journal*, 35 (1993).

Dahlerup, D., 'Three Waves of Feminism in Denmark', in G. Griffin and R. Braidotti (eds), *Thinking Differently: A Reader in European Women's Studies* (London: Zed Books, 2002).

Darling, E., '"Enriching and Enlarging the Whole Sphere of Human Activities": The Work of the Voluntary Housing Sector in Housing Reform in Inter-war Britain', in C. Lawrence and A. Mayer (eds), *Regenerating England: Science, Medicine and Culture in Inter-War Britain* (Atlanta: Editions Rodopi B. V., 2000).

——, '"A citizen as well as a housewife": New Spaces of Domesticity in 1930s London', in H. Heynen and G. Baydar (eds), *Negotiating Domesticity: Spatial Productions of Gender in Modern Architecture* (London: Routledge, 2005).

Davies, R., 'Marking the 50th Anniversary of the Platt Report: From Exclusion, to Toleration and Parental Participation in the Care of the Hospitalised Child', *Journal of Child Health Care*, 14:1 (2010).

Davin, A., 'Imperialism and Motherhood', *History Workshop Journal*, 5 (1978).

Evans, T., 'Stopping the Poor Getting Poorer: The Establishment and Professionalization of Poverty NGOs, 1945–95', in N. Crowson, M. Hilton and J. McKay (eds), *NGOs in Contemporary Britain: Non-State Actors in Society and Politics since 1945* (Basingstoke: Palgrave Macmillan, 2009).

Finch, J. and Summerfield, P. 'Social Reconstruction and the Emergence of Companionate Marriage, 1945–59', in D. Clark (ed.), *Marriage, Domestic Life and Social Change: Writings for Jacqueline Burgoyne (1944–88)* (London: Routledge, 1991).

Giles, J., '"Playing Hard to Get": Working Class Women, Sexuality and Respectability in Britain, 1918–40', *Women's History Review*, 1:2 (1992).

——, 'A Home of One's Own: Women and Domesticity in England, 1918–1950', *Women's Studies International Forum*, 16:3 (1993).

Gittins, D., 'Married Life and Birth Control between the Wars', *Oral History* 3:1 (1975).

Hall, C., 'The History of the Housewife', in E. Malos (ed.), *The Politics of Housework* (London: Allison and Busby, 1980).

Harris, J., 'Political Thought and the Welfare State, 1870–1940', *Past and Present*, 135 (1992).

Harrison, B., 'For Church, Queen and Family: The Girls' Friendly Society 1874–1920', *Past and Present*, 61 (1973).

——, 'Women in a Men's House: The Women MPs, 1919–1945', *The Historical Journal*, 29:3 (1986).

Hinton, J., 'Women and the Labour Vote, 1945–50' *Labour History Review* 57:3 (1992).

——, 'Militant Housewives: The British Housewives' League and the Attlee Government', *History Workshop Journal*, 38 (1994).

Hufton, O., 'What is Women's History', *History Today*, 35 (1985).

Hunt, K., 'Negotiating the Boundaries of the Domestic: British Socialist Women and the Politics of Consumption', *Women's History Review*, 9:2 (2000).

Hunt, K., 'Women as Citizens: Changing the Polity', in D. Simonton (ed.), *The Routledge History of Women in Europe Since 1700* (London: Routledge, 2006).

Innes, S., 'Constructing Women's Citizenship in the Inter-war Period: The Edinburgh Women's Citizens' Association', *Women's History Review*, 13:4 (2000).

Koven, S. and Michel, S., 'Womanly Duties: Maternalist Politics and the Origins of Welfare States in France, Germany, Great Britain, and the United States', *American Historical Review*, 95:11 (1990).

Land, H., 'The Family Wage', *Feminist Review*, 6 (1980).

——, 'Eleanor Rathbone and the Economy of the Family', in H. Smith (ed.), *British Feminism in the Twentieth Century* (London: Edward Elgar, 1990).

——, 'Motherhood, Race and the State in the Twentieth Century: An Introduction', *Gender and History* 4:3 (1992).

Langhamer, C., 'The Meanings of Home in Postwar Britain' *Journal of Contemporary History*, 40:2 (2005).

——, 'Adultery in Post-War England', *History Workshop Journal*, 62 (2006).

Levine, P., '"Walking the Streets in a Way No Decent Woman Should": Women Police in World War I', *Journal of Modern History*, 66:1 (1994).

Lewis, J., 'The Ideology and Politics of Birth Control in Inter-War England', *Women's Studies International Quarterly*, 2 (1979).

——, 'In Search of a Real Equality: Women between the Wars', in F. Gloversmith (ed.), *Class, Culture and Social Change: A New View of the 1930s* (Brighton: Harvester Press, 1980).

——, 'Dealing with Dependency: State Practices and Social Realities, 1870–1945', in J. Lewis (ed.), *Women's Welfare/Women's Rights* (London: Croom Helm, 1983).

——, 'Mydral, Klein: Women's Two Roles and Post-war Feminism 1945–1960', in H. Smith (ed.), *British Feminism in the Twentieth Century* (London: Edward Elgar, 1990).

——, 'Mothers and Maternity Policies in the Twentieth Century', in J. Garcia, R. Kilpatrick and M. Richards (eds), *The Politics of Maternity Care: Services for Childbearing Women in Twentieth-Century Britain* (London: Clarendon Paperbacks, 1990).

——, 'Models of Equality for Women: The Case of State Support for Children in Twentieth-Century Britain', in G. Bock and P. Thane (eds), *Maternity and Gender Policies: Women and the Rise of European Welfare States, 1880s to 1950s* (London: Routledge, 1991).

Lister, R., 'Citizenship: towards a Feminist Synthesis', *Feminist Review*, 57 (1997).

McCarthy, H., 'Parties, Voluntary Associations and Democratic Politics in Interwar Britain', *Historical Journal*, 50 (2007).

——, 'Service Clubs, Citizenship and Equality: Gender Relations and Middle-class Associations in Britain between the Wars', *Historical Review*, 81 (2008).

McCarthy, H. and Thane, P., 'The Politics of Association in Industrial Society', *Twentieth Century British History*, 22 (2011).

Macnicol, J., 'The Effect of the Evacuation of Schoolchildren on Official Attitudes to State Intervention', in H. Smith (ed.), *War and Social Change: British Society in the Second World War* (Manchester: Manchester University Press, 1986).

Marks, L., 'Mothers, Babies and Hospitals: "The London" and Provision of Maternity Care in East London, 1870–1939', in V. Fildes, L. Marks and H. Marland (eds), *Women and Children First: International Maternal and Infant Welfare, 1870–1945* (London: Routledge, 1992).

Mason, F. M., 'The Newer Eve: The Catholic Women's Suffrage Society in England, 1911–1923', *Catholic History Review*, 4 (1986).

Meehan, E., 'British Feminism from the 1960s to the 1980s', in H. Smith (ed.), *British Feminism in the Twentieth Century* (London: Edward Elgar, 1990).

Meyerowitz, J., 'Beyond the Feminine Mystique: A Reassessment of Post-war Mass Culture, 1946–1958', *The Journal of American History*, 79:4 (1993).

Morgan, M., 'Jam Making, Cuthbert Rabbit and Cakes: Redefining Domestic Labour in the Women's Institutes, 1915–60', in *Rural History*, 7:2 (1996).

Offen, K., 'Defining Feminism: A Comparative Historical Approach', *Signs*, 14 (1988–89).

Pateman, C., 'The Patriarchal Welfare State', in A. Gutmann (ed.), *Democracy and the Welfare State* (Princeton, Princeton University Press, 1988).

——, 'Equality, Difference, Subordination: The Politics of Motherhood and Women's Citizenship', in G. Bock and S. James (eds), *Beyond Equality and Difference* (London: Routledge, 1992).

Pedersen, S., 'The Failure of Feminism in the Making of the British Welfare State', *Radical History Review*, 43 (1989).

——, 'Gender, Welfare, and Citizenship in Britain during the Great War', *American Historical Review*, 95:4 (1990).

Peretz, E., 'A Maternity Service for England and Wales: Local Authority Maternity Care in the Inter-war period in Oxfordshire and Tottenham', in J. Garcia, R. Kilpatrick and M. Richards (eds), *The Politics of Maternity Care: Services for Childbearing Women in Twentieth-Century Britain* (London: Clarendon Paperbacks, 1990).

——, 'The Costs of Modern Motherhood to Low Income Families in Inter-war Britain', in V. Fildes, L. Marks and H. Marland (eds), *Women and Children First: International Maternal and Infant Welfare 1870–1945* (London: Routledge, 1992).

Perriton, L., 'Forgotten Feminists: The Federation of British Professional and Business Women, 1933–1969', *Women's History Review*, 16:1 (2007).

Phillips, A., 'Citizenship and Feminist Theory', in G. Andrews (ed.), *Citizenship* (London: Lawrence and Wishart, 1991).

——, 'Must Feminists Give Up on Liberal Democracy', in D. Held (ed.), *Prospects for Democracy: North, South, East and West* (Cambridge, Cambridge University Press, 1993).

Potter, A., 'The Equal Pay Committee: A Case Study of a Pressure Group', *Political Studies*, 5 (1957).

Prochaska, F., 'A Mothers' Country: Mothers' Meetings and Family Welfare in Britain, 1850–1950', *History, The Journal of the Historical Association*, 74 (1989).

Pugh, M., 'Domesticity and the Decline of Feminism, 1930–1950', in Smith (ed.), *British Feminism in the Twentieth Century* (London: Edward Elgar, 1990).

Rathbone, E., 'Changes in Public Life', in R. Strachey (ed.), *Our Freedom and Its Results* (London: Hogarth Press, 1936).

Ravetz, A., 'A View from the Interior', in J. Attfield and P. Kirkham (eds), *A View From the Interior: Feminism, Women and Design* (London: The Women's Press, 1989).

——, 'Housing the People' in J. Fyrth (ed.), *Labour's Promised Land? Culture and Society in Labour Britain 1945–51* (London: Lawrence and Wishhart, 1995).

Riley, D., 'War in the Nursery', *Feminist Review*, 2 (1979).

——, 'Some Peculiarities of Social Policy Concerning Women in Wartime and Post-War Britain', in M. R. Higonnet, J. Jenson, S. Michel and M. C. Weitz (eds), *Behind The Lines: Gender and the Two World Wars* (New Haven: Yale University Press, 1987).

Robinson, S., 'Maintaining the Independence of the Midwifery Profession: A

Continuing Struggle', in J. Garcia, R. Kilpatrick and M. Richards (eds), *The Politics of Maternity Care: Services for Childbearing Women in Twentieth-Century Britain* (London: Clarendon Paperbacks, 1990).

Rowan, C., 'Women in the Labour Party, 1906–1920', *Feminist Review*, 12 (1982).

Scott, G., '"A Trade Union for Married Women": The Women's Co-operative Guild 1914–1920', in S. Oldfield (ed.), *The Working Day World: Women's Lives and Culture(s) in Britain 1914–1945* (London: Taylor and Francis, 1994).

——, '"Workshops Fit for Homeworkers": The Women's Co-operative Guild and Housing Reform in Mid-twentieth Century Britain', in E. Darling and L. Whitworth (eds), *Women and the Making of Built Space in England 1870–1950* (Aldershot: Ashgate, 2007).

Smart, C., 'Disruptive Bodies and Unruly Sex', in C. Smart (ed.), *Regulating Womanhood* (London: Routledge, 1992).

Smith, H., 'The Problem of "Equal Pay for Equal Work" in Great Britain during World War II', *Journal of Modern History*, 53 (1981).

——, 'The Effect of the War on the Status of Women', in H. Smith (ed.), *War and Social Change: British Society in the Second World War* (Manchester: Manchester University Press, 1986).

——, 'British Feminism in the 1920s', in H. Smith (ed.), *British Feminism in the Twentieth Century* (London: Edward Elgar, 1990).

——, 'The Politics of Conservative Reform: The Equal Pay for Equal Work Issue, 1945–1955', *The Historical Journal*, 35:2 (1992).

——, 'British Feminism and the Equal Pay Issue in the 1930s', *Women's History Review*, 5:1 (1996).

Smith Wilson, D., 'A New Look at the Affluent Worker: The Good Working Mother in Post-war Britain', *Twentieth Century British History*, 17:2 (2006).

Summerfield, P., 'Women, War and Social Change: Women in Britain in World War II', in A. Marwick (ed.), *Total War and Social Change* (Basingstoke: Macmillan, 1988).

——, 'Women in Britain since 1945: Companionate Marriage and Double Burden', in J. Obelkevich and P. Catterall (eds), *Understanding Post-war British Society* (London: Routledge, 1994).

Thane, P., 'Women of the British Labour Party and Feminism, 1906–45', in H. Smith (ed.), *British Feminism in the Twentieth Century* (London: Edward Elgar, 1990).

——, 'Towards Equal Opportunities? Women in Britain since 1945', in T. Gourvish and A. O'Day (eds), *Britain Since 1945* (Basingstoke: Macmillan, 1991).

——, 'Visions of Gender in the Making of the British Welfare State: The Case of Women in the British Labour Party and Social Policy, 1906–1945', in G. Bock and P. Thane (eds), *Maternity and Gender Policies: Women and the Rise of European Welfare States, 1880s to 1950s* (London: Routledge, 1991).

——, 'Women in the British Labour Party and the Construction of State Welfare, 1906–1936', in S. Koven and S. Michel (eds), *Mothers of a New World: Maternalist Politics and the Origins of Welfare States* (London: Routledge, 1993).

——, 'Women, Liberalism and Citizenship', in E. Biagini (ed.), *Citizenship and Community: Liberals, Radicals and Collective Identities in the British Isles, 1865–1931* (Cambridge: Cambridge University Press, 1996).

——, 'Family Life and "Normality" in Post-War British Culture', in R. Bessel and D. Schumann (eds), *Life After Death: Approaches to a Cultural and Social History of Europe during the 1940s and 1950s* (Cambridge: Cambridge University Press, 2003).

——, 'Women and Political Participation in England, 1918–1970', in E. Breitenbach and P. Thane (eds), *Women and Citizenship in Britain and Ireland in the Twentieth Century: What Difference Did the Vote Make?* (London: Continuum, 2010).

Turner, B. S., 'Outline of a Theory of Citizenship', *Sociology*, 24:2 (1990).

Walby, S., 'Is Citizenship Gendered?', *Sociology*, 28:2 (1994).

Welshman, J., 'Evacuation, Hygiene and Social Policy: The *Our Towns* Report of 1943', *Historical Journal*, 42 (1999).

Woodesen, A., 'The First Women Police: A Force for Equality or Infringement?', *Women's History Review*, 2:2 (1993).

Woollacott, A., '"Khaki Fever" and Its Control: Gender, Class, Age and Sexual Morality on the British Homefront in the First World War', *Journal of Contemporary History*, 29 (1994).

Wright, V., '"Education for Active Citizenship": Women's Organisations in Inter-war Scotland', *History of Education*, 38:3 (2009).

Yuval-Davis, N., 'Women, Citizenship and Difference', *Feminist Review*, 57 (1997).

Zweiniger-Bargielowska, I., 'Bread Rationing in Britain, July 1946–July 1948', *Twentieth Century British History*, 4:1 (1993).

——, 'Rationing, Austerity and the Conservative Party Recovery after 1945', *Historical Journal*, 37:1 (1994).

——, 'Explaining the Gender Gap: The Conservative Party and the Women's Vote', in M. Francis and I. Zweiniger-Bargielowska (eds), *The Conservatives and British Society, 1880–1990* (Cardiff: University of Wales Press, 1996).

——, 'Housewifery', in I. Zweiniger-Bargielowska (ed.), *Women in Twentieth Century Britain* (London: Palgrave Macmillan, 2001)

Books

Adam, P. (ed.), *Women in Council: The Jubilee Book of the National Council of Women of Great Britain* (Oxford: Oxford University Press, 1945).

Alberti, J., *Beyond Suffrage: Feminists in War and Peace, 1914–28* (Basingstoke: Palgrave Macmillan, 1989).

Alfred, M., *During Six Reigns: Landmarks in the History of the National Council of Women of Great Britain* (London: NCW, 1955).

Andrews, M., *The Acceptable Face of Feminism: The Women's Movement as a Social Movement* (London: Lawrence and Wishart, 1997).

Banks, O., *Faces of Feminism: A Study of Feminism as a Social Movement* (Oxford: Blackwell, 1981).

Beddoe, D., *Back to Home and Duty: Women Between the Wars, 1918–1939* (London: Pandora, 1989).

Beveridge, W. and Wells, A. F., *The Evidence for Voluntary Action* (London: Allen and Unwin, 1949).

Bourke, J., *Working-Class Cultures in Britain 1890–1960* (London: Routledge, 1993).

Bowlby, J., *Childcare and the Growth of Love* (London: Penguin, 1953).

Braithwaite, C., *The Voluntary Citizen: An Enquiry into the Place of Philanthropy in the Community* (London: Methuen, 1938).

Braybon, G. and Summerfield, P., *Out of the Cage: Women's Experiences in Two World Wars* (London: Pandora, 1987).

Bristow, E., *Vice and Vigilance: Purity Movements in Britain since 1700* (Dublin: Gill and Macmillan, 1977).

Brookes, B., *Abortion in England 1900–1967* (London: Croom Helm, 1988).

Bruley, S., *Women in Britain Since 1900* (Basingstoke: MacMillan, 1999).

Burnett, J., *A Social History of Housing 1815–1985* (London: Methuen, 1986).

Caine, B., *English Feminism 1780–1980* (Oxford: Oxford University Press, 1997).

Campbell, B., *The Iron Ladies: Why Do Women Vote Tory?* (London: Virago, 1987).

Carrier, J., *The Campaign for the Employment of Women As Police Officers* (Aldershot: Avebury, 1988).

Cook, H., *The Long Sexual Revolution: English Women, Sex and Contraception 1800–1975* (Oxford: Oxford University Press, 2004).

Conekin, B., Mort, F. and Waters, C. (eds), *Moments of Modernity: Reconstructing Britain 1945–1964* (London: Rivers Oram Press, 1999).

Courtney, J., *Countrywomen in Council* (Oxford: Oxford University Press, 1933).

Cowman, K., *Women in British Politics, c.1689–1979* (Basingstoke: Palgrave Macmillan, 2010).

Davies Llewellyn, M. (ed.), *Maternity: Letters from Working Women* (London: Bell, 1915).

Dyhouse, C., *Feminism and the Family in England, 1880–1930* (Oxford: Oxford University Press, 1989).

Ferguson, M., *Forever Feminine: Women's Magazines and the Cult of Femininity* (London: Heinmann, 1983).

Fisher, K., *Birth Control, Sex and Marriage in Britain, 1918–1960* (Oxford: Oxford University Press, 2006).

Gibson, L., *Beyond Jerusalem: Music in the Women's Institute, 1919–1969* (London, Ashgate, 2008).

Gittens, J., *Fair Sex: Family Size and Structure, 1900–39* (London: Hutchinson, 1982).

Glick, D., *The National Council of Women of Great Britain: The First One Hundred Years* (London: NCW, 1995).

Glucksman, M., *Women Assemble: Women Workers in the New Industries of Interwar Britain* (London: Routledge, 1989).

Goldsmith, M., *Women and the Future* (London: Lindsay Drummond Ltd, 1946).

Goodenough, S., *Jam and Jerusalem* (Glasgow: Collins, 1977).

Gordon, P. and Dougan, D., *Dictionary of British Women's Organisations 1825–1960* (London: Woburn Press, 2001).

Griffith, E. F., *Modern Marriage and Birth Control* (London: Gollancz, 1935).

Hall, L. A., *Sex, Gender and Social Change in Britain since 1880* (Basingstoke: Macmillan, 2000).

Hall, R., *Marie Stopes: A Biography* (London: Virago Ltd., 1978).

——, *Dear Dr. Stopes: Sex in the 1920s* (London: Deutsch, 1978).

Harrison, B., *Prudent Revolutionaries: Portraits of British Feminists between the Wars* (Oxford: Oxford University Press, 1987).

Herbert, A. P., *Holy Deadlock* (London: Methuen and Co., 1934).

——, *The Ayes Have It: The Story of the Marriage Bill* (London: Methuen and Co., 1937).

Hilton, M., *Consumerism in Twentieth Century Britain* (Cambridge: Cambridge University Press, 2003).

Hinton, J., *Women, Social Leadership, and the Second World War: Continuities of Class* (Oxford: Oxford University Press, 2002).

Hollis, P., *Women in Public Life: The Women's Movement 1850–1900, Documents of the Victorian Women's Movement* (London: George Allen and Unwin, 1979).

——, *Ladies Elect: Women in English Local Government 1865–1914* (Oxford: Oxford University Press, 1987).

The Hutchinson Woman's Who's Who (London: Hutchinson, 1934).

Jackson, L., *Women Police: Gender, Welfare and Surveillance in the Twentieth Century* (Manchester: Manchester University Press, 2006).

Jenkins, I., *The History of the Women's Institute Movement of England and Wales* (Oxford: Oxford University Press, 1953).

Jephcott, P., *Rising Twenty: Notes on Some Ordinary Girls* (London: Faber and Faber, 1948).

Kitchen, P., *For Home and Country: War, Peace and Rural Life as Seen through the Pages of the Women's Institutes' Magazine, 1919–1959* (London: Ebury, 1990).

Law, C., *Suffrage and Power: The Women's Movement, 1918–1928* (London: I. B. Tauris, 1997).

Lewis, J., *Women in England 1870–1950: Sexual Divisions and Social Change* (Brighton: Wheatsheaf, 1984).

——, *Women in Britain Since 1945: women, family, work and the state in the post-war years* (Oxford: Blackwell, 1992).

—— (ed.), *Women's Welfare/Women's Rights* (London: Croom Helm, 1983).

—— (ed.), *Labour and Love: Women's Experience of Home and Family 1850–1940* (Oxford: Oxford University Press, 1986).

Lister, R., *Citizenship: Feminist Perspectives* (Basingstoke: Palgrave, 1997).

Loudon, I., *Death in Childbirth: An International Study of Maternal Care and Maternal Mortality, 1800–1950* (Oxford: Clarendon Press, 1992).

Macnicol, J., *The Movement for Family Allowances* (London: Heinemann, 1980).

Marshall, T. H., *Citizenship and Social Class* (Cambridge: Cambridge University Press, 1950).

Merz, C., *After the Vote: The Story of the National Union of Townswomen's Guilds in the Year of Its Diamond Jubilee 1929–1989* (Norwich: National Union of Townswomen's Guilds, 1988).

Mowat, C., *Britain Between the Wars, 1918–1940* (London: Methuen, 1955).

Moyse, C., *A History of the Mothers' Union: Women, Anglicanism and Globalisation* (London: The Boydell Press, 2009).

Myrdal, A. and Klein, V., *Women's Two Roles: Home and Work* (London: Routledge and Kegan Paul Ltd, 1956).

National Federation of Women's Institutes, *Keeping Ourselves Informed: Our Concerns, Our Resolutions, Our Actions* (London: NFWI, 1981).

Noakes, L., *War and the British: Gender, Memory and National Identity 1939–1991* (London: I. B. Tauris, 1998).

Offen, K., *European Feminisms, 1700–1950* (Stanford: Stanford University Press, 2000).

Parker, O., *For The Family's Sake: A History of the Mothers' Union 1876–1976* (Folkstone: Bailey and Swinfen, 1975).

Pateman, C., *The Disorder of Women* (Cambridge: Cambridge University Press, 1989).

Phillips, R., *Putting Asunder: A History of Divorce in Western Society* (Cambridge: Cambridge University Press, 1988).

Pugh, M., *Women's Suffrage in Britain 1867–1928* (London: Historical Association, 1980).

——, *The Tories and the People* (Oxford: Oxford University Press, 1985).

——, *Women and the Women's Movement in Britain, 1914–1999* (2nd ed; Basingstoke: MacMillan, 2000).

Rathbone, E., *The Disinherited Family* (London: E. Arnold and Co., 1924).

Roberts, E., *A Woman's Place: An Oral History of Working-Class Women, 1890–1940* (Oxford: Blackwell, 1984).

Robertson Scott, J. W., *The Story of the Women's Institute Movement* (Kingham: Village Press, 1925).

Rose, S. O., *Which People's War? National Identity and Citizenship in Britain 1939–45* (Oxford: Oxford University Press, 2003).

Ryan, M., *Yesterday Recalled: A Jubilee History of the Catholic Women's League 1906–1981* (London: Catholic Women's League, 1981).

Scott, G., *Feminism, Femininity and the Politics of Working Women: The Women's Co-operative Guild, 1880s to the Second World War* (London: University College London Press, 1998).

Segal, L., *Straight Sex: The Politics of Pleasure* (London: Virago, 1994).

Sheridan, D. (ed.), *Wartime Women: An Anthology of Women's Wartime Writing for Mass Observation 1937–45* (London: Phoenix, 1990).

Soloway, R., *Birth Control and the Population Question in England 1877–1930* (Chapel Hill: University of North Carolina, 1982).

Spring Rice, M., *Working Class Wives* (London: Penguin, 1939).

Stone, L., *The Road to Divorce: England 1530–1987* (Oxford: Oxford University Press, 1990).

Stott, M., *Organisation Woman: The Story of The National Union of Townswomen's Guilds* (London: Heinemann, 1978).

Strachey, R. (ed.), *Our Freedom and Its Results* (London: Hogarth, 1936).

Summerfield, P., *Women Workers in the Second World War: Production and Patriarchy in Conflict* (London: Routledge, 1984).

Sutton, M., *'We Didn't Know Aught': A Study of Sexuality, Superstition and Death in Women's Lives in Lincolnshire during the 1930s, '40s and '50s* (Stamford: Paul Watkins, 1992).

Tancred, E., *Women Police 1914–1950* (London: NCW, 1950).

Vincent, D., *Poor Citizens* (London: Longman, 1991).

Weeks, J., *Sex, Politics and Society: the Regulation of Sexuality since 1800* (London: Longman, 1981).

Weinberger, B., *The Best Police in the World: An Oral History of English Policing* (Aldershot: Scolar Press, 1995).

White, C. L., *Women's Magazines, 1693–1968* (London: Joseph, 1970).

Wilson, E., *Only Halfway to Paradise: Women in Post-War Britain: 1945–1968* (London: Tavistock, 1980).

Winnicott, D., *Getting to Know Your Baby* (London: Heinemann, 1945).

Zweiniger-Bargielowska, I., *Austerity in Britain: Rationing, Controls and Consumption 1939–1955* (Oxford: Oxford University Press, 2000).

Unpublished sources

Blackford, C., 'Ideas, structures and practices of feminism, 1939–1964' (Ph.D. dissertation, University of East London, 1996).

Clements, S., 'Feminism, citizenship and social activity: the role and importance of local women's organisations, Nottingham 1918–1969' (Ph.D. dissertation, University of Nottingham, 2008).

Davidson, R., 'Citizens at last: women's political culture and civil society, Croydon and East Surrey, 1914–39' (Ph.D. dissertation, Royal Holloway, University of London, 2010).

Field, J. and Weller, P., 'The association for education in citizenship, 1935–1955', unpublished paper presented to 'The Left and Citizenship in the 1940s and After', a workshop held at the University of Warwick, 7 November 1991.

Freeguard, J., 'It's time for women of the 1950s to stand up and be counted' (Ph.D. dissertation, University of Sussex, 2004).

Kent, J., 'The attitudes of the British churches to citizenship and national identity 1920–1960, with special reference to the work of William Temple', presented to 'The Right to Belong: Citizenship and National Identity', a conference held at the University of London, 7 May 1994.

Morgan, M., 'The acceptable face of feminism: the Women's Institute movement 1915–1960' (Ph.D. dissertation, University of Sussex, 1992).

Noble, V., 'A mission for women: a reflection on the history of women's organisations in the Catholic Church and their relevance within the contemporary Church' (Diploma dissertation, University of London, 1991).

North, D. L., 'Middle class suburban lifestyles and culture in England 1919–1939' (Ph.D. dissertation, Oxford, 1989).

Richie, R., 'The housewife and the modern: the home and appearance in women's magazines, 1954–1969' (Ph.D. dissertation, University of Manchester, 2010).

Index

Lightning Source UK Ltd.
Milton Keynes UK
UKOW04f1031220315

248238UK00002BA/33/P